TRENDYVILLE

ABOUT THE AUTHORS

Renate Howe is an urban historian with publications on Melbourne's inner city, public housing and heritage. She has actively participated in Victoria's planning system as a member of Planning Panels Victoria and the Heritage Council. She is currently an Honorary Associate Professor at Deakin University and Adjunct Research Associate at Monash University.

David Nichols lectures in urban planning at the University of Melbourne. He is the author of *The Bogan Delusion* (2011) and co-editor with Hannah Lewi of *Community: Making Modern Australia* (2010). His fields of research include community development, culture in urban societies, Australian popular culture and planned urban form, particularly the 'internal reserve' public-private space.

Graeme Davison is Emeritus Professor of History at Monash University. His previous books include *The Rise and Fall of Marvellous Melbourne*, *The Use and Abuse of Australian History*, *Car Wars: How the Car Won Our Hearts and Conquered Our Cities* and, as co-editor, *The Oxford Companion to Australian History*. His most recent book, *University Unlimited: The Monash Story* (with Kate Murphy) appeared in 2012.

TRENDYVILLE

THE BATTLE FOR AUSTRALIA'S INNER CITIES

Renate Howe, David Nichols and Graeme Davison

MONASH University
Publishing

Monash University Publishing
Building 4, Monash University
Clayton, Victoria 3800, Australia
www.publishing.monash.edu

Monash University Publishing brings to the world publications which advance the best traditions of humane and enlightened thought.

Monash University Publishing titles pass through a rigorous process of independent peer review.

http://www.publishing.monash.edu/books/trendyville-9781921867422.html

Series: Australian History

Design: Les Thomas

National Library of Australia Cataloguing-in-Publication entry:

Author:	Howe, Renate, 1939– author.
Title:	Trendyville : the battle for Australia's inner cities / Renate Howe, David Nichols and Graeme Davison.
ISBN:	9781921867422 (paperback)
Subjects:	Urban renewal--Australia--History.
	Urban renewal--Australia--Citizen participation.
	Housing--Australia.
	City planning--Australia.
	City planning--Australia--Citizen participation.
	Australia--Social conditions--1965–
Other Authors/ Contributors:	Nichols, David, 1965– author.
	Davison, Graeme, 1940– author.
Dewey Number:	711.40994

Printed in Australia by Griffin Press an Accredited ISO AS/NZS 14001:2004 Environmental Management System printer.

The paper this book is printed on is certified against the Forest Stewardship Council ® Standards. Griffin Press holds FSC chain of custody certification SGS-COC-005088. FSC promotes environmentally responsible, socially beneficial and economically viable management of the world's forests.

CONTENTS

ABBREVIATIONS AND ACRONYMS

ALP	Australian Labor Party
ANU	Australian National University
APPLE	Albert Park Protection League
BFPCC	Brisbane Freeway Protest and Compensation Committee
BLF	Builders Labourer's Federation
BOMA	Building Owners and Managers Association
BSL	Brotherhood of St Laurence
BTPS	Beaumaris Tree Protection Society
CA	Carlton Association
CAN	Citizens' Action Plan for North and West Melbourne
CBD	'central business district'
CBR	Commonwealth Bureau of Roads
CHP	Concrete Housing Project
CPA	Communist Party of Australia
CRAG	Coalition of Residents' Action Groups (NSW)
CRB	Country Roads Board (now VicRoads)
CSHA	Commonwealth-State Housing Agreement
CUA	Committee for Urban Action
CURA	Centre for Urban Research and Action
DURD	(Federal) Department of Urban and Regional Development (1973–1975)
DLP	Democratic Labor Party (1955–1978)
EHA	Emerald Hill Association (South Melbourne)
EMC	Ecumenical Migration Centre
FEC	Fitzroy Ecumenical Centre
FILEF	Federazione Italiano Lavoratori Emigrati e Famiglie (Federation of Italian Emigrant Workers and their Families)
FRA	Fitzroy Residents' Association
HCV	Housing Commission of Victoria
KSAG	Kensington Social Action Group (Victoria)
MATS	Metropolitan Adelaide Transportation Scheme
MCC	Melbourne City Council
MMBW	Melbourne and Metropolitan Board of Works

NFRA	North Fitzroy Residents' Association
NGO	non-government organisation
NIMBY	'not in my back yard'
NMA	North Melbourne Association (also known as North Melbourne Community Development Association; North and West Melbourne Association)
NSWHC	New South Wales Housing Commission
NWMA	see NMA
OYO	'own your own'
PACAB	Parents and Citizens' Association of Beaumaris
RAG	Residents' Action Group
RAIA	Royal Australian Institute of Architects
SAHT	South Australian Housing Trust
SCC	Sydney City Council
SCM	Student Christian Movement
SEC	State Electricity Commission (of Victoria) (1921–1993)
SPO	Social Planning Office
TCF	'textile, clothing and footwear' (industries)
TCPA	Town and Country Planning Association (of Victoria)
TRG	Town Planning Research Group
UNSW	University of New South Wales
VCOSS	Victorian Council of Social Services
WEL	Women's Electoral Lobby
YCW	Young Christian Workers

INTERVIEWEES AND INFORMANTS

All uncredited quotes attributed to those listed below are from interviews and/or discussions conducted with participants between 2003 and 2012. Parenthetical descriptions refer to roles played by interviewees during the period under discussion.

Geoff Baker (North Melbourne Association and Committee for Urban Action) interviewed by D. Nichols 2003

David Beauchamp (Carlton Association) interviewed by Cameron Tait 2003

Nigel Buesst (filmmaker) interviewed by D. Nichols 2003

Bret Christian (editor Subiaco *Post*) interviewed by D. Nichols 2003

Richard Diggins (former Mayor of Subiaco) interviewed by D. Nichols 2003

David Eyres (architect) interviewed by D. Nichols 2007

Peter Gray (filmmaker) pers. comm. with D. Nichols 2012

Rupert Hamer (Premier of Victoria) interviewed by D. Nichols and Cameron Tait 2003

Bruce Hanford (journalist) interviewed by D. Nichols 2003

Lorna Hannan (educator and activist) interviewed by J. Yule 2003

Caroline Hogg (politician) interviewed by J.Yule 2003

Tom Hogg (economist) interviewed by D. Nichols 2003

Peter Hollingworth (minister) interviewed by D. Nichols 2004

Betty Hounslow (activist) pers. comm. with D. Nichols 2012

Brian Howe (minister, activist and politician) and Renate Howe (activist and academic) interviewed by G. Davison 2004

Alan Hunt (politician) interviewed by D. Nichols 2003

Norah Killip (activist) interviewed by J.Yule 2003

Tony Knox (newspaper proprietor) interviewed by J.Yule 2003

Anne Latreille (journalist) interviewed by D. Nichols 2003

Jane Lennon (activist and heritage expert) interviewed by D. Nichols 2003

Miles Lewis (academic) interviewed by D. Nichols 2003; pers. comm with G. Davison 2009

Harold Mackrell (Mayor of Fitzroy) interviewed by D. Nichols 2003

Ray Marginson (former registrar, University of Melbourne) interviewed by S. Pascoe 2010

Andrew McCutcheon (architect and politician) interviewed by J. Yule 2003

Annemarie Mutton (activist) interviewed by D. Nichols 2004

Barbara Niven (activist) interviewed by J. Yule 2003

Kaye Oddie (activist) interviewed by J. Yule 2003

Ann Polis (newspaper editor) interviewed by D. Nichols 2003

David Scott (Brotherhood of St Laurence) interviewed by D. Nichols 2003

Giovanni Sgro (politician) interviewed by D. Nichols and V. di Campli san Vito 2004

Pete Steedman (editor and politician) interviewed by D. Nichols 2003

INTRODUCTION

Trendyville appears on no map. It was, as a contemporary might have said, not so much a place, more a way of life. In coining the word as a title for this book we sought to evoke, rather than define, a distinctive phase in the recent history of Australia's seaboard cities, still close enough to stir strong feelings, yet far enough away to permit a critical distance. Trendyville stands at the junction between geography, culture and politics, on the road between memory and history.

Trendyville was the home of the 'trendies' – the generation of students and young university-educated professionals who colonised the former working-class suburbs of Australia in the 1960s and 70s. The word 'trendy' first appeared in England in the early 1960s as a term for the fashionable clothes and other articles of consumption among the young in swinging London. By the early 1970s it had broadened its meaning to encompass these 'lifestyles' (another word of the era) and the people who adopted them. According to the journalist Donald Horne, the word arrived in Australia around 1967 or 1968, but by 1971 it also denoted a 'concern' (yet another vogue expression) for such radical leftist political issues as Aborigines and the environment.[1] Eventually the trendies appropriated the word themselves, adding further variations. People occasionally spoke of 'trendyism', and later still the geographer William Logan and architectural historian Miles Lewis suggested 'trendification' as a word for the permeation of the working-class suburbs by middle-class professionals, a process known elsewhere as 'gentrification', but inappropriate, they argued, in a country with no real gentry.[2]

'Trendy' was not a neutral term, and trendies seldom applied it to themselves, unless ironically. It was the slightly scornful label used by outsiders to characterise people whose politics were seen, Horne noted, as mere 'matters of consumer fashion, like shopping bags or types of trousers'.[3] The educationalist W. F. Broderick's 1974 caricature of Melbourne's trendies is a good example:

---

[1]   Donald Horne, *Time of Hope: Australia 1966–72* (Sydney: Angus and Robertson, 1980), 7–8.

[2]   William Stewart Logan, *The Gentrification of Inner Melbourne: The Political Geography of Inner City Housing* (St Lucia: University of Queensland Press, 1985), 52; Miles Lewis, in conversation with Graeme Davison, 2009.

[3]   Horne, *Time of Hope*, 7.

They proliferate in advertising, television, progressive schools, art departments and arty-crafty shops. Their habitat is in Carlton, South Yarra, Toorak and the more salubrious eastern suburbs. Your trendy is youngish, bearded, modishly dressed or in shabby jeans. He talks in the fashionable jargon that he's picked up from art critics about the latest exhibition of abstracts. He is knowledgeable about absurd drama and incomprehensible literature ... Some of my best friends are trendies. They live in Victorian terraces that are crumbling into decay, and they delight in restoring them to their former grandeur. Their trendy wives go about in smocks, make pots, talk about sex and creativity all day and look like Virginia Woolf in one of her off days.[4]

That the trendies saw themselves as setting, or following, a trend, were often interested in fashion, and that their behaviour and tastes reflected a shift in contemporary culture, is not in doubt. They were responding to perhaps the most profound generational change in twentieth century history, and their embrace of new fashions in dress, housing and politics was but one manifestation of its depth. 'Every generation sees the world as new', historian Tony Judt observes, but the 'generation gap' between parents who had experienced depression and war and their 'prosperous, pampered, self-confident and culturally autonomous' children was wider than previous generational shifts. The exaggerated attention the post-1960s generation paid to matters of style, whether in dress, housing or politics, he warns, should not be dismissed as 'mere froth and show'. It was the surface manifestation of deeper, tidal changes in values and world-views.[5]

In reclaiming the crumbling Victorian terraces of the inner suburbs, for example, the trendies often ostentatiously rejected the modernist dreams and conservative politics symbolised by the suburban brick veneer houses and gardens of their parents' generation. 'Trendy' was often defined dialectically in opposition to the conventional 'life-styles' and beliefs it sought to supersede. It overlapped with, but was not synonymous with, what earlier generations called Bohemia and contemporaries called the 'counter-culture'.[6] But while the counter-culture often veered towards the playful, anarchic, and rebellious, the tone of inner-city politics, at least in Melbourne, was

---

[4]   W. F. Broderick, 'Of Ockers, Trendies and Larrikins' Melbourne *Age*, 6 July 1974.

[5]   Tony Judt, *Postwar: A History of Europe since 1945* (London: Vintage Books, 2005), 390–395.

[6]   Compare Tony Moore, *Dancing with Empty Pockets: Australia's Bohemians* (Sydney: Pier 9, 2012), 247–270.

often earnest and politically strategic. It generated hard-fought struggles as well as spontaneous demonstrations. Common to many of the radicals was a belief in the city as a social ideal, and in urban planning as a way of realising it.

Trendyville was a diverse community spanning a range of lifestyles and beliefs. Not all its inhabitants were 'into' smocks, pots (or pot), sexual emancipation or leftish politics. As we show, they included backward-looking 'patricians', revolutionary Marxists and liberal Christian radicals as well as children of the 'Age of Aquarius'. Some were pre-babyboomers or even pre-pre-babyboomers. Many were eager to embrace 'alternative' thinking, but the alternatives could be as different from each other as they were from the conservative 'mainstream'. What they had most in common was a desire to celebrate, enhance and defend the values they perceived as inherent in the inner-city neighbourhoods they were busily transforming into self-conscious communities. In valuing density, diversity, proximity, historical character and 'community' they were partly rediscovering what the nineteenth century makers of the inner suburbs had built into their fabric, and what their immediate predecessors, the European migrants of the 1950s, had imported into them from the cities of Italy and Greece. They became the first generation of young city-dwellers to turn their backs on what had hitherto been regarded as the *summum bonum* of the Australian way of life, the low-density, house-and-garden suburb. In Melbourne, in particular, they joined with proponents of the city's diverse social reform tradition.

But the values they espoused were not only *inherent* in the places they inhabited; they were also *invested* in them. The transformation of slums into trendy suburbs was an act of cultural imagination and political will, informed by ideas that were imported as well as home-grown. The 1960s urban radicals were the first generation to be widely exposed to the influences of foreign travel and university education. Their visions of Carlton, Paddington and North Adelaide were shaped by experiences of foreign travel and the writings of urban radicals in London and Paris, Chicago and New York. The influences were as diverse as Sir John Summerson's writings on Georgian London, Andre Malraux's renewal of central Paris, George Macleod's Christian socialist vision of Glasgow and Saul Alinsky's 'reveille' for the urban radicals of Chicago. Adelaide historian Hugh Stretton, whose book *Ideas for Australian Cities* (1970) brought the future of the cities to national attention, singled out the American social critic and urban radical Jane Jacobs, who had led protests against freeways in New York, as an influence on Australian urban radicals. Her best selling book *The Death and Life of Great American Cities* (1961) was a stinging critique of the failures of modernist city planning, with its slum clearances, high-rise projects and urban freeways, and a robust defence of the organic life of dense, diverse inner-city neighbourhoods. 'Lively, diverse, intense cities contain the seeds of their own regeneration', she declared.[7] The inner-city neighbourhood, with its narrow streets, pubs, corner shops and immigrant sub-cultures was a sympathetic setting for the kind of personal self-discovery, social experiment and political activism that characterised the generation of the 1960s and 70s. Jacobs was the best-known, but far from the only, advocate of such a perspective.

Jacobs' book, as Stretton noted, became 'the bible of the Carlton and Richmond intellectuals who read claret-stained copies of it (sometimes, I do hope, by the light of candles stuck in bottles) in their refurbished terrace houses under the long shadow of the Housing Commission towers'.[8] Jacobs had not persuaded the trendies to adopt a new fashion for inner-city living – that was something they worked out for themselves – but, as Stretton argued, she provided a theoretical rationale and the authority of an international expert for a local politics of resistance grounded, ultimately, in the very traditional desire of householders to defend their own place.

The stereotype of the 'trendy' insinuated another criticism: that the newcomers were essentially self-seeking upwardly-mobile professionals with a keen eye for real estate trends who acquired valuable inner-city property in order to 'do it up', and take a profit. The 'trendy', according to this view, morphed into the 'yuppy'. Were the 'trendies' displacing working-class families and immigrants dependent on access to the labour market of the inner city? Or were they simply taking advantage of the desire of older residents to move out to the suburbs? Were the trendies motivated by the prospect of speculative profits, or was the rapid increase in the value of terrace houses an unforeseen consequence of their successful defence of their home turf? As it is difficult to generalise about the social complexion of the new residents, so it is difficult to generalise about their motivations. The historian must be careful not to succumb to the vices of self-deception, on the one hand, or the distortions of hindsight, on the other.

---

[7]   Jane Jacobs, *The Death and Life of Great American Cities* (New York: Vintage Books, 1961), 448.

[8]   Hugh Stretton, *Ideas for Australian Cities* (Adelaide: The Author, 1970), 217.

In a recent study of inner-city politics in Sydney, Tony Harris warns against the pitfalls of reductionist accounts of their motivation.

> Conflict over urban space and power in Australian inner cities in this period was complex, many faceted and contradictory and has too easily been implicitly ascribed to the imposition of middle class values and economic benefit which has obscured the ambiguities and contradictions of these inner city struggles and the real issues at stake.[9]

By insinuating superficial and self-interested motives, the term 'trendy', it might be argued, succumbs to just such reductionist thinking. It filters out the strains of strongly-held conviction, fiercely-argued principle, and personal self-sacrifice that inspired new social movements, radical experiments in community building, and forceful interventions in urban planning and politics. As one pioneer activist noted, inner-city living could entail significant personal strains and bitter conflicts in which 'you had to put yourself and your family on the line'.

It also fails to register the political and institutional legacy of this era. Inner-city residents pioneered grassroots participation in planning and governance and established the importance of heritage and environmental regulation for the future of the city. They prevented the destruction of large sections of the inner city for the building of high-rise public housing estates and the construction of freeways. The social and economic strength of Melbourne's inner city owes much to the residents' associations and urban activists.

But if 'trendy' is an inappropriate term, what is the alternative? A recent study of the movement to establish the Fitzroy and Collingwood Community Health Centre ascribes its origins to 'missionaries, radicals and feminists'.[10] But not everyone who participated in inner-city politics would be characterised in this way. In later chapters of this book, we have teased out the relationships between the university and the inner-city residents' associations by distinguishing 'patricians', 'trendies' and 'radicals'. For lack of a better term, we have generally described the participants in inner-city politics as 'activists', a term that has the merit of remaining neutral in relation to ideology and method, even if it occasionally includes some whose activism was relatively passive.

---

[9]   Tony Harris, *Basket Weavers and True Believers: Making and Unmaking the Labor Left in Leichhardt Municipality, 1970–1991* (Newtown: Leftbank Publishing, 2007), 3.

[10] Hamish Townsend, *Missionaries, Radicals, Feminists: A History of North Yarra Community Health* (Collingwood: North Yarra Community Health, 2012).

Fifty years on, the first of the inner-city activists are often rueful spectators of the recent history of Melbourne's inner suburbs. The world they have inherited is not the one that, as young activists, they envisioned. In April 2000 Renate Howe and Graeme Davison invited a range of former activists to a conference on 'The Challenge of the Inner Suburbs: Social Inquiry and Community Action' at the Richmond Town Hall. They testified to the sense of excitement, comradeship and political struggle that had characterised their lives, often contrasting it with the lives of the latte-drinking, BMW-driving, yuppies who had since invaded 'their' neighbourhoods. They found it ironic, when they were not disappointed, that the process of 'trendification' was now seen as the result, or even perhaps the goal, of their commitment to the urban social movements of the time.

The time was obviously ripe for a more extended historical inquiry that would draw both on the memories of activists and the growing archive of personal and institutional papers. Howe and Davison, together with geographer William Logan, a pioneer student of gentrification in inner Melbourne, later made a successful application to the Australian Research Council for a study of Melbourne's urban activists. David Nichols, who was appointed research director, carried out many of the interviews and gathered material from archival collections at the University of Melbourne Archives and Victoria University's Crow Collection as well as other interstate repositories. Several former activists also made available their personal collections of papers and memoirs. This archive of interview transcripts and documentary material forms the basis of this book, and will remain as a permanent legacy of the ARC's generous funding.

We are Melburnians with a due sense of local loyalty, but we have sought to place the experience of the city's activists in the context of international urban protest movements and of movements in other Australian capital cities. Our perspective has been sharpened by a series of valuable studies of urban social movements in Sydney, the other main centre of protest. Perceptions of urban activism in Sydney are dominated by the famous Green Bans imposed by the NSW Branch of the Builders Labourers' Federation (NSW BLF) led by Jack Mundey and Joe Owens and the subject of Meredith Burgmann and Verity Burgmann's excellent book *Green Bans, Red Union* (1998).[11] By comparison, Melbourne's urban protest movement was neither as red nor

---

[11]   Meredith Burgmann and Verity Burgmann, *Green Bans, Red Union: Environmental Activism and the New South Wales Builders Labourers' Federation* (Sydney: UNSW Press, 1998).

as green as Sydney's. Except for the involvement of the breakaway BLF's Norm Gallagher and John Cummins in the battle over railway land in North Carlton and in the successful campaigns to save Tasma Terrace and the Regent Cinema, trade unions played a relatively minor and less aggressive role in Melbourne's urban protest movement. More significant, argues Richard Roddewig in his 1978 study of the impact of urban protests on environmentalism in Sydney and Melbourne, was the comparative strength and resilience in Melbourne of community activism represented by resident action groups (RAGs).[12]

Roddewig's observation invites deeper reflection on how the style of urban activism was grounded in the distinctive cultures of the capital cities. Contemporaries sometimes contrasted the secular liberationist flavour of Sydney radicalism, as exemplified by the Andersonian Sydney Push, with the liberal meliorism, flavoured by liberal Protestantism, in Melbourne's.[13] Others have remarked on the strength of local suburban loyalties, as evidenced by a vigorous tradition of local history, as a feature of Melbourne's culture. How far, we may speculate, did these more general features of the civic culture shape the protest movements of the inner suburbs? In seeking to explore this important, if elusive, dimension of urban activism, we have made occasional comparisons with other Australian capitals including Brisbane, Adelaide and Perth.

In the following chapters we have sought to explore the diverse, complex, and conflicting motivations of the new residents of the inner suburbs, and evaluate the outcomes of Melbourne's urban protest movements. As authors, we came to this task with different generational, geographical and political perspectives. We are each in part, participants, observers, historians and critics. Renate Howe was a participant with Brian Howe in the Fitzroy Residents' Association and the Centre for Urban Research and Action and has written widely on the history of public housing, social welfare and the inner suburbs. She has practical experience of the urban development process as a part-time member of the Victorian Administrative Appeals Tribunal. David Nichols brings the perspective of a later generation. He has written widely on Melbourne's architectural and planning history. His experience as a middle-class, academic émigré to working-class Broadmeadows is reflected in his recent book *The Bogan Delusion*. During the 1970s Graeme

---

12 Richard J. Roddewig, *Green Bans: The Birth of Australian Environmental Politics; A Study in Public Opinion and Participation* (Sydney: Hale and Ironmonger, 1978).

13 For example Vincent Buckley, 'Intellectuals' in *Australian Civilization*, ed. Peter Coleman (Melbourne: Cheshire, 1962), 101–2.

Davison taught at the University of Melbourne, close to the events and many of the participants in this story, but lived in the city's eastern suburbs and later moved to Monash University. As chair of the Historic Buildings Council, he was a pioneer of heritage regulation in the inner city. His more recent book *Car Wars* examines the political response of inner-city residents to the building of Melbourne's freeway network. This book is the product of our collaborative research, discussion, writing and revision. While we all participated in the discussions of the shape of the book and the overall themes, and commented on each other's drafts, our personal perspectives and emphases are reflected in the chapters we each wrote: Renate Howe in chapters 2, 5, 8 and 10 and David Nichols in chapters 1, 4 and 9. Renate Howe and David Nichols are joint authors of Chapter 6, Graeme Davison and David Nichols of Chapter 7. Graeme Davison wrote Chapter 3 with the assistance of Stephen Pascoe.

Trendyville remains contested territory. Memories fade and already several of the key figures whose actions and writings we discuss in this book have left the scene. One of our goals in writing it is to bring the witness of the past to counter the distortions of the present. The image of the inner suburbs is now not of diversity and inclusiveness but of a distinct and privileged middle-class enclave of coffee drinking residents who wield extensive political and social influence. In offering an account of the first generation of urban activists we hope to ensure that knowledge of what they achieved in community vitality and social progress is transmitted to later ones. As Melbourne again enters a period of rapid social and economic change, and its inner suburbs undergo a new phase of intensive development, questions of scale, economic diversity, sense of place and the need for a transparent planning process return to the fore. The stories in this book offer a timely reminder of the power of citizens, inspired by humane values and a generous social vision, to resist the interests of developers and arrogant government decision-making.

Chapter 1

PRECURSORS

MELBOURNE IN THE POSTWAR PERIOD

The generation of inner-city residents and activists who created Trendyville often looked back to the 1940s and 50s as a dark age from which the city only awakened in the 1960s and 70s. They saw themselves as the main agents of change, often contrasting their radicalism and cosmopolitanism with the insular conservatism of their parents' generation and the suburbs in which some of them had grown up. Yet like the activists, the movement that they created owed more than they sometimes acknowledged to social forces and movements already in train during the dark age, often in the very suburbs they denigrated. This chapter looks back to the city from which the transformations of the 1960s and 70s sprang, identifying some of the surprising seedbeds of change.

Modernism and the Inner Suburbs

The end of World War Two, and hopes for a New World Order, inspired many Australians with an enthusiasm for modern forms of architecture, transport and design. The first modern high-rise buildings appeared. The impact of the car, so long anticipated, was finally felt in the 50s, and city expansion, freed from the restraints of fixed-rail transport, began to accelerate. In some cities – Perth and Melbourne for example – metropolitan planning schemes prioritised 'growth and the need to arrange an orderly sequence of development' based on road-based transport infrastructure.[1]

Within this modernist paradigm of growth, Melbourne's inner-industrial suburbs were often seen as legacies of the old era, a 'slum' region of deteriorating housing, poverty, red light areas, homelessness and crime. In the

---

[1]   Robert Freestone, *Urban Nation: Australia's Planning Heritage* (Collingwood: CSIRO, 2010), 149.

1930s, Oswald Barnett, Methodist layman and social reformer, had surveyed these areas of poor housing and depressed living conditions and proposed their reform. But after the war public housing authorities set aside the redevelopment of inner-city housing in favour of new housing estates near suburban industry and in regional areas.[2] Traditional industries in the inner suburbs of Sydney had also lost employment, bleeding population from areas such as Leichhardt, Balmain, Paddington and Surry Hills. Older areas such as The Rocks and Kings Cross became synonymous with poverty, prostitution and crime. In short they were seen as yesterday's city, not tomorrow's.

The only answer for the inner cities was to remake them. Planners and politicians looked to the ambitious postwar programs of urban regeneration in the war-scarred cities of Europe and Britain. They were also attracted to models of urban renewal in the racially divided cities of America where downtown areas had been depleted by the move of people and jobs to the suburbs. International experience suggested that Australia's two largest capital cities needed to increase population densities in the central and inner-city areas in order to contain 'urban sprawl' and discourage the movement of households to the suburban fringe.

Graeme Shaw, architect for the Housing Commission of Victoria (HCV), argued that inner-city landscapes were prime candidates for renewal. The average life of a dwelling, Shaw estimated, was seventy years; thus, in inner Melbourne, 'at least 10,000 dwellings should be demolished each year'.[3] Urban redevelopment was 'the process whereby a city renews itself in those sections which have become obsolete and/or from which a more attractive return on investment can be obtained'. Urban redevelopment, in his perspective, was a social, as well as economic, necessity: a remedy for the worn-out and decayed housing identified by Oswald Barnett and other slum reformers.

Sydney led the movement to redevelop the inner city. American-based commercial and financial institutions flocked to the harbour-side city rather than to Melbourne, the traditional financial centre. The property boom reached its zenith between 1968 and 1974. Observers feared the city 'would never be the same again'. Much of Sydney's central area was demolished to make way for multi-storey commercial building while many middle-class areas were transformed by the appearance of high-rise apartments made

---

2   Renate Howe, 'From Rehabilitation to Prevention: The War Years' in *New Houses for Old: Fifty Years of Public Housing in Victoria 1938–1988*, ed. Renate Howe (Melbourne: Ministry of Housing and Construction, 1988), 45–68.

3   Anon, 'Housing' in *Policies for Progress: Essays in Australian Politics*, ed. Alan Davies and Geoffrey Serle (Melbourne: Fabian Society, 1954), 140.

possible by the introduction of new building materials and construction methods.[4] The peak of this modernising thrust was the 1968 scheme to largely demolish and redevelop the Rocks district.

Melbourne stumblingly followed suit. The City Development Association supported by the Melbourne City Council (MCC), central city retail and financial interests and by the Town and Country Planning Association (TCPA) urged redevelopment in inner-city areas to revitalise the CBD. Modernist architects joined the chorus.[5] Bates, Smart and McCutcheon's 20-storey ICI building (1958) was Melbourne's first modernist multi-storey commercial building. It inspired a rush of other sleek cuboid office towers along Collins Street and a sprinkle of high-rise apartments in East Melbourne and South Yarra, but no boom.[6] Concerned by the continuing lag in private investment, public authorities stepped in to foster the redevelopment of inner Melbourne.

During the 1950s and 60s most inner suburbs underwent an unplanned demographic revolution that would have profound consequences for the character of the activist movements that arrived a generation later. Many of their former working-class residents retreated from the inner areas – often with relief, and in pursuit of a cleaner, quieter, less stigmatised life in new suburbs. Meanwhile government authorities began to act on decades-long commitments to raze 'slums' in order to accommodate new roads and higher density housing. By the time these plans were put into action, many of the circumstances and assumptions that had inspired them had begun to change. Now, in the second decade of the twenty-first century, young students marvel at the apparent perversity of government policies designed to raze picturesque historic housing in order to accommodate working-class tenants in what they assume was always prized inner-city real estate.

Until the mid-1960s politicians, planners, developers and even local residents viewed Melbourne's inner city as a classic 'zone in transition', to use the term coined by Chicago sociologist Ernest Burgess. Burgess saw the inner city, the zone immediately outside the CBD, as a holding space, and point of diffusion, for new arrivals whose aspirations would gradually lead them into

---

4   M. T. Daly, *Sydney Boom, Sydney Bust: The City and its Property Market 1850–1981* (Sydney: Allen and Unwin, 1982), 1–25.

5   Peter Mills, *Refabricating the Towers: The Genesis of the Victorian Housing Commission's High-Rise Estates to 1969* (PhD Thesis, Monash University School of Philosophical, Historical and International Studies, 2010), 39.

6   Philip Goad, *Bates Smart: 150 Years of Australian Architecture* (Fishermans Bend: Thames and Hudson, 2004), 146–213.

the suburban mainstream. According to his theory, the zone in transition was characterised by transience and a degree of social disorganisation, or even deviance. This theory had seemingly been confirmed by recent social trends in inner Melbourne, especially by the tendency of newly arrived migrants to settle in the inner city.[7] It was a theory that meshed nicely with contemporary assumptions about migrant assimilation.

Bureaucrats and sociologists, however, were not the only ones to misunderstand social change in inner-city neighbourhoods. Middle-class pioneers, who we would now see as early gentrifiers, did not at first recognise the social forces their arrival had unleashed. They would have been incredulous if someone had suggested that living (much less purchasing real estate) in a decayed nineteenth-century building could be a profitable choice. On the contrary, they had chosen to live in the inner city precisely because it was not like other parts of the city. Living there was a risky, unfashionable experiment, 'an adventure ... hitherto unknown to the bourgeoisie or the detached rich'.[8]

The resident action movements of the 1960s and 70s evolved in a complex dialectical relationship with the forces of modernisation, outlined in the preceding paragraphs. Most obviously, they contested them: by resisting slum clearance, defending historic neighbourhoods, blockading freeways, questioning the aesthetic and political values that inspired them. But their relationship with the modernist movement was more complex than this, for the activists' ideals of personal growth, self-realisation and experiment were essentially modern in spirit. Many of them were the natural or intellectual children of parents who had espoused modernist ideals, conducted their own experiments in urban or suburban living, and nurtured the spirit of experiment in their children. When they came to form radical organizations of their own they often drew, consciously or unconsciously, on models created by their suburban predecessors. The modernist experiments of the 1950s and 60s were conducted within certain economic and political limits, which the radicals of the 1960s and 70s challenged in their turn. In explaining the growth of the radical movements of the 1960s and 70s, therefore, we must first examine the soil in which they were planted and the seed from which they grew.

---

[7] A striking application of this kind of theorising is the report for the Melbourne and Metropolitan Board of Works by F.M. Little and Associates, *Social Dysfunction and Relative Poverty in Metropolitan Melbourne, Research and Development Division*, MMBW, 1974.

[8] Vanne Trompf, 'Inner Man' in *Melbourne University Magazine*, 1964, 14.

Migrants and Cosmopolitans

A crucial role in the remaking of the inner cities was to be played by recent European immigrants, but it was not the role that the modernist planners envisaged for them. In Europe, where the urban bombsite was a familiar sight, the phrase 'postwar reconstruction' had a literal application. Yet 'reconstruction' also encompassed a social element that went beyond re-making or replacement of buildings. Curtin, Chifley and Menzies anticipated that the new nation would be 'reconstructed', in large part, by migrants. They would supply the labour to carry out much of the physical reconstruction but, in the process, they would themselves be remade. Nino Cullota, the building worker in John O'Grady's assimilationist fable *They're a Weird Mob*, personifies this relationship.

Successive Australian governments introduced and expanded large-scale immigration programs. Beginning in 1947 it widened the zone of recruitment from Britain, to northern Europe, the Baltic states, Romania, Bulgaria, Hungary and Italy. An agreement with the Maltese government in May 1948 was the first of several arrangements made with European governments to expand the intake.[9] In his 1953 assessment of 'New and Old Australians', W. D. Borrie tartly described immigration policy as operating on a 'boa constrictor principle'. The nation 'would periodically grasp a large quantity of migrants, crush them into a shape which would permit of their digestion, and then swallow them'.[10]

The migration program was founded on the premise that the migrants would become Australian, rapidly shedding their Old World culture and embracing that of the New. According to the Burgess model, they would aspire to migrate from the inner city, or 'zone in transition', to the suburbs. To the consternation of some observers, however, they showed a regrettable tendency to congregate in particular areas, some of which began to take on aspects of their homeland culture. Borrie – who espoused mutual respect between 'new and old' – noted:

> So long as they are under Government contract there is little
> opportunity for them to band together, but now that thousands of
> them are settling in capital cities and towns of Australia there will

---

[9]   Anon, *1788–1978, Australia and Immigration: A Review of Migration to Australia, Especially since the Second World War* (Canberra: Australian Government Publishing Service, 1978), 14.

[10]   W. D. Borrie, 'New and Old Australians' in *Taking Stock*, ed. W. Aughterson (Melbourne: Cheshire, 1953), 169.

be a tendency for them to revive some element of their national life and culture.[11]

Neighbourhoods such as Lygon Street, Carlton, just beyond Melbourne's central grid, quickly became known as Italian, Greek, Maltese, or just 'migrant' areas, a reputation many have retained for more than half a century.

These migrant areas were often seen as an affront to a society still consciously British in stock and character. The cities were still recovering from the housing shortage created by a decade and a half of depression and war, and the entry into the nation of new adults and their families seemed unfair and perhaps even unwarranted. In 1952, the Melbourne *Argus* trumpeted a 'housing scandal' in Collingwood, where a 'population artificially boosted by migration' was putting 'strain on such accommodation as exists'.[12] More seriously, the immigrant enclaves offended against the assumption of rapid assimilation. New migrants were supposed to forget their origins, rather than flaunt them, according to the 'Good Neighbour' movement, a community-focused assimilation organisation. 'Australians cannot remain unaware of the presence amongst them of non-British settlers', Borrie observed.[13] Colin Clark, Director of the Queensland Bureau of Industry and a fervent decentralist, proposed the 'scientific redistribution of Australia's population' by 'strict governmental control over the location of industries' across a network of regions and new urban neighbourhoods.[14]

Some observers feared that new migrants would revive historic ethnic hostilities and indulge in radical politics, a tendency exacerbated by their concentration in 'ghettoes'. Italian arrivals after the mid-1960s were sometimes branded 'impegnati': 'socially and politically sensitised and more formally educated ... individuals ... who have clear ideas about workers' rights, social justice and the need for community participation'.[15] Others, by contrast, characterised them as uneducated peasants: in a study of Darlington in inner-city Sydney, K. R. McInnes highlighted the lower

---

[11] Borrie, 'New and Old Australians', 183.

[12] Anon, 'Housing Scandal' Melbourne *Argus*, 18 June 1952, 2.

[13] Borrie, 'New and Old Australians', 174.

[14] Colin Clark, 'Have We the Sense?' in *The 1951 Federal Congress on Regional and Town Planning: Record of Proceedings* (Canberra: Federal Congress, 1951), 53–9.

[15] Lidio Bertelli, 'A Social-Cultural Profile of the Italian Community in Australia' in *Espresso, Corretto or White? Some Aspects of the Italian Presence in Australia* (Melbourne: Catholic Intercultural Resource Centre, 1986), 92.

education standard of post-1955 immigrants.[16] Too radical in the eyes of some, too ignorant in the eyes of others: all that hostile observers could agree upon was that the migrants, especially in the mass, were a problem.

These attitudes, reinforced by the assimilationist assumptions of the postwar immigration program, competed, however, with a slowly emerging cosmopolitanism. The theory was that the migrants would absorb the values of the host culture; but by the 1960s there was mounting evidence of an opposite tendency, for the host culture to absorb elements of the migrants'. Servicemen returned from World War Two having seen a wider world and with increased respect for European standards of cuisine, dress, and urban living. Younger Australian tourists in the Europe of the 1950s came to appreciate the charms of close-knit, culturally homogenous continental European communities. These experiences made locals increasingly receptive to the transplanted cuttings of continental Europe springing up in their midst. Miles Lewis, who grew up in Parkville near the University of Melbourne, remembers that academics moved to Carlton in the mid-century not just 'because it was close to the University' but also because 'it began to develop as a left bank coffee shop sort of milieu' through its Italian flavour. The Mediterranean atmosphere of Carlton's main shopping street was a magnet for students and staff of the University. Newtown, south of the University of Sydney, had a similar exotic appeal. Most of the migrants were not actually cosmopolitans themselves, or even bourgeois, but transplanted peasants from Calabria or the Greek Islands. To Australians, reared on meat-and-three-veg British cooking, however, the immigrants' spaghetti Bolognese, pizza and souvlaki seemed like an invitation to a larger world. Their ways of inhabiting the squares and streets of the inner city, and the opportunities they found in them for play, gossip, and conviviality, daily inspired uptight Anglo-Saxons to do likewise.

New Visions of the Inner City

In the 1960s and 70s cheap housing and a raffish atmosphere made the inner city a natural focus of artistic and cultural life. In turn, the newcomers began to look upon their environment with new eyes, discovering beauty

---

16   K. R. McInnes, 'Sydney University Expansion: Site Acquisition' in *Urban Redevelopment in Australia: Papers Presented to a Joint Urban Seminar Held at the Australian National University October and December 1966*, ed. P. N. Troy (Canberra: Research School of Social Sciences ANU, 1967), 342–381.

where modernist planners and engineers found only ugliness and decay. Students of gentrification speak of a process of 'aestheticising' the urban environment, rendering it as a kind of art object. The pioneers of this movement, such as the founders of the National Trust (the Victorian branch of which was founded in 1956) included people like Miles Lewis's father, Professor Brian Lewis and architect Robin Boyd. Both, ironically, were leading advocates and exponents of architectural modernism. On 6 November 1960 Lewis urged members of the Bread and Cheese Club, a society devoted to antiquarian literary and artistic pursuits, to preserve the legacy of nineteenth century architecture still visible all around them:

> He deplored the expedient activity in bulldozing so many old buildings of historical and architectural worth, and the industry fabricating antiques ... It is impossible to hold all we would like to keep, but the grading of buildings by the National Trust according to historical and architectural worth was invaluable.

Robin Boyd, the most influential contemporary historian and critic of Australian architecture, had surprisingly little to say in either of his classic books, *Australia's Home* (1954) and *The Australian Ugliness* (1960), about the fabric of the inner cities. There is much about the qualities of the suburban villa and city skyscraper, but hardly a word or illustration devoted to the terrace house. Only in his 1962 book for children, *The Walls Around Us*, did he briefly and dismissively mention 'cast iron terraces'. 'Nobody loved these terrace houses greatly. They were slung together quickly, like the pink flats of a century later, to make money for an owner who would never live in one.'[17] By the end of his life, however, Boyd had become less confident about the promise of architectural modernism, more appreciative of Melbourne's nineteenth century architectural legacy, and more insistent on urban values of density, heterogeneity and nonconformity.[18]

By the early 1960s the inner suburbs had also caught the eye of young independent filmmakers. Once again it was their contrast with mainstream Australia, and the region's associations with low life and crime, that attracted them. In films like *The Spag*, set in the stony streets of Carlton and Fitzroy, George Mangiamele portrayed the migrants' plight in the face of Australian

---

[17]   Robin Boyd, *The Walls Around Us: The Story of Australian Architecture* (Melbourne: Cheshire, 1962), 42–3.

[18]   See Geoffrey Serle, *Robin Boyd: A Life* (Carlton: Melbourne University Press,1995), 277–279.

racism and indifference. The spareness of the landscape reflects the inherently noble and tragic fate of his protagonists. Nigel Buesst had studied at the University of Melbourne in the early 1960s and became part of a nascent local film scene based on the Olinda – later Melbourne – International Film Festival.[19] He was drawn to the inner city partly in reaction against the prevailing assumption that Australian cities were too bland to provide a background for a national cinema:

> Melbourne was regarded, particularly in the '50s, as a bit of a desert and a lot of people reacted against our perceived blandness ... [O]utsiders took a look at us and said, 'You people are boring', which was never really true.

His film *The Rise and Fall of Squizzy Taylor* (1969) told inner-Melburnians a sordid 'true crime' tale from their history. The film enjoyed a sell-out season at the Carlton Cinema.

Political scientist and short story writer Alan Davies was one of the first academics to move into Carlton, an area he depicted in bleak imagery evocative of Burgess's 'zone in transition':

> A great arc of the city, a sea of broken brick of a desolation that only a hundred thousand houses together can effect, welled out over the plain towards two neat stone-blue hills due north and east. Three streets forked down into this from where he stood but they did not carry far ... Rathdowne Street, frayed at the edges with shops, rolled like rotten lino gently away out of focus, the old elms in its little squares towering above their houses.[20]

As in his sociological studies of class divisions in the city, Davies, like the film-makers, continued to see the inner city in terms very similar to the modernist planners and architects.[21] If they viewed it romantically, it was because its rundown, decaying and unfashionable qualities appealed to their own self-perception as rebels and outsiders. There was little sense, as yet, that the inner city might be a desirable, much less a fashionable, place to live. If the inner suburbs eventually became 'trendy' it was because the outsiders increasingly became insiders. How that transformation occurred is the subject of later chapters.

---

19   F. D., 'Rare Films Will Be Shown at Hills Festival' Melbourne *Argus*, 19 January 1952, 13.
20   A. F. Davies, *A Sunday Kind of Love and Other Stories* (Melbourne: Cheshire, 1961), 4.
21   A. F. Davies, *Images of Class* (Sydney: Sydney University Press, 1967).

Getting Organised: Progress Associations, Preservation Societies and the Resident Action Groups

Inner-city activism was an organisational, as well as an ideological, development. It built upon models of political action that were international and local, some of them already flourishing in other parts of the city. In the 1940s, inspired by ideals of postwar reconstruction, citizens in suburbs and country towns banded together in support of 'community centres', sometimes incorporating play centres, kindergartens, sporting and cultural facilities.[22] Their ideals of community action were often explicitly socialist in inspiration and always bravely modernist in architectural expression, framed in sympathetic response to central government, rather than against it. Other citizens, inspired by liberal ideals of mutual self-interest, formed progress associations to push for better roads and community facilities. The residents' associations formed by inner-city activists in the 1960s and 70s were different from either of these earlier organizations, although they built on aspects of each, especially in how they utilised media and political lobbying at the local level.

In 1995 Patrick Mullins admonished urban scholars for neglecting the influence of progress associations. 'Understanding these voluntary associations is critical if we are to fully comprehend urban development', he insisted.[23] Progress associations had been a common feature of the political landscape in Australian towns and suburbs since the late 19th century.[24] They gave residents a voice on local councils, and acted as a recruiting ground for future councillors. They generally conducted their dialogue with local authorities in civilised tones. Inspired by ideals of voluntary service, they sometimes banded together to provide services that would now be seen as the responsibility of councils, such as the construction of community buildings or playgrounds. As the name suggests, they were motivated by a sense of 'progress', an ideal they conceived in largely material terms as a steady advance towards prosperity, comfort and respectability, although they might also lobby for services, such as when the Garden City Progress

---

[22] Kate Darian-Smith, David Nichols and Julie Willis, 'The Community Can Do It! Planning for the New Civic Centre' in Hannh Lewi and David Nichols (eds) *Community: Building Modern Australia*, (Kensington: UNSW Press, 2010), 169–190.

[23] Patrick Mullins, 'Progress Associations and Urban Development: The Gold Coast, 1945–79' *Urban Policy and Research* 13 (2) (1995), 67.

[24] See for instance Anon, 'Clackall Coach Service' Rockhampton *Morning Bulletin*, 8 November 1879, 2.

Association wrote to the HCV in mid-1940 about the provision of a bus service in their newly-constructed area.[25]

The orientation and style of the residents' associations of the 1960s was different from that of the progress associations: they were more combative, more radical and more holistic in their concerns. In rediscovering community, especially through their engagement with their nineteenth century townscape, they differed from the development ethos and modernising assumptions of the suburban progress associations. Yet they had affinities, too, with the ideals of community vested by their parents' generation in postwar reconstruction. Their community ideal was that of a village, intimate, cooperative in spirit. Those who had 'fled' the suburbs in pursuit of closer, less individualistic life sometimes contrasted the anonymity and conservatism of the suburbs with the organic community of the inner suburbs. 'The suburbs are feminine', political scientist Alan Davies observed in 1972. 'Lose yourself on foot in one, looking (say) for a son's Saturday hockey pitch, and you find yourself dreaming you're trapped in a women's dormitory. Did suburbia breed conservatism as links snapped with the old working-class cultures of the inner city?'[26]

The alignment of suburbia with conservatism, and by implication with passivity, was part of the rhetoric of inner-city activism. It reinforced their idealism and the conviction that in reclaiming the old they were making the new. But it failed to recognise the conservative elements in the activists' own outlook – for example in their desire to conserve their nineteenth century streetscapes – as well as significant strains of activism already present in the suburbs.

Suburban activism was more inclined to focus on the conservation of the natural environment or on the provision of community resources than on the preservation of historic townscapes. In 1954, for example, 'Housewives of Neerim-rd, Murrumbeena, Vic'

> turned out in force on the morning when axemen of Caulfield Council arrived with orders to remove all the street trees. The axemen lamely returned to the town hall without chopping another tree.[27]

In 1949 residents of Beaumaris formed the Parents and Citizens' Association of Beaumaris (PACAB) in an effort to influence the shape of

---

25   HCV Minutes, 25 July 1940, PROV 8212P1.

26   A. F. Davies, *Essays in Political Sociology* (Melbourne: Cheshire, 1972), 36.

27   Anon, Untitled item, *Cross-Section* 15 (1) (January 1954), 3.

development in an area previously identified for industrial and community development by the tyre-maker Dunlop-Perdriau. In a scheme strongly influenced by garden-city ideals, the company had originally planned in the 1940s to move its industrial workforce, along with its factory, from Montague in the inner city to a new model community in the seaside suburb.[28] When the company dropped the scheme, however, middle-class local residents became anxious that land originally allocated for Dunlop's 'model factories' might be filled by less desirable activities. Yet some of the idealism invested in the original scheme remained alive among locals. PACAB listed education, 'benevolence', transport, drainage, open space, streets and clubs among its interests. It promised to publish a newspaper 'of a non-political and of a non-sectarian nature'.[29] Above all it was concerned that the Dunlop land would be 'subdivided in such a manner as to be detrimental to the rest of the district'.[30] On 1 January 1950 PACAB approached Brian Lewis to ask if he would use Beaumaris as a planning case history. Within a decade, Beaumaris boasted a scout hall, six-court tennis club, bowling club, two playgrounds and numerous streets of comfortable, large blocks of middle-class housing. Through local advocacy, lobbying and publicity, PACAB had helped to create a comfortable, amenity-rich suburb from the ruins of a projected model industrial town.

Meanwhile the Beaumaris Tree Preservation Society (established 1953)[31] was seeking to conserve the area's natural environment. Following in the footsteps of the Save the Dandenongs League established by retired kinder-garten teacher May Moon in 1950[32], the Society pressured local councils – particularly the City of Sandringham – to stop removing trees along the foreshore. 'Beaumaris or Bare-maris'? naturalist Crosbie Morrison asked in his regular *Argus* column in 1956. The pretty seaside suburb risked the fate suffered by country towns in which 'the bulldozer' was 'the first of the builder's tools. Row after row of bare boxes ... ugh!' Another supporter of the cause, architect Robin Boyd, 'judged Beaumaris to have ... preserved

---

28   W. A. Bartlett, Letter to J. S. Gawler, 22 November 1943, NAA Series A11677/1.

29   Parents and Citizens' Association of Beaumaris, *Planning in Beaumaris* (Beaumaris: The Association, 1960), npn.

30   Anon, 'Executive Grasped the Chance for Sound Town Planning' in Parents and Citizens' Association of Beaumaris, *Planning in Beaumaris*, npn.

31   Valerie Tarrant, *The Public Education Enterprise of the Port Phillip Conservation Movement 1965–75* (Master of Education Thesis, University of Melbourne, 1984), 10–11.

32   Anon, 'League for Preservation of Dandenongs' Melbourne *Age*, 10 May 1951, 2; Betty Hotchin, ed., *May Moon: A Conservation Pioneer* (Monbulk: Monbulk Historical Society, 1999).

more native foliage than any other suburb'.[33] The history of the Beaumaris Tree Preservation Society – later the Beaumaris Conservation Society – formed a bridge between the community activism of the 1940s and the environmental activism of the 1960s and 70s. By the 1960s it was mobilising the local community to resist new commercial incursion on the foreshore such as an 'Oceanarium' at Ricketts Point, a project apparently designed for 'captive penguins' and 'performing seals'.[34]

Local activism is a tender plant, subject to the vagaries of voluntary effort. Once its immediate objectives have been attained, it is prone to decline. In 1957 the Deepdene Progress Association disbanded. It had come into being to serve the interests of a middle-class area, a small sub-section of the old, wealthy suburb of Camberwell, but there was no longer any need of such an organisation: 'Members, past and present', it was reported, 'are well satisfied with their accomplishments, which has [sic] brought their district to a stage where they believe there is no longer any need for their association'.[35] Their experience confirms Mullins' observation that progress associations prosper only in developing regions. By the 1960s PACAB had seemingly reached a similar point when it presented the State Library of Victoria with a volume commemorating its achievements.

Cultural Antecedents: From Eltham to Carlton

When the suburbanites of Beaumaris battled to preserve their bushland, they were fighting for a lifestyle that combined rural and modern urban life. A decade before Carlton became a centre of the 'counter-culture', Eltham, twenty-seven kilometres from central Melbourne, had emerged as an alternative to conventional suburbia. 'There's no reason', writes Jenni Mitchell, 'why "bohemian" should necessarily be associated with inner-metropolitan areas, though these have provided the classic location, in popular mythology at least, for the lives of most bohemians'.[36] From the 1940s residents of the semi-rural outpost of Melbourne—mostly graziers, orchardists and townsfolk—were joined by an influx of artists, writers, academics and other unconventional types. The magnet for much of the bohemianism was Montsalvat, a mock-mediaeval castle built in the 1930s as the centre of an artists' colony led by Justus Jorgensen. 'Everything was

---

[33] Geoffrey Serle, *Robin Boyd: A Life* (Carlton: Miegunyah Press, 1995), 125.

[34] W. Ridland, 'Oceanarium at Ricketts Point' Melbourne *Age*, 7 July 1966, 2.

[35] Anon, 'Deepdene Progress Assoc. Disbands' *Outer Circle Mirror*, 17 December 1957, 5.

[36] Jenni Mitchell, 'Bohemia in Eltham' *Meanjin* 64 (1–2) (2005), 77–84.

built of mud-brick except for the Great Hall, which had bodgie-tudor beams made of gumtree logs painted black', jazz musician John Sangster recalls.[37] The personal and cultural links between Eltham and Carlton were strong. Filmmaker Tim Burstall saw Eltham as 'a rural Bloomsbury'; his wife Betty became the founder of La Mama, an experimental theatre off Lygon Street, Carlton, inspired by an off-Broadway New York theatre of the same name.[38] Tony Knox, son of Eltham architect and community activist Alistair Knox, turned the *Carlton News* into the *Melbourne Times* – the inner-city activists' newspaper of record. 'There was always activism in Eltham', he believed, characterising the area as an 'enclave of rejects from society, "the arties." Barry Humphries, another Melbourne Bohemian of the pre-Carlton era, recalled Eltham as a 'picturesque riverside hamlet where, in adobe houses amongst the eucalypts dwelt painters, potters and artistically minded and free thinking academics and civil servants'.

> Until the small hours the blaring gramophones filled the bush with the voices of Dylan Thomas, Lotte Lenya, Harry Belafonte and Bill Haley and his comets; frightening the wallabies and traumatising the kookaburras. Within the house, the flagon claret flowed as beard, sandals and sheepskin vest discussed Arthur Koestler, Jackson Pollock, Stan Frieberg, Saul Bellow and himself with a long-haired, chain-smoking, breast-feeding, unmarried ceramicist.[39]

Songwriter and bass player Greg Macainsh, who emerged from a 1950s–60s upbringing in Eltham and Warrandyte to attend Swinburne Film and Television School, became the creative force behind the 1970s rock group Skyhooks. Skyhooks debuted at St Jude's Hall, Carlton in 1973. Macainsh's first song was 'I Went Down To Eltham To Get Me A Job In A Band'. His more famous compositions include 'Carlton (Lygon Street Limbo)'.

What Was New?

The links between Eltham and Carlton, like those between the progress and preservation associations of the 1950s and the resident action groups of the 1960s and 70s, were often stronger than the inner-city activists

---

37 John Sangster, *Seeing the Rafters: The Life and Times of an Australian Jazz Musician* (Ringwood: Penguin, 1988), 37.

38 Alistair Knox, *We Are What We Stand On: A Personal History of the Eltham Community* (Eltham: Adobe Press, 1980), 76.

39 Barry Humphries, *More Please* (Ringwood: Viking, 1992), 176.

acknowledged. Yet many remained convinced that the 1960s had brought a shift in both the tempo and character of inner-city politics that was more than a matter of degree. When Barbara Niven, who would later become active in the Emerald Hill Association, moved from Beaumaris to Middle Park in 1969, she noticed a marked difference in the attitudes of residents in the two suburbs.

> I didn't like the community attitudes [in Beaumaris]. There was an active thing going on down there about a development at Ricketts Point and I got involved in that to some extent … but the attitudes of the people involved in the protest I thought were just dreadful. They were so completely self-interested and there was a kind of attitude towards anyone who might disagree with them on even the smallest detail that meant you were sort of on the social outer if you did that … Later on I realised it was characteristic of the kind of society that Beaumaris had at the time.

Her perspective contrasts with that of Val Tarrant who saw 'a significant number' of Beaumaris residents 'seeking … to educate the public, including relevant authorities' on wider issues. Niven had perhaps been born too late to experience the excitement of the PACAB's early days but Tarrant may have overlooked the core of self-interest that often overtook local activism after its first flourish.

Yet the differences between the urban politics of the 1950s and the 1960s and 70s were not simply a matter of generational perspective. Something different had entered the atmosphere of the city with the advent of the resident action groups. They were the response, not just to a new stage in the development of the city, but to new ideals and the arrival of a new generation of university-educated professionals attuned to international, as well as Australian, movements. If the activists looked back with disdain upon the suburbs from which they had come, it was not so much because of the limitations of the suburbs, or even of the organizations they had inherited, so much as the new possibilities which the inner city had inspired in them.

Chapter 2

A DECADE OF TURBULENCE

1965–1975

In the mid-1960s, Melbourne's inner suburbs entered a period of tumultuous change. The social and political movements of the era were both cause and effect of profound structural changes in the city's inner suburbs, a region that had been the focus of Australian manufacturing industry since the 1880s.

In 1965 the inner city's geography was still a recognisable product of the Victorian era of coal and steam and sweated labour. Large foundries and engineering works clustered in South Melbourne, Kensington and North Melbourne, shipyards and railway workshops near the port in West Melbourne and Port Melbourne while medium and smaller size textile, clothing, footwear and food producing industries gravitated to Carlton, Fitzroy, Richmond and Collingwood. Each locality had a distinct identity. People knew the Irish Catholic clans of Richmond, the wharf labourers of Port Melbourne, the slaughterers and packers in the Flemington-Kensington meatworks, indigenous casual labourers in Fitzroy, the boot and shoe workers of Collingwood and women home workers in the textile industry. Yet by 1975 this intertwining of work and social life had unravelled. The RAGs established over the decade in all the inner suburbs did not draw support from the factory workers or labourers of the inner suburbs but from new middle-class residents employed in service industries, public service, education, professional and financial firms, tertiary institutions and hospitals.

Turning Melbourne Inside Out

The inner city had begun to de-industrialise in earnest in the early postwar period when the northern, western and south-eastern suburbs of Melbourne attracted both new industries and old ones seeking to rebuild their plants and update machinery. Returned servicemen and their families, along with former inner-city workers, settled nearby. In the inner-city postwar migrants – men and women mainly from Greece, Italy and Yugoslavia who found employment in service positions, labouring, or working in older uncompetitive factories – were drawn to the low rents and cheap housing of the inner suburbs. Following the withdrawal of protective tariffs by the Whitlam ALP government in 1973 many of these factories closed as competition from the Asian region intensified. The inner suburbs of Sydney, Melbourne and Adelaide lost on average one third of their people, 'a total loss of well over a quarter of a million'.[1] In his aptly named book *Melbourne Remade* urban historian Seamus O'Hanlon describes this change as part of a global movement marking 'the end of the industrial age', a 'terrible decade for Western cities in which the collapse of manufacturing saw economic and social tensions rise'.[2]

This crisis in the inner suburbs led to increasing interest from governments and planners in the ambitious postwar programs of urban regeneration in the war scarred cities of Europe and Britain. There was also interest in urban renewal programs in the racially divided cities of America to rebuild downtown areas depleted by the move of population and employment to the suburbs. International experience suggested that Australia's two largest capital cities required modernisation through urban renewal to increase population densities in the central and inner-city areas. By increasing densities at the centre, policy makers hoped to contain 'urban sprawl' by discouraging the movement of households to the suburban fringe.

Proposals for the redevelopment of the CBD and inner areas had political support from the city councils of Sydney (SCC) and Melbourne (MCC), most inner-city municipal councils, from state governments and some welfare agencies. In Victoria the Liberal Country Party government led by Henry Bolte succeeded the ALP government led by John Cain in 1955. David Scott, former director of the Brotherhood of St Laurence (BSL), recalled the somewhat accidental circumstances that led the incoming government to embrace urban renewal:

> The Liberal Party became strongly committed to slum clearance and other things we'd recommended, not believing that they were likely to be in government for some time. Then there was the split in the Labor Party and so the Liberals found themselves in government ... with this

---

[1] Hal Kendig, *The Changing Role of the Inner Suburbs* (Canberra: Australian National University, Research School of Social Sciences, Urban Research Unit, 1977), 1.

[2] Seamus O'Hanlon with Tony Dingle, *Melbourne Remade: The Inner City since the 1970s* (Melbourne: Arcade Publications, 2010), 9.

recent and very strong commitment to doing something about getting on with the job of clearing slums.

Ten years later a Liberal Party government led by Robert Askin was elected in New South Wales on a similar platform for urban redevelopment of Sydney.

The planning infrastructure of Australian cities was ill-equipped to meet the growing pressure for development. The Commonwealth government's power over the planning of cities was limited to funding state infrastructure and housing projects through the National Investment Fund and the Commonwealth State Housing Agreement (CSHA). There was no national urban planning department or policy coordination except for a brief period from 1972–1975 when the Whitlam ALP government established the Department of Urban and Regional Development (DURD). Despite the concentration of population in capital cities there was little focused metropolitan planning by state governments. An analysis of the development pressures on Sydney during the boom period describes the city's planning as 'atrocious' and a major explanation for the rise of residents' associations and the widespread imposition of Green Bans by the New South Wales branch of the Builders Labourers' Federation (BLF).[3] The State Planning Authority of New South Wales was largely funded by levies on local government and did not have a strong metropolitan focus. Local councils had minimal planning capacity; this was true even of councils in areas under development pressure such as the City of Sydney and North Sydney.

Although it included the inner-city areas of Carlton, North and East Melbourne and parts of Kensington, South Yarra and Parkville, the Melbourne city council overwhelmingly represented the financial and retail interests of the CBD. Inner suburban councillors exerted little influence on decisions. 'It's just them sitting down there in the Town Hall with their knighthoods and us sitting up here wondering what they will do next', Carlton Association founder David Beauchamp recalled. Residents of the inner suburbs also had feeble representation on the Melbourne and Metropolitan Board of Works (MMBW), the water and sewerage authority which had become the city's main planning body following its 1954 Plan for Melbourne.[4] Although all metropolitan municipalities

---

3   Daly, *Sydney Boom, Sydney Bust*, 1.

4   Tony Dingle and Carolyn Rasmussen, *Vital Connections: Melbourne and Its Board of Works, 1891–1991* (Ringwood: McPhee Gribble, 1991).

appointed commissioners to the Board, the greater population and wealth of suburban councils outweighed the influence of inner-city commissioners. The representation of local government on the MMBW and the Board's increasing role in infrastructure provision and planning led to a tense relationship with the state government and Premier Bolte made several attempts to turn the Board into a commission. This relationship further deteriorated in 1966 after the appointment as MMBW chair of Alan Croxford, a lawyer who had been a commissioner for the Shire of Doncaster and Templestowe. Croxford moved quickly to expand the planning powers of the MMBW. In 1967 the Board published *Living City*, a substantial report on the future growth of Melbourne. Two years later the government released the *Melbourne Transportation Plan* outlining plans for an extensive freeway network, an underground city railway loop and new rail lines to Doncaster and Monash University.

A distinctive feature of Melbourne planning was the power wielded by the interlocking and often competing interests of special-purpose statutory authorities such as the MMBW, the SEC, the Harbour Trust, the Victorian Railways and especially the HCV and the Country Roads Board (CRB). Established during the era of 'state socialism', and run at arm's length from government, these authorities were repositories of great technical expertise, public trust and both formal and informal power. In the early twentieth century their heads, men like Sir John Monash, Sir Harold Clapp and Sir Ronald East, enjoyed as much prestige as state premiers. By the 1960s, however, these bodies had often become bureaucratic silos, unresponsive to democratic influences. They were predominantly staffed by men with a technical background, many of them returned servicemen.[5] The looming clash between the state bureaucrats and the inner-city trendies was grounded in the cultural divide between old-fashioned, hard-nosed technocrats and a younger generation of university-educated professionals attuned to ideals of personal self-discovery and democratic decision-making. The inner suburbs became their battlefield.

The state bureaucracies were often poorly equipped to meet the needs of the time. While HCV staff had expertise in tenant selection and management neither the HCV nor CRB had adequate capacity for economic and social impact planning. In keeping with their original function – building country roads – the engineers who ran the CRB were often country boys themselves,

---

5   Tony Dalton, 'Architects, Engineers and Rent Collectors: An Organisational History of the Commission' in *New Houses for Old*, 45–68.

educated in regional technical colleges.[6] The first CRB working group focused on urban roads was formed in the mid-1960s in response to increased traffic congestion in Melbourne and to design and build the Clifton Hill overpass but it had no capacity to evaluate the impact of projects. It was a similar story in other states. In 1970 engineer and economist Tom Hogg was appointed to the newly established Commonwealth Bureau of Roads (CBR) to undertake a cost benefit analysis of national road building programs. He found a 'fairly authoritarian culture' in the state road authorities, 'which were bastions of macho engineering, hard-edged, no-nonsense stuff and to say that some of them had delusions of grandeur would not be at all exaggerated'. It was a culture sympathetic to the large-scale development of American style urban freeways. As Hogg observes, road and freeway planning proceeded without cost-benefit analysis and without consideration of community impacts. It was not until the late 1960s that 'there was a growing social awareness in the wider community about social costs and benefits of whatever, not just road projects but the Housing Commission and government budgets and a whole range of things'.

The lack of coordination between three levels of government and the various statutory authorities bedevilled planning in Melbourne and in other capital cities. Brisbane City Council was the one municipality in Australia to represent almost an entire metropolitan area but its influence was limited by the autocratic powers of the state government of National Party Premier Joh Bjelke-Petersen (1968–1987). With a power-base in rural Queensland, the Nationals were often deaf to metropolitan interests. One indication of the low priority given to planning was that among the minor portfolios of Russ Hinze, Minister for Racing, were Local Government and Main Roads. This was the closest the government came to recognising planning as an area of state responsibility. The 'Colossus of Roads', the stoutly-built minister was also known, jocularly, as 'Minister for Everything'.

Conflicting Views

The largest urban renewal developments in Melbourne were undertaken by the HCV. In responding to the postwar need for public housing and with a waiting list of thousands, the HCV looked to overseas models for public housing provision. Following a tour of developments in America and Britain in 1958 the *Bulletin* reported that J. P. (Jack) Gaskin, deputy director

---

6   Graeme Davison with Sheryl Yelland, *Car Wars: How the Car Won Our Hearts and Conquered Our Cities* (Crows Nest: Allen and Unwin, 2004), 174–5.

of housing and Ray Burkitt, chief technical officer, had plans for 20 storey flats. 'Their reasons' it explained 'are very much the same as those given by all other public-housing authorities who have seen recent developments in America and Europe, that is locating maximum numbers of people in close proximity to services and employment. Multi storey flats are the only way of economically developing sites with high site values'.[7] The same *Bulletin* article also reported that 'the HCV has the building capacity for high rise residential flats'. In 1960 Chief Commissioner V J Bradley and F S Howell, manager of the Concrete Housing Project (CHP) travelled overseas to investigate the latest design and construction techniques for new multi-storey developments in Britain and Europe. The CHP had already successfully developed the modular concrete slabs initially produced to construct mass produced homes for building the HCV 3 and 4 storey walk-up flats. The CHP was now in the process of further developing its technical ability and capacity to build high-rise buildings with modular components produced at the Holmesglen factory.

These overseas visits influenced a change in HCV objectives. Following Gaskin's appointment as Director of Housing in 1966 the Commission's raison d'etre moved from slum reclamation to implementing a large-scale urban renewal agenda. An outcome of the 1958 Gaskin-Burkitt tour had been the building of 'mixed estates' on the British model which included both walk-up and high-rise flat buildings at a housing density of 200 persons per acre.[8] Planning for mixed estates in the early 1960s involved consultation with Melbourne architects Bernard Evans, Bates, Smart and McCutcheon and Leslie Perrott and Partners all of whom contributed to the design and development of HCV estates.[9] The Commission's experience that single tower developments did not provide sufficient density to be cost effective was confirmed by interstate examples such as the 10 storey tower at Rosebery designed by Harry Seidler for the NSW Housing Commission and the 10 storey Wandana flats at Subiaco, in Perth.

However, the mixed estates developed in 1962 and 1963 did not achieve the density benchmark of 200 people per acre and this together with the increasing costs of obtaining inner-city land led the HCV to develop high-rise only estates. There had been little new research on inner-suburban

---

7   *The Bulletin*, 18 March 1959, 7.

8   J. P. Gaskin and R. Burkitt, 'Report on Some Aspects of Housing Overseas' (Melbourne, HCV, 1959).

9   Peter Mills, *Refabricating the Towers*, 167.

housing since Barnett's prewar report and the Commission instigated a review in 1965 by two of its architects, Graham Shaw and J. H. Davey, to identify areas for demolition and redevelopment. The Shaw-Davey review recommended the demolition of 1000 acres of inner-suburban housing.[10] Perhaps unfairly dubbed 'the second gear windscreen survey' – it was mainly undertaken by car – the report was nevertheless an inadequate research basis for the large-scale redevelopment program planned by the Commission.

The HCV moved rapidly to reclaim large areas of inner-city land for slum clearance. By the beginning of 1965 six reclamation projects were under way and ten high-rise towers were under construction including 20 storey blocks at the Debney Park estate, 22 storey blocks at the Carlton estate and the 32 storey Emerald Hill Tower on Park Street, South Melbourne. By 1969 the HCV claimed to have acquired some 251 acres 'of run down obsolete housing and had created open space and rehoused elderly and families'.[11] This scale of demolition and redevelopment had not been envisaged in the 1930s Barnett study which had recommended the redevelopment of carefully selected 'slum pockets' and the relocation of families in suitable accommodation. Not long before his death the 85-year-old Barnett attended a conference held to mark the opening of the 32 storey Park Towers in South Melbourne and perceptively noted that the HCV pioneers had been 'more concerned with social issues' whereas the HCV of the late 1960s were 'engineers and builders – very efficient ones. They've gone in for highrise. Our thinking was for homes'.[12] Architectural and engineering consultants had contributed to the design and construction of Melbourne's tallest multi storey residential building and the Park Towers development was the pride of the HCV. As the lift doors opened on the executive floor of the Commission's headquarters in central Melbourne, visitors were confronted with an illuminated model of Park Towers in a glass case. On its completion a ring of HCV high-rise flats dominated Melbourne's low density inner-city landscape.

This extensive development of inner-city high-rise public housing estates was a Melbourne phenomenon, its rapidity made possible by the CHP modular construction techniques. The South Australian Housing Trust's inner-city redevelopments were medium-density in scale. The NSWHC built some high-rise towers well before Victoria but increasingly preferred

---

[10]   Anne Tyson, *Activism, Conservation and Residents' Associations* (Master of Public History Thesis, Monash University, 2000), 5.

[11]   Mills, *Refabricating the Towers*, 293.

[12]   Renate Howe, *The Inaugural F. Oswald Barnett Oration: Housing and the Church; A Vision and Challenge* (Melbourne: Ecumenical Housing Inc., 1994), 21.

more family-friendly medium-density developments and the building of large suburban housing estates to the south and west of the city.[13] Sociologist Michael Jones found that NSWHC tenants preferred suburban villas to high-rise flats, that it was cheaper to house low-income families in the suburbs than pay the heavy costs of requisitioning land in the inner city, that block clearing destroyed many houses in good condition and that manufacturing jobs were moving from the inner to the outer suburbs.[14] The same was true of Victoria but Jones' research was vehemently rejected by the HCV.

The appearance of high-rise towers looming over the city's low-rise inner suburbs provoked a strong public reaction. More than any other single factor, it goaded local residents into action. 'Fucking monster blocks went up', journalist and student activist Pete Steedman recalled, 'and I think it was only when a couple of them went up that people suddenly realised, shit, what this was doing and people started to have an understanding'. HCV renewal projects became local battlegrounds. By 1965 the North Melbourne Association (NMA) had led protests over the high-rise development at Debney Park while the Carlton Association (CA) vigorously opposed de-velopment of the Carlton estate, the densest at 267 persons per acre.[15] Opposition to large-scale HCV redevelopment in Fitzroy of four 20 storey blocks at Atherton Gardens in 1969 and in Richmond led directly to the formation of RAGs in those suburbs.

These battles crystallised conflicting views about the future of the inner suburbs. Melbourne's planning authorities were convinced they needed to be modernised to overcome the twin problems of de-industrialisation and de-population. The MMBW's *Living City* (1967) predicted that inner Melbourne was on the American path to becoming an area of poverty, neglect and decay. The HCV's high-rise flats aimed to reverse this trend by boosting the supply of labour and low-cost housing. However, these policies misread the nature of changes in the inner city. A study of change in Australia's three largest cities by Hal Kendig underlined the differences between Australian experience and that of Britain and America, especially the more rapid suburbanisation of residences, shopping and industry and

---

[13]   Renate Howe, 'Housing Commissions' in *The Encyclopedia of Australian Architecture*, ed. Philip Goad and Julie Willis (Port Melbourne: Cambridge University Press, 2012), 343–344.

[14]   Michael A. Jones, *Housing and Poverty in Australia* (Carlton: Melbourne University Press, 1972).

[15]   Mills, *Refabricating the Towers*, 290.

related freeway construction in American cities. Australian cities were not afflicted with the concentration of social problems and disinvestment in American cities. They had nothing like the huge burden of deteriorated housing that Britain had inherited from the war years. Kendig concluded that Australian 'inner areas have neither declined nor stagnated' and that 'there was no evidence of dramatic increases in vacancy rates that would suggest the American experience of abandonment of housing'.[16]

There was frustration that the rapid development of high-rise public housing towers in Melbourne took place just when they were being abandoned elsewhere. By 1965 the Robert Taylor homes on the near north side of Chicago, which had impressed the HCV visitors in 1958, were recognised as a social disaster, while the high-rise public housing developments lining State Street on the south side of the city were the focus of racial riots in 1966. Overcrowded with black immigrants from the south they were popularly regarded as 'ghettos'. In Britain two classical sociological studies by Michael Young and Peter Wilmott contrasted the supportive networks of family and neighbourhoods in London's East End neighbourhood of Bethnal Green with the more alienated lives of those uprooted and transplanted to the new industrial suburb of Dagenham. The HCV seemed impervious to the mounting evidence that 'slum clearance and the concept of redeveloping large areas of housing (read: bulldozing them) was an utter disaster'.[17] Peter Hollingworth observed that 'in 1967–68 when the Fitzroy estate was being developed they were already demolishing them in New York, an example of how action can be ten years behind the world trends, yet still not learn from the mistakes of overseas'. In 1971 Melbourne *Herald* reporter John Sorell conducted a rare interview with Jack Gaskin, now HCV Chief Commissioner, described as an ex-builder 'big, tough, forthright, aggressive'. 'I know I'm doing the right thing,' Gaskin insisted. 'I am proud of my flats'. He acknowledged that overseas the trend had changed – 'they are not putting them up in other cities at the rate of a few years ago' – and that the HCV was now considering more terrace house type development which, he admitted, 'reflects a slight change in our thinking'. Nevertheless, he insisted, 'our campaign to rid Melbourne of its slums will continue'.[18]

---

[16]   Hal Kendig, *New Life for Old Suburbs: Post War Land Use and Housing in the Australian Inner City* (Sydney: Allen and Unwin, 1979), 8.

[17]   Amos Rappaport, 'Surgery for the Slum' *The Australian*, 5 June 1972, 6.

[18]   John Sorrell, 'He's Proud to Reshape Our City' Melbourne *Herald*, 18 August 1971, 7.

His perspective was not shared by the new young, diverse workforce attracted by cheap property prices and employment opportunities in the inner city, who marked a cultural generational shift from the view of inner-city decline held by the postwar generation leaders in politics and public administration.

Who Were the Activists?

Melbourne's residents' associations inherited a tradition of local activism, grounded in the city's political past. Observers as different as Vincent Buckley and Manning Clark had sought to define the blend of religious social and literary influences that had contributed to its distinctive liberal, democratic political culture. The men and women who made up the resident action groups were often tertiary educated; in most cases they had worked, lived or studied overseas, usually in the US and Britain, and travelled in continental Europe. The radical traditions of the inner suburbs, the stamping grounds of the trade unions and the Australian Labor Party, were among their attractions. In his study of political change in Balmain, Tony Harris emphasises the 'political aspects to the shifts of the complex assortment of largely tertiary educated individuals who began to rent or buy the old worker housing of inner-city suburbs from the 1960s, aspects located in the historical context of political radicalisation and social movement activism'.[19] Caroline Hogg, who had studied at the University of Adelaide, where she 'managed to get myself involved in the only demonstration that occurred in the four years I was there', had no sooner arrived in Melbourne than she recognised the relative strength of political activism. Her participation in demonstrations against capital punishment and the Vietnam War led on to wider social and political involvements.

The resident action of the 1960s and 70s grew out of earlier protest movements, especially the anti-nuclear and peace marches organised by groups such as the Congress for International Cooperation and Disarmament in the late 1950s and by Student Action, a coalition of student groups formed in 1961. Demonstrations opposing Australia's involvement in the Vietnam War gathered momentum following the introduction of 'ballot-box' conscription in the late 1960s and spawned street marches, radical newspapers and sit-ins. The largest anti-Vietnam War demonstration in Australia, the first Moratorium, was held in Melbourne in 1970, when over 100,000 participated in the Collins Street march and sit-in.

---

[19]   Tony Harris, *Basket Weavers and True Believers*, 4.

The protest movements of the late 1960s and 70s drew their inspiration from diverse sources, ranging from Freudian psychology to liberationist Marxism, and from Reich's *The Greening of America* to Mao's *Little Red Book*. A decade earlier, however, in the era of JFK's New Frontier and the anti-hanging and anti-Apartheid campaigns, students were often taking their cue from a very different range of sources, theological as often as political. Their heroes were the apostles of non-violence, such as Gandhi and Martin Luther King. Many were inspired by a rush of books urging the engagement of churches with inner-city poverty and powerlessness such as the American theologian Harvey Cox's *The Secular City* (1967) or *Only One Way Left* (1956) by George McLeod, the Glasgow-based Church of Scotland minister and founder of the Iona Community.[20] In a study of the North Melbourne Association, David Moloney identifies two developments that led to its formation in 1966 – the threat to local communities posed by the advent of a new type of high-rise, high density redevelopment and the leadership provided by the emerging social activism among local Protestant churches. Their influence was apparent in the numbers of clergy and laity among influential members of the association. Annual meetings of the NMA continued to be held at the North Melbourne Methodist Mission until 1981.[21] Many of the leaders and members of residents' associations, especially in Richmond, Fitzroy and Collingwood were ministers and laity influenced by new theological trends and new directions for ministry in Britain and America. Peter Hollingworth, who was actively involved in urban issues following his appointment to the North Melbourne Anglican parish in the early 1960s, and later at the BSL in Fitzroy, had visited housing estates in London and New York and Chicago's Ecumenical Institute in 1966. He had returned to Melbourne 'understanding the importance of urban theology, urban mission, urban renewal and how you relate that ministry to the whole issue of justice and change'. Andrew McCutcheon's experience as an assistant at George McLeod's church in the Gorbals area of Glasgow inspired the direction of his community-based ministry in Collingwood. Clergymen, it has sometimes been observed, often assume the role of protectors or enablers of local community. Several of those who took the lead in inner-city activism would later become leaders in a wider sphere.

---

20 Harvey Cox, *The Secular City* (New York: Macmillan Company, 1967); George Macleod, *Only One Way Left* (Glasgow: Iona Community, 1956).

21 David Moloney, 'The North Melbourne Association, 1966–1984: An Introduction' (Honours Thesis, Melbourne University History Department, 1984), 3.

The first generation of Australians to enjoy the benefits of state-funded higher education were also the first to experience the benefits of relatively cheap foreign travel. Going to Europe or America was as much a part of their education as the lectures they listened to or the books they read.[22] For young women especially, these experiences had a transformative effect. It inspired new ideals of neighbourhood and community, and nourished the leadership skills and capacity to realise them. Kaye Oddie of the NMA observed that 'a lot of these people had lived overseas, because it was just the normal thing to go overseas once you got your degree, so people had got that very strong feeling of living in close communities from overseas and liked it'. Women composed the majority of resident association members, not only in Melbourne but also in New York, Toronto and Sydney. Melbourne women's participation in the RAGs built on a long-standing tradition of women's leadership in local council politics, schools and churches. The new model of community participation was influenced by the emerging women's movement in Melbourne and changed views of women's activism in communities and families, especially relevant to the many RAGs members who were women with young families.[23]

Although sparsely represented in the official leadership of residents' associations, women activists did not feel gender discrimination by male office bearers. Ann Polis of the Carlton Association recalled that 'I actually didn't feel anything like that [discrimination]. It was really odd you know'. Kaye Oddie 'never got the feeling that there was any kind of difference. Perhaps that was a sign of the times. Perhaps that was a sign of the fact that a lot (of RAG members) were professionals working in universities where there was less discrimination'. If not office bearers, women found their role in running most of the organisational side of the associations and protests, both influential and satisfying.

The urban activists of this decade were a new generation drawn to the physical and social environment of the inner city for a diversity of reasons. A desire to be free of the constraints associated with Melbourne's postwar 'cream brick' suburban ethos perceived as restrictive, conforming and

---

22   Graeme Davison, 'Tourists, Expats and Invisible Immigrants: Being Australian in Britain in the 1960s' in *Australians in Britain: The Twentieth Century Experience*, ed. Carl Bridge, Robert Crawford and David Dunstan (Monash University ePress, 2009), 1–14.

23   Renate Howe, "Nobody but a Bunch of Mothers': Grassroots Activism and Women's Leadership in 1970s Melbourne' in *Australian Women Leaders in Politics, Workplaces and Communities*, ed. Rosemary Francis, Patricia Grimshaw and Ann Standish (The University of Melbourne: eScholarship Research Centre, 2012), 331–340.

dominated by traditional gender roles was, arguably, a push factor. More intangible factors also influenced those early residents who chose to live in run-down suburbs with few community facilities, dilapidated houses without modern conveniences and neighbours with whom they had little in common. For many, residence was a commitment – a commitment driven by a mixture of ideals and aspirations aimed at protecting the heritage of the built environment, tackling conditions of poverty and disadvantage and valuing the community and radical political traditions of the inner suburbs. In the end, most decisions were driven by the usual reasons for urban location choice – affordability, employment, and convenience. The importance of property investment as an influence on inner-city location choice came to prominence towards the end of this decade.

Urban Renewal

The growing momentum of social and economic changes in the inner city intersected with plans by the Bolte government for large-scale urban renewal. In 1969 Ray Meagher, the Minister for Housing, introduced legislation into the Victorian parliament appointing the HCV as the Urban Renewal Authority for Melbourne. During debates on the bill, Meagher stated that the HCV had been selected as the urban development authority over the MMBW as there was no difference between slum clearance and urban renewal. Architecture lecturer Miles Lewis, who acted for the residents' associations in monitoring the bill, was critical of its failure to distinguish between the provision of low-income housing and urban renewal and also of the lack of adequate provision for public participation. Although there was provision for the appointment of an advisory committee, Lewis described the appointees as unlikely to represent community interests.

In revolting against the plans to 'modernise' the inner city, Melbourne's urban activists were joining an international trend. An influential and well known critique of modernist development was Jane Jacobs' book, *The Death and Life of Great American Cities*, based in large part on her experience as leader of a citizens movement to save New York's Greenwich Village from the redevelopment proposals of the New York Port Authority under the leadership of Robert Moses. The book was widely read not only in the USA but also around the world and 'became an inspiration, guidebook and bible for not only a new generation of planners but ordinary citizens as well'.[24]

---

[24]   Anthony Flint, *Wrestling with Moses: How Jane Jacobs Took On New York's Master Builder and Transformed the American City* (New York: Random House, 2009), 129.

For Jacobs, urban renewal was 'not the rebuilding of cities but the sacking of cities'. Like the East End London studies, she recognised the importance of close-grained 'organic' urban communities in providing social advantages such as networks of friends and relatives, access to transport and low rents. She advanced a new view of planning based on communities and networks and respecting the historic built environment. Jacobs' ideas on the importance of preserving and rehabilitating traditional urban neighbourhoods inspired Melbourne's inner-city residents opposed to the HCV's urban renewal program.

Within the fortress of the Housing Commission, the modernisers grew increasingly resentful of the well-organised, but in their eyes misguided and self-interested opposition of the residents' associations. In early 1970, Ray Burkitt, former Chief Technical Officer and now a Commissioner, accepted an invitation from the Carlton Association to debate the urban renewal program. Renate Howe recalls the meeting was held at the Carlton Methodist Mission (later the Church of all Nations) in Palmerston Street under the shadows of the high-rise towers on the Carlton estate. The CA was represented by George Tibbits, lecturer in architecture at the University of Melbourne and with a growing public profile for his opposition to the HCV program. Neatly attired in a grey suit, Tibbets read in measured tones from carefully prepared speaking notes. Ray Burkitt, son-in-law of Oswald Barnett, was as much a product of Melbourne's tradition of liberal reform as those he confronted. He saw himself as a link with the founding aspirations of the HCV and believed urban renewal, by replacing old housing with new, was in the Barnett tradition: new neighbourhoods and new communities would be rebuilt in inner areas. Despite the high density necessitated by economics the new flats would be an improvement on slum life for the elderly and for families. Harking back to the rhetoric of his father-in-law, he concluded with a description of the shocking living conditions in the reclaimed area compared with the improved accommodation for those resettled in the new flats.

For his part, Tibbits argued that high-rise estates housing low-income residents would be the 'slums of the future' pointing to examples in American and British cities. Melbourne did not need them and, taking a page from Jacobs, they would destroy the inner-city fabric and disrupt community networks. He questioned Burkitt's view that existing inner-city housing would continue to decay and was not worth repairing, pointing to signs of regeneration in Carlton such as the building of flats by private developers and the renovation of houses by migrant families and new residents. Tibbits argued that the HCV-forced resumption of housing in reclamation areas denied home owners their basic rights and that migrant home owners who had undertaken extensive DIY renovations had been especially harshly treated. The inner city would regenerate naturally and urban renewal was unnecessary.

The exchange encapsulated opposing and irreconcilable views on the future of the inner city. To the audience of Carlton and inner-city residents there was no doubt of the verdict. Tibbits' presentation was received with acclamation while Burkitt angrily accused the audience of having an unrealistic and romantic view of the inner city gained from reading claret-stained copies of Jane Jacobs' book.

These two irreconcilable views were fundamental to many battles over the future of the inner areas of Melbourne during the turbulent decade of urban transformation. However, although not represented by the speakers at this meeting, there was an influential third view developing and later articulated by reform-minded local government councillors, NGOs and within the residents' associations. This view favoured neither large-scale 'slum' clearance nor unfettered market-led regeneration but advocated planned urban regeneration sponsored by government that built on the obvious strengths of the inner suburbs such as location, population diversity and a strong sense of community.

Chapter 3

PATRICIANS, TRENDIES AND RADICALS

THE UNIVERSITY AND URBAN ACTIVISM

The middle-class professionals who led the movement into the inner city seldom anticipated, or even welcomed, its results. Yet the 'trendies', as they were called, set trends that captured the imagination of later generations. Radical experiments in community living and grassroots politics matured into fashionable 'lifestyles'. The 'alternative' became 'mainstream'. The current landscape of the inner cities, dominated by university graduates, Green voters and secular humanists, is the legacy of a cultural revolution led by the trendies, the first generation of Australians to enjoy the benefits of mass higher education. 'It was a time of great hope', Fitzroy activist Jane Lennon recalls. 'We thought we were very privileged, us Commonwealth Scholarship students, first in our families to go to uni and I think we had this great sense, well I did … that we were going to take on and save things and create a new order'. In the 1960s and 70s the universities were transformed from privileged enclaves to centres of social criticism and experiment, a revolution in outlook that also changed the relationship between the university and its environs.

By the 1960s, the waves of European immigrants drawn to the inner city by low rents and unskilled factory employment had been joined in the suburbs closest to the campus by students unable or unwilling to find accommodation in colleges and hostels, the traditional places of student residence. Inhabiting and adapting its nineteenth-century streets and terrace housing, the migrants had modelled patterns of community living that began to influence others alert to the possibility of more 'urbane' ways of life. Meanwhile the pressures of growth were forcing the university to expand into the adjoining suburbs, generating conflict with local residents, including its own students and staff.

The university also provided much of the intellectual capital required to re-make the inner suburbs. It transmitted and adapted international models of urban living. It provided the professional expertise in architecture, planning, history and sociology required to challenge outmoded political and bureaucratic structures. And it acted as an informal power-base for a new style of resident politics. There was no single model for these engagements. Each university and suburb developed its own style of urban activism, shaped by the ethos of the suburb as well as the ideologies and interests of those who came to live there.

In this chapter we explore these relationships, seeking to understand how changes on the campus influenced urban activism in the surrounding suburbs, particularly in Melbourne. By the early 1970s, the politics of the inner suburbs had become a subject of academic analysis. In one of the keenest contemporary appraisals, Sydney sociologist Andrew Jacubowicz portrayed the 'cosmopolitan lifestyle' of the inner suburbs as the creation of a 'new class' of university-educated professionals and of their search for 'a place with a particular image which encompasses both the physical structure and design, and the sorts of people with whom they like to associate'.[1]

Jacubowicz's emphasis on image, urban design and peer influence captures the salient characteristics of the 'trendy'. Assumed rather than stated in Broderick's caricature, quoted in the introduction to this book, is the trendies' adherence to intellectual as well as material fashions, and to the life of the campus as well as the art studio. The influence of the university on the society and politics of the inner suburbs went deeper, however, than fashion or lifestyle. The inspiration for urban change often came from abroad, as Australians pondered the relevance of European and American models of urbanity to the Australian context. Each new theory or technique was adapted and tested against local conditions. In the following pages, we sketch three patterns of activism we call, for heuristic purposes, the patrician, the trendy and the radical. Each was shaped by particular ideas, social groups and academic disciplines and flourished in distinctive inner-city locales. In practice these patterns often merged and overlapped with each other. They represent tendencies within a more general movement rather than distinct forms.

---

[1]   Andrew Jakubowicz, 'The Ideology of Urban Change' *Ekstasis*, no. 4 (December 1972), 8.

Town and Gown

The relationship between the city and the university – between 'town and gown', as it was traditionally known – had long been problematic. Academics had often aspired to the quiet and seclusion of the cloister, and held aloof from the town. Yet from the beginning the spirit of the Australian universities had been more utilitarian than their European counterparts. Melbourne's nickname 'The Shop' captured something of its ethos. The first universities were located on the perimeter of the capital cities: Sydney (1850) about two kilometres south of the centre of town, between Glebe and Newtown; Melbourne (1853) a little further to the north of its CBD between Carlton and Parkville; Adelaide (1874) on North Terrace, alongside some of the city's other main cultural institutions. The younger foundations of Tasmania (1890), Queensland (1909) and Western Australia (1911) began in modest premises in their central business districts but later moved to park-like campuses in the suburbs: Western Australia to Crawley in 1932, Queensland to St Lucia in 1938 and Tasmania to Sandy Bay from the early 1960s.

While the physical distance between the older universities and the city remained small, the social distance was greater. Until 1938 the Melbourne campus was encircled by an iron fence, 'It stands in a green oasis in a somewhat unfashionable inner suburb', the philosophy professor A Boyce Gibson observed, 'but its grounds are large enough to save it from its environment, and have, hitherto, sufficed for all expansions, as well as to accommodate seven professors' houses'.[2] Adding to the sense of academic seclusion were the denominational colleges ringing the campuses along Melbourne's College Crescent and Sydney's Carillon Avenue. Unlike Oxford and Cambridge, where students lived in college, most Australian students were day-trippers forced, as Boyce Gibson noted, to live 'between two worlds, separated by the daily purgatory of train or tram'. In the eyes of traditionalists, the college, with its Gothic revival architecture and quasi-parental discipline and tradition, offered a bridge between the infant world of home and school and the adult world of business and the professions. As late as 1960, Dimity Reed recalls, 'the university was a contained thing ... gracious and green'.[3]

---

2   A. Boyce Gibson, 'To Birmingham from Melbourne' *Birmingham Gazette*, 2 July 1938, University of Melbourne news cuttings, UMA 73/9.

3   Dimity Reed, 'Carlton – A Memory' in *Carlton: A History*, ed. Peter Yule (Melbourne: Melbourne University Press, 2004), 137.

The Crowded Campus

The first breach in the container occurred soon after the war when exservicemen and women, sponsored through the Commonwealth Reconstruction Scheme, arrived on the campus. Older, more worldly, and often more critical of their society, they were a restless presence among the callow school-leavers. In 1945 the the University of Melbourne Student Representative Council, under the leadership of Ian Turner, a Communist, established a student hostel in a de-licensed pub in proletarian Fitzroy. Amirah Gust, who would become Turner's wife, remembered it as 'the place for parties, meetings and assignations'. 'For me', she wrote, 'it became a home from home'. Hurrying back to her parents' house in Elwood along broken streets lined with decrepit houses, dingy shops and unkempt gardens, and frequented by drunks and prostitutes, she experienced both the fear and thrill of life on the city's wild side.[4] Her friend and fellow communist Stephen Murray-Smith rented a loft above an old stable just south of Grattan Street, where the campus adjoined a neighbourhood identified by a 1937 housing inquiry as a slum. 'The Loft, in its glory, was entered through a hole in the floor, a hole through which a policeman's helmet once rose slowly during a noisy party', he recalled. Like an artist's garret, the loft, with its cobwebs, tiny windowpanes and homemade bookcase was a symbol of privation in the cause of revolutionary purity. By the late 1950s, however, as the pressure for residential accommodation on the campus grew stronger, the numbers of students resorting to 'Carlton's damp and cheerless lodgings' (as Geoffrey Blainey described them) began to grow.

Between 1957, when the Murray Commission system recommended a major expansion in the university system, and 1972, the student populations of Australia's two oldest universities approximately doubled.[5] In 1964 the University of Melbourne's Student Housing Board reported that about a quarter of the student population lived away from home during term but less than one-eighth had access to supervised accommodation in a college or hostel, a similar proportion to Sydney's students.[6] Most of the overflow occupied rooms or shared houses in Carlton and Parkville, Newtown and

---

[4] Amirah Inglis, *The Hammer & Sickle and the Washing Up: Memories of an Australian Woman Communist* (South Melbourne: Hyland House, 1995), 22–3.

[5] John Poynter and Carolyn Rasmussen, *A Place Apart, The University of Melbourne: Decades of Challenge* (Melbourne: Melbourne University Press, 1996).

[6] Compare University Senate, Preliminary Report of the Committee to survey and report on students' living arrangements compared by Prof. A. P. Elkin, Senate Minutes 7 June 1965, University of Sydney Archives.

Glebe, often under conditions that, according to Melbourne's student counsellor Ray Priestley, threatened their physical and mental health. 'They become particularly vulnerable to the temptations of the bottle, the pep pill, and in extreme cases to the dope pedlar', he warned. Despite the fears of university authorities few of the students considered themselves at risk. 'So many students have now fended for themselves in flats and sub-divided houses that many speak in favour of such independence', the board admitted.[7]

Until the mid-1960s, undergraduates living at home with their families generally remained satisfied with their lot, but five years later a survey revealed that more than half preferred to live away from home if they could. Thirty-nine percent said they would prefer to live with parents (about fifty-five percent actually did), eighteen percent in college or hostel and twenty-five percent in a private flat or house. If cost were not a factor, however, the numbers wishing to stay at home fell to thirteen percent, while those preferring college rose to thirty percent, and flats and houses to about thirty percent (twenty-two percent had no definite preference).[8] 'Too many students live at home with their parents out in the suburbs', a Melbourne law student declared. 'I think they have to get right away from their parents in order to think for themselves'.[9] The university's Housing Officer, Beth Robieson, had noticed a definite shift in student preferences.

> Five years ago when I first interviewed freshers who were not going into some form of supervised residence it was apparent that they themselves usually felt the need of a substitute for home. But needs can change in the short span of five years. Today's young people entering university are far more independent and self-reliant. Above all they want to live where they can associate freely with fellow students.[10]

'The college has lost out to Carlton', the political scientist Graham Little noted in a contemporary study of Melbourne undergraduates. The group house, rather than the college or the flat, had become 'the favoured style'. Students expressed 'a quite specific idealism about what is wanted: an ideal of community. Of living together somewhat separate (in one's room) but joined

---

7   Minutes of the University of Melbourne Student Housing Board, 30 July 1965, University of Melbourne Archives.

8   D. S. Anderson, *Carlton Redevelopment Survey*, July 1965, University of Melbourne Archives.

9   Ben Boer, 'What digs?' *Farrago*, 1 May 1970.

10   Beth Robieson to Chair, Student Housing Board, 23 February 1970, Student Housing, University of Melbourne Archives.

in mutual knowing and exploration'. The university, he argued, mirrored a much broader change in attitudes towards greater self-determination and self-realisation.[11] The openness to experience, to intellectual and social difference, to communal values and shared living, first articulated in relation to the student house, would later – with necessary adaptations – shape their ways of inhabiting the inner city.

Beyond the Campus

At the moment when students were looking beyond the campus and the college to spread their wings, the university was also seeking breathing space. In 1960 the 50-acre (20 hectare) rectangle of the University of Melbourne's campus was land-locked on all four sides. To the west, wedged between the leafy boulevard of Royal Parade and Flemington Road, close by the Royal Melbourne Hospital, was the tiny, somewhat exclusive residential enclave of Parkville. To the south, beyond Grattan Street, the precincts of the University merged into the commercial and industrial outskirts of the CBD. To the east, across Swanston Street, the university adjoined the area's main shopping street, Lygon Street, which was already beginning to acquire its present character as Melbourne's 'Little Italy'. Further east and extending south were the terraces and cottages along and behind Drummond, Rathdowne and Canning streets, the centre of the emerging student city of boarding, rooming and group houses. College Crescent, the northern perimeter of the campus, took its name from the denominational colleges, home to a privileged minority of undergraduates and to an older, usually less privileged, group of theological students. Further north, beyond the Melbourne General Cemetery, lay the still-ungentrified streets of North Carlton and Princes Hill.

In its submission to the Murray inquiry, the university had argued that it simply could not accommodate the expected influx of students on its already crowded Parkville campus. It had considered and rejected a scheme to construct a ribbon of high-rise buildings along its borders, arguing that the student population should be pegged at 10,000 and that urgent consideration must be given to the establishment of a new university to accommodate the overflow.[12] A decade later, however, after the opening of Monash and

---

[11]   Graham Little, *Faces on the Campus: A Psycho-Social Study* (Carlton: Melbourne University Press, 1975), 4, 137, 235.

[12]   Poynter and Rasmussen, *A Place Apart*, 174; Graeme Davison and Kate Murphy, *University Unlimited: The Monash Story* (St Leonards: Allen and Unwin, 2012), 3–6.

La Trobe, the situation was no better. The University was 'a community of 15,000 crowded into a jumble of buildings, from tin huts to skyscrapers, that covers almost every square foot of the original site, and spills into the surrounding area'.[13] The pressure to find living space was becoming urgent.

Parkville Patricians

First to feel the pressure was the dormitory suburb of Parkville. During the Second World War officers from the nearby American base at Camp Pell in Royal Park had taken over flats and houses in the area and the opening of the nearby Royal Melbourne Hospital had further swelled the demand for accommodation. Some owners took the opportunity to move out to the eastern suburbs and convert the spacious terraces into guesthouses for students. 'Colourful Parkville has flavour of Bohemia', a 1948 profile of the area began, claiming that 'many a thesis' had been written in its 'garrets'.[14] In the first of several spot-purchases, the University acquired a block of flats on the corner of Morrah and Park Streets for staff accommodation. By 1960, about thirty academics and a similar number of students appeared on the local electoral roll. They included several professors: educationalist George Browne, botanist Brian Capon, physiologist Douglas ('Panzee') Wright and architect Brian Lewis, as well as a number of lecturers and demonstrators clustering in the suburb's two widest and most attractive streets, The Avenue and Park Drive.

With the rapid expansion of the University, the pressure on its traditional dormitory suburb became intense. Already near saturation point, the number of academic residents increased only marginally over the decade. In 1965 fifteen students shared a Royal Parade terrace house with one single tiny bathroom. 'This a shocking place to live in', a 20-year old woman student admitted, 'but accommodation at anything approaching reasonable terms is so hard to come by, that I can't afford to be thrown out'. In July of that year the University floated plans to acquire 65 acres of land in Parkville and Carlton, the suburbs designated for university expansion under the 1954 metropolitan planning scheme.[15] Two years later a scheme to resume

---

13 Carlton Redevelopment Scheme, Draft Report to Planning Consultants, 1965, David Saunders papers, 73/1 University of Melbourne Archives.

14 Jack Richards, 'Colourful Parkville has Flavour of Bohemia' Melbourne *Argus Weekend Magazine*, 11 September 1948, 2.

15 Anon, 'Varsity "must buy more land"' Melbourne *Age*, 8 July 1965, 7; Anon, 'Housing Minister's Tour' Melbourne *Age*, 16 July 1965, 3.

Ievers Reserve, a wedge of green space between Gatehouse Street and Park Drive, for redevelopment, prompted local residents, led by defence scientist Stan Dean, social administrator Eric Benjamin and architects Brian and Hilary Lewis and David Saunders, to form the Parkville Association.

The Lewises had met in Liverpool in the early 1930s where Australian-born Brian and English-born Hilary were students in the school of civic design founded by the famous town planner Patrick Abercrombie. During the war Hilary worked on Abercrombie's 1944 Greater London Plan and after their return to Australia in 1947, when Brian became professor of architecture at the University of Melbourne, she arranged for Abercrombie to visit Melbourne on a lecture tour. They lived in Parkville – the nearest Melbourne afforded to the kind of urban residential neighbourhoods they had known in England – and, along with other Melbourne academics, became founding members of the Victorian branch of the National Trust in 1958. Saunders, a student and defender of terrace house architecture, had built his own modern terrace house in Gatehouse Street, backing onto the threatened Ievers Reserve.

In 1970 a more formidable threat appeared when 89 houses in Storey and Morrah Streets were slated for demolition to provide University High School with playing fields to replace those marked for confiscation by the hospital. Once again the Parkvillians sprang to the defence of their 'delightful suburb'.[16] A detailed illustrated book, *South Parkville*, written and illustrated by Hilary and including advice from cast-iron decoration expert Dr E Graeme Robertson, persuaded the National Trust to classify the entire suburb. A prototype of other local 'heritage studies', like Bernard and Kate Smith's *The Architectural Character of Glebe Sydney* (1973), the book evoked the historical interest, architectural taste and social exclusivity of the area. After being 'entertained by a charming hostess in a delightful Parkville home with a carefully chosen group of residents', the responsible state minister aborted the redevelopment scheme and Parkville was saved.[17]

Long-time Parkville Association stalwart Norah Killip personifies the patriarchal sense of history that binds this 'pretty, convenient community'. Her great-grandparents had built the first house in South Parkville in 1872 and as a child she holidayed with her grandparents in The Avenue. The 'Bible Belt' suburbs where she grew up seemed 'boring and mindless' by comparison.

---

16   Leonard Radic, 'A Priceless Piece of Parkville Threatened' Melbourne *Age*, 25 August 1970, 8.
17   Hilary Lewis, *South Parkville*, 2nd edition (Melbourne: Parkville Association, 1996), 59.

After graduation from the University of Melbourne she became a librarian at University High School and later at Ormond College, renting a room in nearby Benjamin Street, before travelling through Greece and Italy to England where she worked as a children's librarian in Norwich and joining the Friends of Rural Pathways. In 1975 she met economic historian and Parkville resident John Killip. 'Please marry me, the Parkville Association needs a historian', he pleaded. 'Besides I live almost back to back with your great-grandfather's house'.

The secret of the association's influence, Norah believes, is its non-party political character. 'We were an association', not a 'residents' action group', she notes. 'It sounds so much more gentlemanly'. Its policy was never to make public statements but to seek private meetings with the candidates for Melbourne City Council and the state government. Its social activities, such as its annual Cup Day champagne party in Royal Park, reflected the upper-middle-class ethos of its members, at least half of whom, Norah estimates, worked at the University. Parkville was not gentrified – or at least not much – for it had never really ceased to be genteel. Nor was it really 'trendified' – its residents were traditionalists more than trendies. It was what it had long been and its activism was dedicated simply to keeping it that way.

Carlton Trendies

Carlton, on the other hand, was the heart of 'Trendyville'. In Lygon Street, two blocks east of the campus, the University met the immigrant sub-cultures established by Jewish and later Italian immigrants. Local landmarks such as King and Godfreys', licensed grocers and Donini's pasta shop, Jimmy Watson's wine cellars, Readings Bookshop, the 'Carlton Bughouse' cinema, University Café and Caffe Sport, La Mama and the Pram Factory symbolise the mix of student raffishness and radical chic that came to define the area.[18]

Thirty years after they arrived, middle-aged trendies were in no doubt about why they came to Carlton. 'I suppose because of the University', replied Ann Polis, who would later become the editor of the influential local newspaper the *Carlton News*. 'I mean, it just was where I thought my spiritual home was. I moved into a house in Rathdowne Street, North Carlton [in 1960]. I liked being able to move around easily on foot and things were happening everywhere, everything was accessible, public

---

[18]   Caitlin Mahar, 'Lygon Street' in *Carlton: A History*, 25–6.

transport was accessible. It was interesting, you know, there were Italians, there were Greeks, all sorts of people, pubs, all that sort of stuff. It was very vibrant'. 'The University was the reason I was there', architecture student Dimity Reed agreed. 'We all lived in a collection of houses along Swanston Street or in the lanes behind ... Our parents all lived in the suburbs or the bush, so my generation at Melbourne washed around Carlton like suds in soft water'.[19] Some students had first glimpsed the inner city as commuters from the suburbs and later came to stay. 'The intensely mixed social fabric of Carlton was a tonic to us suburban types, giving us for the first time the feel of cities where the dreamers of ideas feed their dreams', recalled poet and critic Chris Wallace-Crabbe.[20]

In 1955, two years before the Murray report, the academic presence in Carlton was barely discernible. The electoral rolls listed only 74 students, two professors, both living in houses on University grounds and one lecturer – Alan Davies – living in Rathdowne Street. Five years later, the number of students had increased to 127 and academics to about 77, although it is difficult to distinguish academics from other teachers. Many lived in the University colleges but among the early academic residents were political scientist Jim Jupp, historian Don McKay, art historian Franz Philipp and his wife, Australian historian June Philipp, and English tutor Gay Tennent. Jupp and Philipp were both immigrants, from London and Berlin respectively, who sought traces of the urban sophistication of the cities from which they had come. 'I found Melbourne very parochial', Jupp later admitted. 'It looked very small to someone coming from London ... The only cosmopolitan element available was the migrants from southern Europe'.[21]

By 1970 the numbers of students had grown to almost 400 and the academics and teachers to 229. The proportion listed as living in the residential colleges had decreased and an academic residential enclave had appeared in and around Drummond, Rathdowne, Wilson, Garton, Arnold and Bowen streets in North Carlton. They included psychologist Hal Colebatch, mathematician Roger Grimshaw and his historian wife Patricia, University archivist Frank Strahan and his wife, poet Lyn Strahan, literary critic Robin Grove, English lecturer and later publisher Jennifer Gribble, historian Allan Johnson and classicist Denis Pryor. By 1975 the student

---

19 Reed, 'Carlton – A Memory', 137.
20 Chris Wallace-Crabbe, 'A Mental Carlton', unpublished memoir.
21 Mark Lopez, *The Origins of Multiculturalism*, 93–94.

population had increased to 1056 (largely as a result of the lowering of the voting age from 21 to 18 in 1973), and the academics and teachers to almost 300. They included lawyers Sandy Clark and Gareth Evans, pianist Ronald Farren-Price, psychologist Charles Langley, political scientists Graham Little and Robert Manne, philosophers Lachlan Chipman and Jan Srezedkicki, and linguist Richard Zatorski.

Andrew Jacubowicz portrays the trendies as refugees 'fleeing the suburbs that they dislike'. Yet some had never lived in the suburbs at all. Miles Lewis, architect son of Brian and Hilary Lewis, had grown up in inner-suburban Parkville, later rented rooms in Swanston Street, where he met his wife Mary, and bought a house in Carlton's Drummond Street in 1970 before moving to south Fitzroy in 1976. 'I don't think I can be said to be an incomer', he insists. 'I get agoraphobia if I cross the Yarra'.[22] Others arrived as students from the countryside or abroad, sometimes via the colleges. The academic architect and composer George Tibbits came from Warrnambool while the engineer Trevor Huggard, a leader of the anti-freeway campaigns of the 1970s, had grown up in Cummeragunga, New South Wales, where his father was superintendent of an Aboriginal reserve.[23] David Beauchamp and Roger Grimshaw, successive presidents of the Carlton Association, were New Zealanders.

The Carlton Association, founded in 1968, was the political voice of the new Carlton. Tibbits would later characterise it as the voice of 'working-class families, postwar refugees, southern European migrants, old people, young people, professionals and students', the political extension of a sense of 'neighbourhood built around the street block'.[24] The association strove hard to realise its avowed commitment to 'participatory democracy'.[25] By the mid-1970s, when its membership had risen to about 2000, more than 200 people were actively involved in its myriad sub-committees, taskforces, working groups and community events. It devised an elaborate communication system, based on area convenors, reminiscent of the famous precinct captains of the Chicago Democratic Party machine, who linked

---

22 Miles Lewis, *The Inner Suburbs: Past, Present and Future, Proceedings of a Seminar at the University of Melbourne on World Town Planning Day* (Melbourne: CURA, 1979), 89; and pers. comm.

23 Davison with Yelland, *Car Wars*, 193–4.

24 George Tibbits, The Carlton Association. n. d., 5/3/1 Carlton Association Papers, University of Melbourne Archives.

25 Minutes of General Committee, 6 February 1971, 96/32, University of Melbourne Archives.

local neighbourhoods to the association's executive.[26] Yet, in its founding years especially, the organisation depended heavily on a small circle of academic activists, including the theologian Professor Harry Wardlaw, Presbyterian clergyman Mal Cormack, University archivist Frank Strahan, political scientist Lorraine Benham, administrator Bob Wilson, architect George Tibbits and mathematician Roger Grimshaw, all with strong connections to the University of Melbourne. Almost the entire committee, including engineer David Beauchamp, Dr Len Hartman, teacher Chris Molan and local high school principal Alleyne Sier were university-educated professionals. Although the association strove to enlist migrant groups in its campaigns, it recognised, at least privately, that the Italians were 'unlikely to join a community association'.[27]

Beyond their professional and organisational skills, the academics were engaged in something that was more elusive and important. As intellectuals, they were imaginatively reconstructing – to use Ann Polis's nice phrase – their 'spiritual home'. There were many labourers in this process and they drew upon insights and techniques drawn from disciplines ranging from literature and history to architecture, town planning, engineering and political science. Sometimes they acted collaboratively, as for example in the association's 1972 report on the Carlton Urban Renewal Scheme which drew on advice from a range of academic advisers, including engineer Beauchamp, economist Andrew Burbidge, transport expert Nicholas Clark, town planner Fred Ledgar, architectural historian Miles Lewis, social worker Judith O'Neill and sociologist Brian Howe.[28]

The trendies looked upon the city with new eyes, seeing beauty where earlier generations had seen only ugliness and squalor. The process of gentrification, a Canadian geographer suggests, required the 'aestheticisation of the city'. 'The redemptive eye of the artist could turn junk into art'.[29] Not only visual artists – painters, photographers, architects – but literary ones – writers, poets and historians –combined to turn Carlton from a slum (junk) into a 'historic neighbourhood' (art). In 1961 Alan Davies published a book

---

26   The Block Group, 2/1/5; The Carlton Association, 2/1/5, 'What is the Community Participation Scheme?' 2/1/2, Carlton Association Papers, University of Melbourne Archives. Compare Harold Gosnell, *Machine Politics: Chicago Model* (Chicago: University of Chicago Press, 1937), ch. 4.

27   Minutes, 10 February 1969, 96/32, University of Melbourne Archives.

28   *Urban Renewal, Carlton: An Analysis, Carlton Association Report no. 5*, 25 September 1972, Carlton Association Papers, University of Melbourne Archives.

29   David Ley, 'Artists, Aestheticisation and the Field of Gentrification' *Urban Studies* 40 (12) (2003), 2542.

of short stories, *A Sunday Kind of Love*, set against the background of Carlton and illustrated with charming engravings of its streets. Chris Wallace-Crabbe first ventured into 'pre-yuppy' Carlton as an occasional drinker in Jimmy Watson's famous Lygon Street winebar. 'Wining the cheerful hours out of mind', he recalled, 'we drew closer to Stendhal and Colette, Leopardi and Baudelaire, Lampedusa and "Palinurus". After a few bottles we could almost dream that we had been written by Proust'.[30] His colleague and fellow poet, Vincent Buckley, would later write a cycle of poems, *The Golden Builders* (1976), in homage to the builders of Carlton's terraced streets, now threatened by the bulldozer and the wrecker's hammer.

The hammers of iron glow down Faraday.
Lygon and Drummond shift under their resonance.

In a converted Pram Factory in Drummond Street, playwrights David Williamson and long-time Carlton resident Jack Hibberd created a kind of larrikin Brechtian theatre that dramatised the ideological ferment of the student houses of Carlton. *Stork* (1971), a comic film based upon David Williamson's play, and *Monkey Grip* (1977), Helen Garner's novel of sexual and pharmacological addiction, captured its comic and tragic sides. These literary creations consolidated an image of Carlton as a counter-cultural enclave, a world defined in opposition to the Babbits of North Balwyn.[31]

This oppositional culture emboldened Carlton's determination to defend its territory against the assaults of officialdom. But what exactly were the trendies seeking to defend? At its first meeting, the Carlton Association fell into an argument about whether it should focus its efforts on preserving the local environment or on strengthening its society. The debate was somewhat artificial – in practice, the association was active in both environmental and social matters – but it registered ambivalence at the heart of the movement. While they campaigned strongly for improvements to the standard of local education, especially at the Princes Hill High School, their strongest efforts were directed towards the conservation of Carlton as 'an area ... unique except for New Orleans in the character of its buildings'.[32]

Carlton lacked the architectural distinction and integrity of Parkville. In 1959, the year he completed his master's thesis on terrace architecture, lecturer David Saunders wrote to the Victorian Housing Commission

---

30 Wallace-Crabbe, 'A Mental Carlton'.
31 See for example, *Carlton: A History*, 189–195.
32 Meeting to form a North Carlton Association, Minutes, December 1968.

contesting its decision to declare much of Carlton an urban renewal area.[33] Few local buildings, he conceded, were of such outstanding architectural or historical value as to merit 'unconditional preservation', yet as a whole they exemplified 'an important phase in the development of early Melbourne architecture':

> Inherent in this development is the charm and dignity of an architecture which has grown out of the social conditions of its own time–values which are found no longer in contemporary architecture, and even in contemporary living. If slum reclamation and redevelopment follows the direction it is pointing now – that of complete demolition of all buildings in an ordained area– the loss suffered in later years, in terms of history and architecture, will be irretrievable and most regrettable.[34]

As a member of the university's Student Housing Board, Saunders later argued that a mixture of old and new terrace housing would offer the most suitable remedy for the emerging crisis of student accommodation. 'The terrace type of house', he noted, 'was already one of the most popular types of residence for students'.[35] He was feeling his way towards a more authentically Australian urbanism, one that acknowledged the functional and social, as well as stylistic, advantages of density, and the value of adaptation rather than the creative destruction of contemporary modernism. He was an immediate convert to Jacobs' *The Life and Death of Great American Cities* and its plea for a renewed appreciation of small spaces of the city, its streets, squares, footpaths and neighbourhoods. Australians had been influenced too much by British traditions of urban analysis, he contended. 'A pair of US spectacles is recommended to any such people, as a change worth trying at least until local lenses are made'.[36]

Saunders had helped to show why Carlton was worth saving; but saving it required an understanding of the social and political forces re-making the inner city. After Saunders moved to the University of Sydney his successor George Tibbits, a Carlton resident and founding member of the Carlton Association, introduced a new subject, Urban Studies, embracing urban

---

33   Saunders to Grahame Shaw, 13 November 1959, David Saunders Papers, 73/1, University of Melbourne Archives.

34   Points on the Redevelopment of an Area in Carlton 1959, David Saunders Papers, 73/1, University of Melbourne Archives.

35   Minutes of the University of Melbourne Student Housing Board, 30 July 1965, University of Melbourne Archives.

36   Review in *Australian Planning Institute Journal* 2 (5) (1963), 161–2.

sociology, politics and planning. Students were encouraged to apply their insights to fieldwork projects in the inner city. In 1969 the Association compiled a report, *Housing Survival in Carlton*, analysing the sociological character of the urban renewal area designated by the Housing Commission. Relying on superficial external inspections and standards enshrined in the 1916 Building Regulations, the HCV had classified the area as 'substandard' and in need of renewal. In fact, the association's survey disclosed, the residents included a mix of young professionals, owner-occupying Italian migrants and old pensioners. 'They are not slum-dwellers', it emphatically declared. The regulations reflected an outdated 'cultural prejudice' against terrace housing as a viable form of dwelling unit.[37]

As the battle intensified, Tibbits enlisted his fourth year architecture students as unpaid research assistants in a sociological study of the displacement of residents in the Commission's Carinya Gardens development.[38] With his colleague Miles Lewis, he was a principal author of the report *Urban Renewal, Carlton*, the Carlton Association's most detailed critique of the Commission's operations. Urban renewal, they argued, was a cause of, rather than a remedy for, the displacement of the poor, a problem that could be solved only by social welfare.[39] At the peak of the conflict in 1972 Carlton residents demonstrated outside the HCV offices, burning an effigy of the housing minister Ray Meagher who, according to Carlton Association president Richard Malone, was 'motivated by feelings of revenge against Carlton'; many suspected unconscious motives of pay-back in his attitude towards the inner city, the region from which the Brunswick storeman's son had escaped to suburban Frankston. A 60-year-old balding ex-serviceman (he had been a POW on the Burma Railway), former municipal officer and suburban newsagent, Meagher was a product of the school of hard knocks, a ready-made-symbol for everything the hirsute, smart-arse young Carltonians despised. 'Ray Meagre' was one of their nicknames. According to Miles Lewis, the effigy was the idea of Frank Delmonaco, a Lygon Street tailor. But personalising the enemy was also a measure of growing polarisation of politics in the closing months of the Bolte premiership.

The HCV, Malone declared, had no more right to vent its prejudice against small terrace houses by blitzing Carlton than a follower of the

---

[37]   *Housing Survival in Carlton: Objections to the Housing Commission's Proposal to Reclaim the Block Bounded by Lygon, Lee, Drummond and Princes Streets* (Melbourne: Carlton Association 1969), 8.

[38]   Carlton Association, Committee Minutes, 18 June; 21 October 1970.

[39]   *Urban Renewal, Carlton*.

architectural critic Robin Boyd would have to express his distaste for 'the cream brick deserts of suburbia' by demolishing suburbs like Balwyn.[40]

Melbourne's evening newspaper the *Herald* dubbed the Carlton Association 'the most influential suburban watchdog in Melbourne. It has the biting power of a yard full of Doberman Pinschers'. Some of its bite came from the intellectual expertise mobilised, in their spare time, by its members on the campus of the University of Melbourne. Even the hand that fed many of them was not safe from its attacks. In the late 1960s under vice-chancellor David Derham, the University's vice-principal Ray Marginson, an astute former senior public servant, floated a comprehensive master plan including a proposed 'University City' on its northeastern flank between Swanston, Faraday, Lygon and Elgin Streets. When the news broke, the Carlton Association Committee deputed one of its members, University Archivist Frank Strahan, to arrange an informal meeting with his boss Marginson. Perhaps they hoped informal diplomacy, like the Parkvillians' successful afternoon tea party, would head off the threat. But times had changed. The University could invoke powers of compulsory acquisition, Marginson explained, but was reluctant to do so. It needed more space for academic and residential accommodation, as well as other services.[41] Why? an anonymous local resident asked the new *Melbourne Times*. 'The University is not a car-parking, baby-minding, student-housing, professional preservationist institution and should not become involved in these areas through property acquisition'.[42] Carlton residents had already vowed to oppose the entire process of block clearance and 'urban renewal'. Marginson's implied threat only steeled their resolve.

In 1973 the University returned with a more 'sensitive' mixed-use scheme that would retain more of the area's historic fabric. 'Why should the university expand its size at all?' the association replied. Why not move south into the industrial zone of South Carlton, or make more intensive use of land around the colleges in Parkville?[43] Although personally congenial to many of the Carlton activists – his wife Betty was actually a leading figure in the Hawthorn Residents' Association – Marginson was unable to persuade them of the University's good intentions. 'We had tremendous opposition from

---

40   Richard Malone, 'Carlton Declares War on the Housing Commission' (c 1972), Carlton Association, Urban Renewal.

41   Carlton Association, Committee Minutes, August/December 1969.

42   Letters to the Editor, *Melbourne Times*, 9 June 1971, 2.

43   University Action Group 1973, Carlton Association Papers 84/92. Box 2, University of Melbourne Archives.

the Carlton Association, because they believed we were going to demolish north of Elgin Street, and I could never convince them that the intention was to create a new environment', he recalls.

Carlton inspired the biggest, noisiest, most tenacious and professional of the new bands of urban activists. While the suburb hosted a range of political activists, some well to the left of the Carlton Association, its core supporters, closely connected to the University, exhibited the pattern of 'participatory democracy' in the defence of common interests and territory that came closest to Jacubowicz's model of the new inner-city politics. As with its counterparts in Glebe and North Adelaide, it expressed a politics of community defence, rather than environmental preservation like the Parkvillians, or 'community development' like its neighbours in Fitzroy.[44]

Fitzroy Radicals

A kilometre southeast of the campus, beyond the Carlton Gardens, is 'Melbourne's first suburb', Fitzroy. Originally a middle-class annex of the CBD, by the 1950s it was a notorious slum. In the 1930s Oswald Barnett identified 'The Narrows', a tract of run-down crowded housing between Brunswick and Napier streets, as a target for 'slum clearance', and by the mid-1960s the Housing Commission, the agency he inspired, was poised to begin construction of a complex of high-rise public housing on the site. Ironically, directly in the path of the bulldozers lay the Brunswick Street Methodist Church, once one of the denomination's strongholds, now home to a tiny remnant of elderly parishioners. Rather than resist its seemingly inevitable extinction, the church agreed to sell the property and use the proceeds to continue its mission in a different form.

Accordingly, when the new minister, Reverend Brian Howe, arrived to take up his appointment in 1969, he found himself with neither a church nor a congregation, but with a pot of money and a commission to rethink the place of the church in a diverse, rapidly changing, inner-city environment. He had asked the Methodist Conference to send him to Fitzroy; 'I was very keen on the inner city', he recalls. Fitzroy was the laboratory he and his wife, historian Renate Howe, had selected for a radical experiment in urban inquiry and action. But the path that led them there began several years earlier as a theological student at Queen's College in Parkville where, with Renate, he

---

[44] Compare Benno Horst Engels, *The Gentrification of Glebe: The Residential Restructuring of an Inner Sydney Suburb 1960 to 1986* (PhD thesis, Department of Geography, University of Sydney, 1989), ch.8.

had participated in the debates and conferences of the Student Christian Movement. A decade before the Marxist-oriented student movements of the late 1960s and '70s, the campus religious societies, especially the Catholic Newman Society and the Protestant SCM, captured the idealism of a student generation conscious of the winds of change, yet still uncertain of their strength and direction.

Brian Howe was a child of the suburbs. Raised in Malvern by his grandfather, a former miner and follower of the ALP, and grandmother, a member of the Methodist Church, he absorbed something of the values of both, seeking to combine Christian faith and radical politics. As a 'talkative' young man, he enjoyed the vigorous debates of a Methodist youth group led by teacher and musician Maurice Williams, scion of a famous Methodist family that included theologian Colin Williams and economist Bruce Williams. Under Williams' influence, he read Reinhold Niebuhr's *The Nature and Destiny of Man* and began to think seriously about theological study, although he would work briefly for the Tramways Board and begin a commerce degree before arriving at Queen's in 1957. There he encountered a cohort of like-minded theological students – they included the architect and later politician Andrew McCutcheon – and a talented stable of theologians, historians and biblical scholars, including Colin Williams, George Yule, Harry Wardlaw and Davis McCaughey. Earnest but not solemn, theologically rigorous but undogmatic, this-worldly rather than other-worldly, the ethos of Queen's and Ormond and of their on-campus off-shoot the SCM became a powerful incubator of radical Christian thinking.[45] From the cloistered surrounds of College Crescent, its influence percolated into the inner city where the students engaged in schemes of religious, social and political uplift. McCutcheon spent a summer working with poor residents of North Melbourne while Howe worked with charismatic minister Alf Foote at the nearby Carlton Methodist Mission, later the Church of All Nations.

Among the students of that era, the city emerged as both site and symbol of a new radical Christianity. They heard the prophetic call of American theologian Gibson Winter to escape *The Suburban Captivity of the Churches* (1961) and his Harvard compatriot Harvey Cox's call to enter *The Secular City* (1965). 'The Gospel', Cox declared, 'does not summon man back to dependency, awe, and religiousness. Rather it is a call to imaginative

---

[45] See Renate Howe, *A Century of Influence: The Australian Student Christian Movement 1896–1996*, (Sydney: UNSW Press, 2009), especially chs. 10 and 11.

urbanity and mature secularity'. In 1965 the Howes moved to Chicago where Brian studied at McCormick Theological Seminary on the near-north side and Renate researched a PhD thesis comparing the history of the Protestant churches in Melbourne and Chicago as a visitor at the University of Chicago. They had come to 'an exciting city at exactly the right moment', when the rising hopes of the Kennedy and Johnson presidencies had yet to be dashed by the repressive violence of the 1968 Chicago Democratic Convention. As he investigated the role of the churches in the Johnson Poverty Program, Brian interviewed police and youth workers and pondered the ideas of renowned Chicago 'community organizer', Saul Alinsky. Renate encountered the story of the famous Hull House settlement and its inspiring leader Jane Addams whose democratic creed ('With not For') they would seek to follow back in Melbourne.[46] 'Conversations in Chicago were always about the city', Brian observes. '[You] got to feel that the city was a kind of symbol of modernity, [that] it represented all sorts of possibilities'. 'City' rather than 'suburb' became a keyword in their own thinking.

Back in Melbourne, the Howes were eager to draw on the lessons of their intense Chicago experience. 'Fitzroy is a suitable area for ecumenical experimental ministry to an urban society', they believed. Eschewing older paternalistic patterns of mission, based on service provision and charity, the Fitzroy Ecumenical Centre (later known as the Centre for Urban Research and Action, or CURA) aspired to foster 'freedom, justice and communication in the city'.[47] It was a task that called for a blend of reflection and action, focused policy-related research and political engagement. As well as their own 'churchy network' of worldly theologians and sympathetic academics, the centre soon attracted a wider network of social workers, leaders of immigrant communities, heritage enthusiasts and local politicians. 'I was always a very good networker', Brian reflects, more at home coordinating, energising and politicking than writing or preaching. The centre's cyclostyled journal *Ekstasis* (the name was inspired by the sociologist Peter Berger's celebration of 'ecstasy' – the capacity to stand outside the everyday routines of life) debated urban issues ranging from childcare to low-cost housing, and multiculturalism to homelessness. Its small paid staff – an economist, a community worker and a secretary – coordinated a program of research and action projects including studies of migrant women's employment, ethnic

---

46   'We Have Sought to Work with People Not for Them', Annual Conference Report 1974, *Ekstasis*, no. 10 (November 1974), 4.

47   *Ekstasis*, no. 1 (1971), 2.

rights and housing.[48] Most of CURA's key supporters were graduates and it continued to draw upon the intellectual resources of the campus (both Renate and Brian held academic appointments, at Deakin and Swinburne respectively) but it stood closer, intellectually as well as geographically, to the social welfare, planning, migrant, Labor Party and resident action networks in its own locality, than to the groves of academe. By the mid-1970s, the balance between reflection and action had shifted. 'Change is more likely to be a product of organisation and action than a product of either academic research or reflection', Brian now believed.[49] With his election as federal Labor member for Batman in 1977, it tilted further still, although never losing its theological and academic orientation.

'Trendification' by the mid-1970s had begun to transform the social landscape of Fitzroy. The first arrivals were often students and junior academic staff priced out of the more eligible academic dormitories of Parkville and Carlton. Since the late 60s, the median price of houses in North Carlton had trebled, with the steepest increase in the early 1970s.[50] The golden age of student bohemia had passed. One elder student advised freshers looking for accommodation in 1976 that:

> grotty digs with a Bohemian flavour, adjacent to the seat of learning, are rather difficult to find nowadays. Now, I'd rather not launch into a rave about how the trendies are taking over Carlton and forcing the rents up. Suffice it to say that if you are determined to live in Carlton or Parkville (and let's face it, these areas have many advantages for the student), you are going to have to search hard and be prepared to pay more than the self-respecting, impoverished student should admit to being able to afford.[51]

In 1969 newlyweds Jane and Brian Lennon had barely completed their studies when they bought a rundown cottage in Falconer Street, North Fitzroy, on a deposit of $1000. With silver and turquoise trim and a front garden full of vegetables, it had been the home of an Italian migrant, Romeo

---

[48]   Centre for Urban Research and Action, *The First Decade 1969–1979* (Fitzroy: Centre for Urban Research and Action).

[49]   *Ekstasis*, no. 10 (November 1974), 3.

[50]   The median price in 1966–8 was around $8000; by 1972 it was $12,000 and by 1974, $27,000. Based on data in 'Record of sales of properties' published twice annually by Multiple Listing Bureau of Victoria, East Melbourne.

[51]   Jill Barnard, 'Fun and Nightmares in Your Dreamhouse', *Melbourne University Orientation Handbook 1976* (University of Melbourne: Student Representative Council, 1976), 9–10.

Valotti. Jane first got to know the area as a student boarding at St Mary's College in Parkville. 'I had a bicycle that I'd brought down from Wangaratta ... and so I rode around a lot and knew the inner suburbs'. As a geographer she had a keen interest in the process of urban renewal and helped found an Urban Society to foster discussion among her fellow students. There was a gap, however, between the bland formulations of the urban geographers ('they were sort of surveyors') and Jane's more passionate engagement in urban issues. 'We were all very committed, you know, we were going to be the new Christians'. Fitzroy represented a new ideal of community, of neighbourliness and shared experience. Some residents tore down their back fences to create shared gardens.

When she married, Jane turned down a scholarship to study in America and put her academic ambitions on hold. Soon, however, they found a new channel. Inspired by the example of the Carlton Association, a group of interested residents, led by academics John and Laurie O'Brien, the University of Melbourne protocol officer Tom Hazell, and Brian Howe, formed the Fitzroy Residents' Association. Jane became convenor of its history group, documenting the houses threatened by redevelopment, especially along Victoria Parade in South Fitzroy.[52] After the birth of her son Rory she returned to part-time tutoring. 'Uni hours were pretty flexible', she recalls, and the geography department offered an informal base for her activity. After running off publicity material on the department's gestetner machine, she walked her baby home, pushing leaflets into letterboxes.

Meanwhile her husband Brian had also become immersed in Fitzroy's cause. Later in 1970 Jane returned from an interstate conference to find the house a mess, 'with jars of daffodils as a peace offering'. 'What on earth is going on?' she exclaimed. 'I'm running for council', Brian explained. 'I'm going to clean it up'. Fitzroy, like Collingwood and Richmond, was a fiefdom of the old ALP machine. There had been no election in their ward for more than twenty years. The rolls were full of bogus electors, many long since dead. Assisted by his friends, including sympathetic members of the Carlton Association, Brian door-knocked the area. Old-timers, suspicious of the long-haired bearded student, were outraged to learn that ALP stooges had been impersonating their dead relatives. He gained some credit in their eyes as the son of Tommy Lennon, a well-known local character who ran a two-up school in South Fitzroy in the '30s. He won in a landslide.

---

52   Jane Lennon, 'The Vicpar Case' in *Fitzroy – Melbourne's First Suburb*, ed. Chris McConville (Melbourne: Hyland House, 1989), 310–14.

Resident action in Fitzroy climaxed in the early 1970s, with battles raging over the Housing Commission's schemes in Atherton Gardens and Brookes Crescent[53] and a valiant but doomed campaign to save houses slated for demolition along Victoria Parade. One of the saddest losses, in Jane's re-collection, was the old Methodist Chapel with its picturesque magpie window in South Fitzroy. Sadder still was the break-up of the Lennons' marriage, in part a casualty of the pressures of their unstinting activism. She stayed on in Fitzroy, beginning a new career in National Parks and conservation. Other single women may have been daunted by the suburb's narrow streets and seedy reputation, but having grown up in the bush, the place held no fears for her. 'I was a big strapping country girl in Fitzroy village'.

The Triumph of the Trendies

Old urban activists look back on the struggles of the 1970s as a kind of golden age. They were drawn to the inner city by its otherness: its architectural charm, historical character, 'vibrant' ethnic mix and lively counter-culture, qualities enhanced by proximity to the university, the intellectual powerhouse from which they drew the resources to interpret and defend it. The passion and friction excited by their struggle to save their new home enhanced the pleasure of inhabiting it.

By the late 1970s, however, as trendies began to outnumber the older-timers, migrants, crims and corrupt politicians who gave colour to the area, a tone of anxiety and regret began to enter their conversation. Social researcher Michael Jones, who had helped found the Carlton Association, admitted that he no longer enjoyed visiting the Greek restaurants in Swan Street Richmond because they were 'full of people like me'. 'When you get too many scruffy, deviant people there', he decided, 'you get a slum; when you get too many people from the same high socio-economic status, the area, in fact, loses a lot of its interest to people'. Perhaps, he suggested whimsically, a 'Trendy Appeals Board' should be established to curb the influx of middle-class residents.

To the Fitzroy radicals the loss of local colour paled beside the more serious question of social disadvantage. Were the low-income tenants and migrants who used to live in the inner city being lured away by better prospects elsewhere, or pushed out by the increasing cost of living in a trendified suburb? In 1974 local poet ΠO issued a notice on behalf of the old Fitzroy to the new:

---

53   See Chapter Six.

GET OUT OF FITZROY

You've side-stepped the blood pools

The pus holes and

Raised the rents

Classed the restaurants

Closed down the hamburgers

Gouged out the stomachs of houses

And photoed the bedrooms of drunks

You've made this place hell

WE'LL BURN THE STREET SIGNS

We know our way around

GET OUT OF FITZROY.[54]

CURA, as the social conscience of the inner suburbs, raised its voice in defence of 'the displaced'. The newcomers, Howe argued, were 'unaware ... of the ambiguities implied in their so-called progressive stance. They represent a new breed of residential invaders who contribute through high incomes to the displacement of the lower-income groups to the more spacious, but service-deprived, outer suburbs'.[55] In a later study, *The Displaced* (1977), CURA focused on the threat to vulnerable housing classes such as private tenants and rooming house occupants.[56]

Whether the poor and the migrants had been displaced from the inner city, or had escaped to something better, was not so much a matter of fact as of the value placed upon the facts. The question mattered less if you were looking at the architecture than if you were looking at the society, and if you believed that cities should be left alone rather than managed and planned. 'If the Greek residents of Fitzroy find that they can sell their houses profitably to young middle-class couples, and on the proceeds fund a trip home and buy their dream home in Reservoir, they ... have escaped, not been displaced', insisted Miles Lewis, who had recently purchased his own bit of South Fitzroy. 'The plight of those people who have had money forced down their

---

54   ΠO, 'Get Out of Fitzroy' in *Into the Hollow Mountain*, ed. Mark Gillespie (North Fitzroy: Outback Press, 1974), 96.

55   Brian Howe, 'Conceptualising Values in Urban Society' *Ekstasis*, no. 6 (June 1973), 8.

56   Centre for Urban Research and Action, *The Displaced: A Study of Housing Conflict in Melbourne's Inner City* (Fitzroy: Centre for Urban Research and Action, 1977), 9.

throats against their will agitates me much less than some other problems'.[57]
Displacement was the question of a moment in the mid-1970s when social
and ethnic plurality remained a characteristic of the inner suburbs. A decade
later it was all but forgotten amidst the growing numbers of restaurants, art
galleries, bookshops, winebars, cinemas and other portents of trendification.
The vibrant neighbourhoods that the activists fought to save were a far cry
from the affluent playgrounds they unwittingly created.

Patricians, trendies and radicals – sub-groups within the general movement of tertiary-educated young people into the inner cities of Melbourne
and Sydney – had more in common with one another than with the more
diverse populations among whom they came to dwell. Where they differed
was not so much in their ways of dwelling, as in the intellectual paradigms
they brought with them and the politics they espoused. In the long run, it
could be argued, it was the strong undertow of market forces, represented
by the transformation of the tertiary-educated labour force, the increasing
advantages of central city living, and the prestige attaching to a fixed quota
of 'historic architecture' that shaped the fortunes of the inner suburbs.
But in the short run, during the decade and a half when the future of the
inner suburbs was in the balance, the intellectual energy, imagination and
resources provided by the students and academic staff of the university
played a pivotal role.

At least as important, however, as the activists' influence on the inner
suburbs was the influence of the inner city on the activists. 'We were the
young radicals, asking questions', Jane Lennon recalls. In an era when the
city had become a symbol of modernity, the questions they asked, and
the answers they gave, shaped not only their own locality but, indirectly,
the wider society. They included countless novelists, poets, historians,
geographers, planners, sociologists, architects, engineers and politicians, at
least four state ministers and a deputy prime minister. They nurtured the
modern heritage movement, models of participatory planning, community
health and childcare, and policies of multiculturalism. More than any other
group, the activists of the inner suburbs were prophets of the progressive
ideal of modern Australia.

---

[57]   Lewis, *The Inner Suburbs*, 91.

Chapter 4

WHAT ARE WE FIGHTING FOR?

MELBOURNE'S RESIDENTS' ASSOCIATIONS

You couldn't build a freeway without demolishing the houses, you couldn't build Housing Commission flats without demolishing the houses and I just thought we had lots of really interesting buildings in South Melbourne which, for one reason or another, had been overlooked by the National Trust.

Barbara Niven, an early Emerald Hill Association activist, spoke for many early residents' association members in equating the survival of her community with the preservation of an urban landscape in which, as a refugee from middle-class suburbia, she had come to feel at home. Its material fabric of streets and houses was inseparable from the vitality of the social networks that sprang to its defence. Each association struck a balance between environmental and social objectives according to the personalities and ideologies of its leaders, the social complexion of the suburb and the 'threats' arrayed against it. This chapter examines the emergence of resident action across Melbourne's inner suburbs, weighing the strength of these influences on the character of each. The emergence of the residents' associations as a political force coincided with the advent of 'second-wave feminism', and their successes were often strongly influenced by the organisational skills and passionate commitment to local community of their female members. Defending the neighbourhood, it might be argued, was a logical extension of the traditional female role as defender of home and hearth, but the cause was one that often extended women's political influence well into the corridors of power.

The Emerald Hill Association had been formed in August 1968,[1] succeeding an earlier group established to defend St Vincent Place, an elegant

---

[1]   Susan Priestley, *South Melbourne: A History* (Carlton: University of Melbourne Press, 1995), 391.

park space surrounded by terraces that today enjoys iconic status. Geoff Baker, a member of the North Melbourne Association in the 1960s, agreed that 'community development certainly includes a protection of heritage buildings and the infrastructure and the fabric of a suburb'. The stories told by many urban activists turn around their collective efforts to save the historic fabric associated with a particular class, community or society. They asserted their right to a voice in their own future in the face of the threat posed by indifferent or ignorant state or local authorities. The cause could be as specific and local as an apparently redundant church, a stand of old trees or a street of 'slum' housing, but the motives that inspired it were social as much as material.

The emphasis placed by each group of residents on physical preservation or community networking varied. Some distinctions between the Carlton, Parkville and Fitzroy groups have been canvassed in the previous chapter. The Melbourne-South Yarra Group began in April 1969 as the South Yarra Anti-Highrise Group. Its primary emphasis was on limiting inappropriate (particularly, large-scale) residential developments and preserving a diverse urban environment. The Richmond and North Melbourne associations and the Kensington Social Action Group, on the other hand, were established as community-oriented organisations and stressed the retention of human networks rather than just the built environment. The interest and commitment of key individuals were also important in the fortunes and character of specific RAGs – sometimes as important as the changing demographic character of the suburbs.

This chapter examines the background, operations and intentions of individual RAGs in Melbourne, then turns to discuss the organisation and tactics they adopted in their own regions.

The North Melbourne Association

'In a highly mobile, urbanized society the word "community" means community of interests, not physical community', the Chicago community activist Saul Alinsky observed in 1971.[2] In the forty years since he published *Rules for Radicals* Alinsky's adage has become even more true, but the North Melbourne Association, the first of the Melbourne RAGS, had embraced both ideas from the first. Organisations to promote the interests of local residents, such as Progress Associations and 'Tenants Leagues',

---

2   Saul D. Alinsky, *Rules for Radicals: A Practical Primer for Realistic Radicals* (New York: Random House,1971), 120.

had flourished since the 1940s, but the North Melbourne association represented a new, and more self-conscious, stage in their evolution.

It began in 1965 when 'a group of North Melbourne residents ... met together to discuss community awareness and responsibility'.[3] Most of them were middle-class professionals who had taken up residence in Hotham Gardens, a privately-developed estate of medium-density housing on land previously occupied by 'slum' housing and acquired through compulsory purchase by the Housing Commission. As middle-class newcomers (or perhaps even interlopers, in the eyes of some locals), they may have been conscious of their responsibility to contribute something to the area in which they had come to live.

The lead, in North Melbourne as in several other suburbs, came from clergymen and churches. 'There were very few amenities for the people of North Melbourne', Rev John Goff of the North Melbourne Methodist Church observed, 'no decent restaurants, shopping centre etc and no sense of community'. Goff was one of four representatives of local churches on the provisional committee of the NMA. He regarded the residents of Hotham Gardens, the founders of the association's forerunner, the North Melbourne Community Development Association, as its natural leaders. They included its chairman, lecturer in pediatrics Dr Robert Southby, architect David Eyres and his wife, former nurse but now university student Anthea, and the Rev Barry Martin of St Mary's Church of England.

The committee quickly sought to establish links with Hotham Gardens locals by sending out a questionnaire drawn up by Anthea Eyres. Copying and postage were paid for by the churches involved. Almost ninety percent of respondents were home owners; eighty-seven percent wanted 'more social facilities' and were dissatisfied with the local shopping options; one third were car owners; two thirds believed 'leadership from Hotham Gardens' should extend over the remainder of the North Melbourne community.

While a large majority assumed that the professionals should lead, a few expressed misgivings. 'Leadership is wishful thinking', a university tutor objected. 'People living here before flats were built resent us', a physiotherapist added. 'They feel rates, taxes etc have gone up because of us. Probably would not accept leadership, but perhaps partnership'. Another academic suggested: 'Active encouragement should be given to other

---

3   Robert Southby, from letter accompanying questionnaire included in North Melbourne – Hotham Gardens Project 1965–66 envelope, Richmond Association papers PA 99/25 Box 3, State Library of Victoria.

residents of N. Melb to take part in development of services and activities'. The muted reservations of the few who questioned middle-class hegemony anticipate the more strident, ideologically charged debates of the early 1970s when ideals of participatory democracy and resident action came to the fore. Among the twenty-six respondents who offered written comments, only one mentioned conservation of the built environment. 'Need to preserve original terrace houses. Some excellent early architecture in N. Melb'.[4]

Within a year, the Hotham Gardens group had been absorbed into a larger body covering the entire suburb. In September 1966 a public meeting resolved that a formal association be created 'to promote the development of North Melbourne and the well-being of the community'.[5] Its purpose was:

> To initiate and where necessary implement action which will assist the integration, development or advancement of the communal well-being of the residents of North Melbourne: and to provide effective means of approaching State, Municipal or other public authorities and instrumentalities when considered necessary in the interests of North Melbourne.[6]

From a narrow focus on the leadership pretensions and preoccupations of the new middle-class residents, the association had moved towards a more active political role in defence of the whole area.

In the late 1960s the association was stirred into action by a threat of demolition to a small shopping strip in Abbotsford Street, known as Happy Valley. Although valued by the locals, the Housing Commission regarded it with indifference or even hostility. A group of women – 'The Four Housewives' – led by Communist Party activist Ruth Crow, wrote letters opposing the Commission's action. David Eyres drew up plans for a mixed development of shops and flats reminiscent of cosmopolitan European living. What mattered in the eyes of the Hotham Gardens professionals was the retention of a community facility, not the preservation of the existing buildings.

The Association was quickly coming to a broader understanding of its goals, partly through the energy, idiosyncratic thinking and commitment of Ruth Crow and her husband Maurie. The Crows moved to North

---

[4]   Unlabelled, handwritten notes detailing meeting on 'December 6th 1965 at 8.00 p.m. at St. Mary's Church of England Vicarage Howard St, North Melbourne', Richmond Association papers PA 99/25 Box 3, State Library of Victoria.

[5]   'General Meeting' 1966.

[6]   'Proposed Constitution' 1966.

Melbourne in 1964 and gradually became involved in the activities of the North Melbourne Association, often exerting a strong informal influence on its direction and commitments. Maurie, a lawyer with experience as an organiser in the Clerks' Union, had been born into a wealthy Melbourne family who disowned him when he embraced Communism. His wife Ruth, born Miller, came from a Ballarat family hard hit by the Great Depression, a crisis that no doubt affected her deeply. It crystallised in her ideologically inspired activity beginning with a left-wing breakaway from the ostensibly apolitical Housewives' Association, to form the Union of Australian Women. Already in their fifties when they joined the NMA, the Crows' experience bridged the 1940s era of Stalin's Five Year Plans and the ecological and feminist concerns of the 1960s and 70s. Their *Plan for Melbourne (1969– 72)*, issued under the auspices of the Victorian Communist Party's Town Planning Group, imagined the city's transport, community services and power structures replanned on socialist lines.

As her friend Lorna Hannan observed, Ruth regarded the NMA as 'just another way of doing things':

> Ruth was an immensely generous person who understood how to get other people to do things with her because, however far they'd go with her, that was enough for her. She didn't ever make people feel that they hadn't done enough … She used to walk around in the later period of her life with a bag that usually had three or four different leaflets in it and when she saw you coming she'd work out which leaflet was the one that was appropriate for you.

'Privately', Ruth later recalled, 'Maurie and I regarded the question of what O-Y-O (own-your-own) flat dwellers could do for the community as being rather patronizing'.[7] The Association briefly fell into abeyance in the early 1970s; by 1973 the Crows' involvement saw it restored as a force.

The Crows' political views do not appear to have counted against them (or in their favour). According to Ruth, the NMA had actually sought them out in an effort to 'bridge the generation gap'.[8] Geoff Baker, a strong figure in the RAG coalition the Committee for Urban Action, and a clergyman's son, recalls the Crows as working 'behind the scenes … They weren't the kind of people who pushed to be on the committee of the

---

7   Ruth Crow, 'Early History of the NMA from the mid 1960s to the early 1970s' 1995, Crow Collection, Victoria University, Box 32–37/16 0001.

8   Quoted in Gib Wettenhall, 'Connections' [obituary for Maurie Crow] *Australian Society* 7 (7) (July 1988), 45.

North Melbourne Association, they were quite happy about being in the background to provide information, support, suggestions, to do some of the hard yakka'. The NMA exhibited a breadth of class and political interests that defies any simple categorisation. Historian Colin Long divides the Melbourne RAGs of this time into 'leftish' (the North Melbourne and Carlton Associations) and 'far more conservative' (East Melbourne and 'South Yarra' groups).[9] Yet many of their members would have rejected these categorisations, or indeed any political tag. While the Crows kept a low profile – indeed, Maurie sometimes urged NMA members to drop his name from public announcements lest his Communist affiliations taint the organisation in the eyes of some observers – within the Association, according to Baker, party politics were rarely discussed. Liberals and DLP supporters kept company with Laborites and Communists. By tacit agreement, political labels were for the world beyond the locality.

Ruth Crow campaigned relentlessly on a host of issues, many applicable to her own neighbourhood. Her column, 'Ruth Writes', which appeared regularly in the *Northern Advertiser* in the early 1970s, until its demise in 1974, featured a photograph of Ruth but did not reveal her surname or mention her affiliation with the many organisations she wrote about, much less her connection to Maurie, whom she disingenuously referred to only as a community member she admired. Her commitment to redress educational disadvantage, shared with other NMA activists like Lorna and Bill Hannan, found local expression in the association's campaign to win the right for North Melbourne students to attend the prestigious selective University High School. She kept a keen eye out for urban innovations in other suburbs that might inspire her own community. Could North Melbourne adopt the 'adventure pathway' along the Yarra devised by Bruce Williamson of the Richmond Association?[10] Could the pedestrian mall opened in Footscray be a model for North Melbourne's Errol Street?[11]

The heyday of the NMA in the late 1960s and early 1970s coincided with that of the locality's popular independent newspaper the *Northern Advertiser*. Like its contemporary, the *Carlton News/Melbourne Times*, it was willing to go into 'battle' on behalf of North Melbourne's residents, and its demise in March 1974 was a blow to the independent press in inner-city Melbourne.

---

9   Colin Long, *Global Restructuring and Local Urban Development: Melbourne 1970–1998* (PhD Thesis, University of Melbourne,1999), 240.

10   Ruth Crow, 'Down by the River?' *Northern Advertiser*, 2 September 1971, 2.

11   Ruth Crow, 'Exciting Example' *Northern Advertiser*, 20 May 1971, 7.

From June 1973 it campaigned ceaselessly in favour of a Citizens' Action Plan for North and West Melbourne: the 'CAN' column, carrying news and views of the scheme, and stirring 'ordinary people' to participate, became a regular feature of the paper.

The primary force behind CAN was the ubiquitous and ever-resourceful Maurie Crow, although the final published report was ascribed to 'the efforts of fifty members of the North Melbourne Association'.[12] The first announcement of the plan in the *Advertiser* captures its spirit:

> CAN the area around the Errol Street shops be planned to be a more attractive place for both shopping and recreation? ... CAN the North Melbourne Town Hall be used for more or different purposes? ... CAN greater use be made of existing council facilities such as kindergartens, infant welfare centres, community centre, library, elderly citizens club and swimming pool? ...

> CAN the area around the Moonee Ponds Creek be made less obnoxious? ... CAN a mixed community (this is mixed age groups, mixed income groups, mixed ethnic groups and so on) be retained in our district? ... CAN we retain the Victoria Market on its present site? ... CAN you help us find the answers to these community problems? ... You can make the C.A.N. column your column'.[13]

The campaign peaked in a 'month of meetings' in August 1973 when the NMA and Maurie Crow sought to engage with 'as many people as possible'.[14] The organisers were evidently in a rush to complete their report in time to influence the deliberations of Interplan – the Australian/American consortium contracted by the Melbourne City Council to conceive a future design for the whole of the CBD and the inner city.[15] 'Public participation' was one of Interplan's stated principles and, taking them at their word, the NMA aspired to bring local pressure to bear on the notoriously impervious attitudes of the officials at Town Hall.

'Small is beautiful' was a slogan of the time. The CAN report celebrated the beauties of the North Melbourne community including its pedestrian

---

12   *C.A.N. Report: Citizens Action Plan for North and West Melbourne* (North Melbourne: North Melbourne Association, 1973), iii.

13   Anon, 'Help us with our C.A.N. plan' *Northern Advertiser*, 21 June 1973, 3.

14   Anon, 'It's a month of meetings' *Northern Advertiser*, 26 July 1973, 5.

15   See Long, *Global Restructuring and Local Urban Development*, 222–226, as well as the numerous Interplan reports.

culture and intimate scale. It proposed neighbourhood focal centres, sharing of facilities, engendering of social mix, retention of the existing building stock – primarily for its cheapness ('The existence of ... dilapidated buildings ... is quite an important element in the whole process of generation of new culture').[16] It defended the superiority of terrace housing which enabled high-density living with low maintenance requirements and no loss of privacy.[17] The 'historic' character of the area, it argued, was of cultural, rather than narrowly aesthetic, importance: neighbourhood character reinforced North Melbourne's identity.[18] The report also recommended the creation of new socially-mixed residential areas, notably the 'Newmarket New Town', on the site of the abattoir; a decade later this became the 'new suburb' of Lynch's Bridge.[19] The CAN project manifested the NMA's conviction that their suburb was for everyone, not just homeowners.

Anthea Eyres, Annemarie Mutton and the Richmond Association

Resident action was a movement in tune with the times. From the grassroots, its ideas, organisational models and even its leaders circulated from one inner suburb to another. Long before the CAN report, David and Anthea Eyres, founders of the North Melbourne Association, had moved to Richmond where Anthea helped prime another phase of resident action.

In the twenty-first century, Richmond has become one of Melbourne's most desirable suburbs, but until the 1990s it was regarded as somewhat down-at-heel. The Housing Commission had made inroads into the area in the early 1940s, with the building of three streets of detached bungalows on the site of a racecourse in Bridge Road. A 1988 local history *Copping It Sweet* portrayed the HCV's move into Richmond in the 1960s as an invasion resisted by locals.[20] Yet the main voice of residents, the Richmond Association, is unmentioned in the book; perhaps evidence that a RAG needs local survivors, willing to testify, to maintain a legacy. The Richmond Association adopted a complex attitude to the Commission's presence in the area.

---

16 Anon, 'Very Cheap Premises Needed' in *C.A.N. Report*, 30.
17 *C.A.N. Report*, 31.
18 *C.A.N. Report*, 38–40.
19 'A New Town at Newmarket' in *C.A.N. Report*, 48–9.
20 City of Richmond, *Copping It Sweet: Shared Memories of Richmond* (Melbourne: Carringbush Library/City of Richmond, 1988), 54–60.

The presence of new middle-class residents in traditional working-class suburbs was newsworthy in 1970. When David and Anthea Eyres and Frank and Annemarie Mutton arrived in Richmond the Melbourne *Herald* was tempted 'to speculate whether it will become Melbourne's Paddington'. The area was 'absolutely fantastic', Annemarie Mutton enthused. 'I feel more involvement and identity here than in any place I have lived'.

Annemarie Mutton had arrived in Melbourne in the late 1930s as a Jewish refugee after fleeing her native Vienna with her first husband, Zionist historian Ernest Bowen (born Ernst Boehm). She later taught at Preshil, the progressive Kew school. After their divorce, she met her second husband, Frank Mutton, an Australian-born fitter and turner, trade unionist and Communist activist, through the Peace movement. They married in 1964 and lived for a time in the old Bowen matrimonial house in upper-middle-class Kew. But their address suggested to Frank's unionist associates that he had become a class traitor, and Annemarie's middle-class education and cultural interests compounded their status anxiety. They sold the house in Kew and bought a rather cramped former rooming house in East Melbourne, close to Frank's Union's headquarters. Soon he had found a job as a technical assistant in the the University of Melbourne Engineering Department. Under Annemarie's influence, his cultural interests were broadening as they visited art galleries and attended concerts. They began to look for another house, scouring the inner suburbs from Port Melbourne to Carlton in search of a place that somehow resolved their ambiguous social and political status. One Sunday afternoon, they followed a 'for sale' sign on the corner of Bowen Street, Richmond, to a former brothel – a 'beautiful, attractive' ruin of a house– and bought it on the spot. Soon they had moved in and begun renovations.

> Frank had fixed a contraption under the stairs for cutlery, and crockery, and pots and pans and we had a little stove, an oven in the sitting room that we'd made, you know it looked lovely. Half of it was stored in the storeroom place and this is what we had, and we could entertain and we had an apple tree and a pear tree and everybody came out and sat there … Frank said 'it cost us as much in beer and coffee as a thousand bricks'. All my friends came and said 'What made you do that? You would go to Richmond? Good God! You had this lovely house in East Melbourne, why would you do that?' They could understand that I'd sold Grange Road [in Kew] to go into East Melbourne, but Richmond is *the end*.

There was something daring, but reassuring, about moving into an old working-class, now gentrifying suburb, that appealed to a pair of late middle-aged Leftists. It resolved, or left conveniently unresolved, the status discrepancies and family loyalties they had left behind in Kew. And, as the suburb itself came under threat from hostile commercial and political forces, it opened a challenging new field for radical activism.

For Anthea Eyres, who had previously lived in North Melbourne, it was a second experience of inner-suburban living. 'Richmond is a good place to bring up children', she had discovered. 'It's stimulating, there are many different nationalities, classes of people, variety of houses and it is close to the city'. While 'some re-development' was needed, most locals were 'against the indiscriminate abolition of houses by the Housing Commission', she added. In Richmond, as in North Melbourne, she seldom took a public lead, preferring the vital backroom role as secretary of both the North Melbourne and Richmond Associations. Some of the concerns of the first, especially the emphasis on social networking and working-class welfare, rather than heritage preservation, carried over into the second.

The Eyres had moved into Richmond in 1966 but it was not until 1969 that they began to appreciate the social repercussions of the construction of the Housing Commission's towers in North Richmond – such as the displacement of tenants and the compulsory acquisition of homes – and were goaded into action.

The Muttons immediately took up the cause of residents dispossessed by the Housing Commission's high-rise developments without inadequate compensation. On the first night they slept in their new home a note appeared in their letterbox.

> Would we come to a meeting at Anthea Eyres' – diagonally across to the back gate – to form an Association that would take care of what they're trying to do, the Housing Commission, with land and with cottages of workers ... So anyway we went there and, it was full, doctors and solicitors and parsons. I rang a couple of people and ... we got the people together. That was the deciding moment in our life because we joined this group and we were instantly active. Well of course Frank threw the cat amongst the wolves because he said that his view was that the Housing Commission should not be allowed to have only housing for poor people, it should be mixed instead of creating a ghetto ...

This egalitarian and, to Annemarie, 'revolutionary' approach was to mark the Association's work over its short existence. As in North Melbourne, a clergyman, Ian Ogilvy, 'a parson in East Melbourne and a man of many words', according to Mutton, was to the fore. 'Ian was a very great help because he could reach the people in East Melbourne and he had influence, and he came from the same background you know … And so we were quite broad right from the start'. Ogilvy became Association president in 1970. Like Goff in North Melbourne, he was a pillar of the community with tactical ability to steer around controversy. A later president, John Neill, was more confrontational, describing the demolition of the Richmond Community Health Centre as 'rape'.[21] Perturbed by local government corruption, Neill stood unsuccessfully for council in 1975.

As the HCV development proceeded members of the Association formed a 'High Rise Welcoming Committee' for new residents. 'Would mother be interested in day-time English classes in the Estate?' was one of their standard questions. Welcomers sought to gauge whether particular people seemed 'to be likely "leaders" for social activities, etc'.[22] In May 1970, the Association made frontpage news when it came to the defence of Antonia Georgiopoulos, the final owner-occupier in Mahony Street, Richmond, to be evicted by the HCV. In an article entitled 'The Force Triumphs', Vincent Basile described Georgiopoulos and members of the Richmond Association keeping bailiffs at bay for half an hour – Georgiopoulos even chasing one through the street with a brick in her hand – until five policemen entered the fray and removed her belongings from her house. By 1972 the Richmond Association had 80 members,[23] but rapid changes in the area, the decline of the immediate threat – the HCV curtailed its high-rise building here as elsewhere – and the departure of both Eyres and Mutton (to Kew and South Melbourne respectively) seem to have brought its decline. The organisation did not survive the 70s and is now largely forgotten. Annemarie Mutton reflects:

> It *was* a community and I think that Anthea and I were probably the movers of it, you know? We kept people together and we brought people together, but then new people came in and they had very different views and I grew old and Frank grew old and Anthea went away and lived somewhere else … It was only, I would say, we had three or four years

---

21   Anon, '"Rape" says critic' Richmond *Advocate*, 25 June 1975. This was of course not an uncommon turn of phrase at the time, see e.g. Ron Burke, 'The Great National Park Rape' *Farrago*, 30 March 1972, 17.

22   'High Rise Welcoming Committee' folder, Richmond Association papers PA 99/25 Box 1, State Library of Victoria.

23   Jeff Floyd, *Citizen Participation* (PhD Thesis, University of Melbourne, 1972), 220.

of high activity which got us to all those stratas that you can find in Richmond.

Their experience underlines the importance of the role of individuals, especially of women, in the residents' associations. Even when they were not formal office-holders, it was often they who provided the moral passion, organisational drive and sheer stamina to sustain the reform effort. Eyres was a central figure in the foundation of both the North Melbourne and Richmond Associations. In Mutton she found an ally from a very different background whose interest in community and those disadvantaged by the machinations of an unresponsive and uncommunicative bureaucracy mirrored her own.

The single most important defining feature of the community-based RAGs, like those in North Melbourne and Richmond, was the commitment of its overwhelmingly middle-class members to engage, lead and (though such a term would not have been in use at the time in question) empower the broader community. A critical role in maintaining their radical social orientation was played by older left-wing activists like the Crows and Muttons. Other RAGs effectively turned their back on residents of Housing Commission areas – there is little evidence, for instance, of Carlton or Emerald Hill Associations taking a strong interest in welcoming new Housing Commission tenants as part of their community. In Fitzroy, however, CURA and the BSL were active in supporting the new HCV residents and in encouraging the formation of a Housing Commission Tenants' Union.

Barbara Niven and the Emerald Hill Association

Inner suburban activists can often recall a moment when a threat of some kind – the demolition of a building, the projected widening of a road, the imposition of a high-rise housing estate – provoked them into action. Teachers Barbara and David Niven had moved to Middle Park in 1969. Three months after their arrival 'in the early morning bulldozers came in and bulldozed the complete avenue of plane trees that went the whole length of Canterbury Road [the Nivens' street]. I couldn't get over it', Barbara recalled. As a student, she had belonged to the the University of Melbourne ALP Club and developed a life-long interest in drama. The arrival of the bulldozers on Canterbury Road stirred her indignation against what she saw as wanton destruction by local bureaucracy. After a visit by Ray Wilson of the Emerald Hill Association (formed the previous year), she joined and was soon engaged in some of its ramifying network of affiliated groups and sub-committees. These included the Albert Park Protection League (APPLE), the Canterbury Road Preservation Group, the Perimeter Roads Action Group, the Campaign for a Better Council (formed 1973) and a Historical Buildings sub-committee.[24] There were about 80 members when she joined; the Association had grown to 131 by 1972.

'Protection' and 'preservation' – the watchwords of the Emerald Hill Association – were the defensive stance of the new middle-class residents of an area they prized largely for its accessibility, historic character and aesthetic charm. In reviving the area's picturesque nineteenth-century name, 'Emerald Hill', they underlined their preservationist outlook. Already with a large proportion of managerial and professional residents, South Melbourne 'gentrified' faster than other inner suburbs.[25] An American social scientist discovered that residents of Middle Park, one of its most favoured neighbourhoods, were more inclined than those in North Fitzroy and North Carlton to value the area's environmental attributes, compared with its social character and 'lifestyle'.[26]

Unlike the North Melbourne and Richmond activists, the Emerald Hill Association made little attempt to promote the interests of the suburb's working class. It characterised itself as 'non-political'.

Many of South Melbourne's newcomers were young families, only a few of whom had family ties to the area.[27] The Emerald Hill Association formalised the shared interests and networks of mutual assistance already found, for example, in a cooperative baby-sitting group. As Barbara Niven noted, its political influence grew out of these informal communal relationships:

> The co-op ran without bookkeeping. At that time, most people I knew who were in baby-sitting co-ops had a secretary and it ended up with rows and arguments about who owed what to whom but this token system was invented by one of the people in our group who had access to places where they could manufacture plastic disks and it was a self-regulating baby-sitting co-op. You got a spike with a whole lot of triangular bits, orange for an hour and red for half an hour, or maybe

---

24   Floyd, *Citizen Participation*, 217.

25   William Stewart Logan, *The Gentrification of Inner Melbourne: The Political Geography of Inner City Housing* (St Lucia: University of Queensland Press, 1985), 14–16.

26   Michael Jager 'Class Definition and the Aesthetics of Gentrification: Victoriana in Melbourne' in *Gentrification of the City*, ed. Neil Smith and Peter Williams (Boston: Allen and Unwin, 1986), 154.

27   Jager, 'Class Definition and the Aesthetics of Gentrification', 149.

the other way around, and you were expected to use them plus a list of names. If you had tokens coming off the top, you were expected to go out and use your tokens and if you had a nearly empty spike you'd be ringing around saying, 'Give me some baby-sitting to do'. It was a terribly important network because all of us, I think, were in the Emerald Hill Association.

'One of the local estate agents said [it] was one of the most powerful networks he'd ever encountered', Niven later recalled. 'He said no estate agent in his right mind would offend any member of that group because the whole group would hear about it'.

The core of the new residents' interests was in their family homes, and the main stimulus to their political action was a process of urban redevelopment that threatened the amenity and value of their neighbourhoods. That threat had been quietly growing stronger for more than a decade. The first high-rise public housing had been constructed in South Melbourne in the late 1950s. Private developers often followed the Housing Commission into areas of what were often characterised as worn-out or superseded housing. In 1972 the large real estate developer LJ Hooker purchased, from five different owners, Lanark Terrace, an eighty-year-old row of six terrace houses in Canterbury Road, South Melbourne with the intention of building a 21 storey block of flats on the site. It had no forewarning of the trouble it had bought.

The Nivens, Canterbury Road residents, raised the alarm about the Lanark Terrace plan. Inspired by Merilyn White, an EHA colleague who had knocked on Premier Rupert Hamer's door to discuss his freeway plans, Barbara decided to take a tram to Spring Street and talk to Alan Hunt, the Minister for Planning. Hunt and Premier Rupert ('Dick') Hamer were the most influential members of a Liberal government that had broken with its predecessors, and with most of its interstate counterparts, in taking up 'quality of life' issues in its social programs. Both men were receptive to ideals of 'grassroots democracy' and 'open government'.

That an individual citizen felt able to walk into the office of a minister, and that the minister felt obliged to see her, says something about the political mood of the time. Hunt explained to Niven that her organisation had forfeited its right to object. She replied that, under the by-laws of South Melbourne council, it had never been able to exercise that right.

It was a funny interview because I said, 'The building referees' decision is tomorrow and they are going to come in with a decision and we have had no right of objection'. He said, 'Well, you've had the right to object' and I said, 'No we haven't'. He didn't believe me but I was so adamant about it he finally said, 'Well, just a minute', and he went out of the room and he was away for a few minutes. He came back and he said, 'You're right'.

The next day, the building referees deferred the decision on Lanark Terrace, an action that Hunt vehemently insisted was out of his hands. On 14 August 1973 the council refused Hooker permission to demolish Lanark Terrace and erect flats.

The company's representative at the Town Planning Appeals Tribunal argued that 'representations at a Parliamentary level' were an abuse of process. In his testimony to the Tribunal, George Tibbits described Lanark Terrace as having a 'distinctive and unique design'. 'There is no other building in the Melbourne metropolis quite like it'. Resident and town planner Laurence Wilson criticised the Hooker proposal as a 'gross overdevelopment' of the site, adding further concerns about privacy, shading and wind exposure.[28] Tall buildings, the Tribunal was told, would destroy the sailing on Albert Park Lake. The proposed building, according to one local resident, was 'quite grotesque and quite out of balance, an imbalance, a monster'.[29] In response, the developer's expert witnesses contested both the architectural quality of the terrace and the surrounding landscape. 'There is not really a streetscape as such' in Canterbury Road, they argued, and Lanark Terrace itself was an architectural curiosity rather than a fine example of anything. The streetscape issue – notably, the question of scale – was key.

The Emerald Hill activists presented themselves as the voice of a silent majority of local residents troubled by the prospect of development but too fearful or cynical to speak out. Barbara Niven cited the case of one gentleman who:

> lives right next to the proposed building who has already been effected by the construction of the 10 storey building two houses away from him. He is not here because he has no belief in the system and he just thinks that what he will do is take the action to protect himself if it is necessary when that arises ... very long term residents ... don't like sticking their necks out and they regard any kind of appearance before any kind of

---

28   Testimony of Laurence Wilson, Town Planning Appeals Tribunal Division 'B' Appeal no. 73/782, 11.

29   McIntosh, 'independent objector', Town Planning Appeals Tribunal Division 'B' Appeal no. 73/782, 18.

official body as [a situation in which] if they stick their necks out they are going to get them chopped off ... the fact they are not here does not mean there is no local concern ... I am not in any sense speaking on their behalf ... they haven't authorised me to do so but they know I am here.

The 10 storey apartment block was one of several constructed in the inner-southern suburbs by private developer Nathan Beller. Hooker could possibly have cited them as examples of benign high-rise development, although in the eyes of the EHA they 'contribute nothing to the social fabric of the area; in fact I think they detract from it'. Implied in their stance was an alternative model of development based, not on modern high-rise construction, but on the 'spontaneous regeneration' of Victorians and Edwardian buildings.

Despite the opposition of local activists, Lanark Terrace was demolished in May 1974. Defeat only reinforced their determination to stop the development. When the Tribunal issued a permit for a smaller 14 storey block, the South Melbourne Council, prompted by local residents, appealed to the Supreme Court. The appeal was turned down. Yet, as Barbara Niven relates, the battle was not over. No sooner had the terrace come down and excavation of the site begun, than the developer struck a snag.

Eventually, what happened was they dug a great big hole after they demolished the building and the council made them put very expensive cyclone wire fencing right around the hole to protect the population ... every day of delay was ending up costing them a fortune. Somebody found carp in the ponds that had formed and this became an urban myth, that the carp had swum through from the lake and they were in this pond. Of course, it wasn't. Some kids had thrown them over the fence and then they went fishing for them.

In the battle to save urban neighbourhoods, myth – in this case, that the ground surrounding the lake was merely a 'raft' – was often as potent as fact, and political stamina as indispensable as professional expertise.

LJ Hooker eventually sold the Lanark Terrace site to another developer, AV Jennings, for low-rise housing. The residents' victory, Barbara Niven now believes, was the result of a long war of attrition. Delays on the project were costing the company tens of thousands of dollars a day. The EHA were working within an evolving system, and were able to draw on a sympathetic state government and help create a representative local one.

The EHA regarded itself as 'apolitical', in the sense of being unaligned with either of the main political parties, although, as Niven explained, in the municipal context its stance on issues of conservation and development pitted it against some well-entrenched local business interests:

> It was interesting. It was political in the sense that there was a universal objection to the fact that we had councillors who lived in Brighton and [other] places. They were absentee and they were businessmen in South Melbourne. That had been the way of the South Melbourne Council for years. It had a sort of ALP ruck and then sort of quasi-Liberal Party councillors who lived out of town and were making decisions, or really didn't care about the decisions.

In the mid-1970s residents began to challenge the hegemony of these non-resident pro-development businessmen who, as Niven perceived, were 'pro-pulling down buildings and all sorts of things'. The critical moment came when councillors from four of the five wards were tipped out in a single election, largely through the influence of the EHA. 'These out-of-town businessmen didn't stand a chance'. The new council was far more to the Association's liking:

> There was a mayor, oh gosh, Bruce Cormick, he was Labor Party and he was also South Melbourne born and bred and he joined with us as well. So there were local people who'd joined on the issues and who were really very helpful. They were in council on their own account, not because we'd put them there. It just meant that once we'd got rid of the businessmen from out of town there was a nucleus in the council that could actually carry things. They did some very brave things really. In days when technically you weren't allowed to refuse a demolition permit, there was this farce where it had to be applied for. The council actually refused it, got itself into some terrible hot water.

South Melbourne Council worked with the EHA to resist the influx of traffic generated by the Westgate Bridge and its freeway approaches. It refused to cooperate with the Country Roads Board and joined with other local bodies to initiate street closures to protect the residential amenity of the area.[30]

By the mid-1970s, the worst of the threats were past and the indignation that had fuelled the EHA began to dissipate. The EHA did not disappear

---

[30]   See David Wilson, 'Council plans to block West Gate traffic' Melbourne *Age*, 10 January 1975, 1; David Wilson, 'Nowhere to go for West Gate's 15,000 cars a day' Melbourne *Age*, 11 January 1975, 3; Anne Latreille, 'South Melbourne wall against West Gate traffic' Melbourne *Age*, 14 January 1975, 4.

entirely, however, but consistent with its preservationist outlook, gradually evolved from political action towards local historical research. Along with other members of the EHA, Niven was recruited by the planning firm Wilson Sayer Corr to document South Melbourne's Victorian streetscapes as part of the council's impact study of the planned freeways. Volunteers equipped with bulk supplies of black and white film surveyed the area, photographing streetscapes and buildings. Each strip of film was contact-printed and labelled by street name and number. The purpose was not to decide which buildings were useful or not, but to assess the heritage value of each precinct. In 1975 Niven became director of a larger project to create photographic strips for inner-city – Richmond, Collingwood, Prahran, Hawthorn – and regional streetscapes.[31]

Here, as in her previous study for the freeway impact study, Niven remained committed to the idea of community involvement. It was important to 'get the local people involved in this process'. She was proud to have evolved a 'survey technique ... which would allow relatively unskilled community groups' to construct 'a picture of those of our historic resources constituted by urban areas of historic character'.[32] The volunteer base of the project had soon extended into other community organisations and schools, even including the elite Melbourne Grammar School.

> That was very funny [she recalled] because some of them turned up in a chauffeur-driven Daddy's car to come to the slums, you know, and do the photography. Some of them went to the top of Park Towers and took arty panoramic views of South Melbourne and the bay, which was not in their brief at all, but that didn't matter.

From her first outraged reaction to the felling of a stand of old trees, Niven's passionate commitment to the conservation of her own neighbourhood had inspired an impressive range of activities that testified to her powers as a communicator and motivator. With the EHA, she later campaigned successfully for the preservation of the South Melbourne town hall and its surrounding buildings. Niven herself attributes some of her success to

---

[31] Anne Latreille, 'Every picture is a memory: As the old makes way for the new residents move to renew the past' Melbourne *Age*, 16 April 1975, 25.

[32] Barbara Niven and Michael Read, 'Surveys of Areas of Historic Character Conducted by the Committee For Urban Action' in Miles Lewis and Alison Blake, *Urban Conservation: Proceedings of a Seminar Conducted at the University of Melbourne, 25th February, 1976*, National Estate Project 130/Urban conservation working papers No. 9, 51–56.

South Melbourne's consciousness of itself as a distinct suburb cut off from its neighbours by a lake, a park and the sea. As late as the 1960s, she believed, it still felt like a country town. Yet like the EHA itself, community consciousness was the product of something more than geography, generational change, or environmental threat. Among the resident action groups that encircled Melbourne by the mid-1970s, the Emerald Hill Association stands out for its strong middle-class base, consistent environmental focus, and its tactical resourcefulness, including its ability to apply pressure directly or indirectly on local and state politicians.

The Carlton Association: Representation and Action

Like North Melbourne, and unlike Richmond or South Melbourne, Carlton was not a municipality in its own right, but a subsection of the City of Melbourne. The fortunes of its residents, so far from being in their own hands, were circumscribed by a range of competing forces, including – besides the City itself – local traders and manufacturers, state bureaucracies and, as seen, the nearby University of Melbourne. The Carlton Association, the voice of local residents, would become the largest, most fissiparous, and most politically tenacious of the resident action groups. Its vigour was a measure, not only of its intellectual and ideological firepower, but of the power of its adversaries.

The most significant of these threats, the HCV's plan for the complete rebuilding of Carlton, known as the 'Perrott Plan', was slow to materialise, allowing a groundswell of resistance to develop. 'It seems unfortunate that a large barrage of Housing Commission flats stands up like a sore thumb dividing an area which was already organising its own renaissance, and which has already, without wholesale redevelopment, great value to this community', Hilary Lewis wrote from her Parkville home in 1966.[33] Her mildy-expressed protest, published in the *Age*, foreshadowed the increasingly vehement objections of the students and young professionals whose homes lay in the Commission's sights on the other side of the campus, in Carlton.

The first steps towards the formation of the Carlton Association came two years later when separate North and South Carlton Associations were formed. According to one of its founders, David Beauchamp, the South Carlton Association was 'intended to assist residents with many different issues … schools, social welfare, the environment and so on … Our original

---

[33]   Hilary Lewis, 'Carlton Redevelopment' Melbourne *Age*, 26 May 1966, 13.

aims had nothing to do with the Housing Commission'. The founders of the North Carlton Association, on the other hand, had taken their lead from other residents' associations in Melbourne and Sydney. Eric Benjamin of the Parkville Association attended the first meeting of its Ad Hoc Committee and, at its first general meeting an invitation was extended to Patricia Thompson, a leading member of the five-year-old Paddington Association in Sydney, to attend.

Thompson undoubtedly had valuable experience to share with the Carlton Association. In the early months of 1968 Paddington residents had protested vehemently against the Department of Main Roads' plans to demolish up to 300 houses, many of them restored by new private residents.[34] In her address, she 'emphasised that power to change or preserve lies with the people who live or work in the area, provided they have a clear idea and are well informed on what they believe is needed'.[35] Mobilising the entire community was an admirable goal, but was it achievable? One member of Thompson's audience considered 'that the Italian community was unlikely to join a community association'. Nevertheless, the Association's members (400 people attended its AGM in 1970) were soon engaged in two major battles which were to define its character in the 1970s. One was a contest over the use of railway land in North Carlton;[36] the other, a fight with the HCV, was the group's first great success.

Resident action was a democratic ideal and most associations aspired to represent their entire local community. Effective social planning, Brian Howe declared in 1970, could only come from the involvement of 'significant numbers of … residents'. He was discussing the lowly but tenacious suburb of Fitzroy. The Fitzroy Residents' Association, formed in the previous year as a result of a report on *Community and Welfare Facilities in Fitzroy*, was created, in Howe's eyes, to promote 'citizen participation in the municipality'.[37] As a clergyman, Howe played a similar role in fostering the community ideal to other inner-city churchmen, such as Methodists John Goff and Andrew McCutcheon in North Melbourne and Collingwood respectively and Presbyterian Ian Ogilvy in East Melbourne.

---

34   Peter Loveday, 'Citizen Participation in Urban Planning' in *The Politics of Urban Growth*, ed. R. S. Parker and P. N. Troy (Canberra: Australian National University Press, 1972), 136.

35   Inaugural meeting 17 March 1969, Minute book Carlton Association 84 (92) Box 1, University of Melbourne Archives.

36   See Chapter Six.

37   Brian Howe, 'Collective Action in Fitzroy' *Action* (December 1970), 3.

In Carlton, Mal Cormack, Presbyterian Minister at the Combined Parish based at the Carlton Methodist Mission, took the first step in enlisting the members of the embryonic Carlton Association on behalf of local residents targeted by the HCV's plans for urban renewal. As David Beauchamp recalls:

> He said that there was a group of residents in the Princes, Lee, Lygon and Drummond Street block who had all been served with slum reclamation notices ... and he asked if we could help those residents. We went and looked at the houses, and decided that they were certainly not slums; they were no different to many of the other houses in Carlton, including the houses that we were living in ourselves. So, a group of us lodged an objection to the Housing Commission on that slum clearance, which was rejected by the Housing Commission.

A four acre (1.6 hectare) block known as the 'Lee Street Block', containing '53 houses, a block of flats, a mixed business, a bakery and a bottle yard' was slated for demolition in June 1969. The Carlton Association (North and South had united in May) responded by holding an open day when anyone in Melbourne could view the 'neatly and proudly kept homes' of the Lee Street Block.

The HCV's plans to 'renew' 200 acres (80 hectares) of Carlton were already well known. By the end of the year, the Melbourne Transportation Study plan to bisect the suburb with a six-lane urban freeway had been announced and other schemes threatening the compulsory purchase and demolition of property, such as in Kay Street, were rumoured to be afoot. The Carlton Association had barely formed before it faced what looked like a concerted bureaucratic assault on the community it represented.[38] Beauchamp declared in 1972:

> I believe that Carlton now faces the most severe crisis in its history. The last one hundred and twenty years have seen many changes, but never has Carlton been threatened with extinction. The combined threats of the Housing Commission, freeways and commercial developments could destroy the Carlton we know.[39]

Even today, veterans of the Carlton Association differ on the balance of self-interest and altruism, defensive preservationism and outward-looking

---

[38] David Beauchamp, letter, *Victorian Historical Journal*, (April 2002), 120.

[39] Carlton Association, Annual Report 1972, University of Melbourne Archives.

social engagement in its multifarious campaigns and social programs. New homeowners in Carlton had an immediate interest in the threat of compulsory acquisition and loss of their scant remaining open space. Historian Pat Grimshaw, who was present at the earliest ad hoc committee meeting, says that the organisation *refused* to become involved in other social issues, such as those involving migrants, schools, high-rise families, or women.[40] Beauchamp, on the other hand, emphasises its inclusive character. From the beginning, it had striven to be so, publicising its activities in the Italian newspaper *Il Globo* and engaging migrant spokesman Giovanni Sgro to address one of its meetings. It formed education and welfare committees as well as architecture and planning committees and made efforts from time to time to realise its declared ideal of 'participatory democracy', for example through a 'Community Participation Scheme' linking residents to the Association via a network of Area Representatives. But Grimshaw is correct in observing that social concerns gradually receded over time, as preservation claimed an increasing proportion of the Association's efforts.

By 1972 the CA had a large membership of around 2000, by far the largest of the Melbourne RAGs. It could, and did, claim to speak on behalf of all Carltonians. According to one of its leaders, Jeff Floyd,

> The Carlton Association ... has conducted fund raising door knocks which have succeeded in raising money from one in three households. As the donation was usually $1.00 one can argue that those donating this sum of money could be included in the membership of the C.A. At least they endorse the activities of its professional executive and thus the group is representative in this sense, which I believe is a valid one. [41]

Size could be a strength. 'An Association like this is strong in proportion as it is big in both senses – that it runs over a wide area and represents everybody and every kind of interest in the area', an astute observer of the North Adelaide Society, historian Hugh Stretton, noted in 1970. 'On the other hand, [he continued], the more all embracing it is, the more internal conflict it is bound to have and the more issues you will find on which it is prudent not to have a policy or on which you are in danger of splitting'. The sheer size of the Carlton Association, as well as the natural argumentativeness of its largely academic base, made tensions, like those already noted

---

[40] Patricia Grimshaw and Katie Holmes, 'A Search for Identity: Carlton's History, Carlton's Residents' *Victorian History Journal* 63 (2–3) (Oct 1992), 164.

[41] Floyd, *Citizen Participation*, 141. This quote corrects a typographical error: 'housholds'.

between Beauchamp and Grimshaw, more or less inevitable. If it gradually tended to focus its efforts more narrowly, it was in part because it was necessary to keep everyone on board. Significantly, Floyd believed that the 'varied background of the people in the area would preclude any attempts to expand the formal part of the C.A. indefinitely'.[42]

The effectiveness of the Carlton Association depended in part on its success in securing the support of other like-minded groups. Well before the halcyon days of the NSW Builders Labourers' Union Green Bans of 1971–74, it secured the support of the union's Victorian branch in its struggle to save a strip of railway land in North Carlton from private development. It also won the sympathy of journalists on Melbourne's three major newspapers, the morning *Age* and *Sun* and the evening *Herald*. No sooner had the Carlton Association looked to Sydney's Paddington than Alan Trengove, a feature-writer in the Saturday *Sun*, advocated it as a model for Melbourne inner suburbs to follow.[43] The *Herald* soon chimed in with a sympathetic editorial:

> It has to be recognized that the reckless, ill-planned suburban sprawl of Melbourne in the post-war decades has brought new problems and done some permanent damage ... in the present Carlton project, serviceable houses which their occupants like are ... marked for destruction ... people are entitled to ask questions.[44]

The same paper had previously suggested, once again on its editorial page, that 'The fight to preserve fifty picturesque old Carlton houses from destruction by the Housing Commission spotlights growing unease about the Commission's policies'.[45] The *Age* had published letters opposing the notion of Carlton as a slum as early as 1966. 'It has many acres of good class, if in some cases old, housing – London and Rome are old, too' wrote the President of the Carlton Business and Property Owners' Association, J W Ridgeway.[46] The paper's own editorial stance was more equivocal. But several of its journalists, especially those with links to the Carlton intelligentsia, were outspoken. Leonard Radic predicted that the Board of Works' freeway plans would 'blaze a trail of destruction' through the inner suburbs.[47] Architecture

---

42   Floyd, *Citizen Participation*, 141.
43   Alan Trengove, '"Paddo" Shows the Way' Melbourne *Sun*, 28 June 1969, 9.
44   Anon, 'Which Way Are We Growing?' Melbourne *Herald*, 13 June 1969, 4.
45   Anon, 'Planning Away Our Charm' Melbourne *Herald*, 9 May 1969, 4.
46   Anon, 'Opposition to the Carlton Scheme' Melbourne *Age*, 29 April 1966, 2.
47   Leonard Radic, 'Ring Road – Is It Worth $200m?' Melbourne *Age*, 5 May 1969, 6.

columnist Graham Whitford questioned the modernist prejudices of the Housing Commission. 'By the commision's standards, most of England's picturesque villages, so necessary to the country's tourist industry, would be demolished', he observed. 'Is their policy more enlightened than ours?'[48]

The RAGs were usually eager to proclaim their 'non-political' character and to stress techniques of persuasion and reasoned argument. 'It is always worth beginning with pleasant, civil approaches ... Don't start abusing them needlessly until they act as if they deserve it', Hugh Stretton advised the residents of North Adelaide. Paper warfare rather than street demonstrations was the RAGs' forte, but the late 1960s and early 1970s was an era of protest. Many of the activists themselves were veterans of radical protest movements, some going back to the peace movements of the 1950s, and many more to the anti-Vietnam war protests that swept the campuses in the late 1960s and culminated in the two Melbourne Moratoriums in 1970–71. The Monash University 'riot' of 1969[49] took place at the very same time as the Housing Commission began to realise its Lee Street plan. Sooner or later the passions and tactics of the anti-war movement were likely to spill over into the resident action movement. RAGs were generally slow to adopt demonstration tactics but, as Stretton recognised, 'peaceful forms of it can be effective if used with care and sufficient numbers'.

Some years later the Richmond Association, headed by Anthea Eyres and Annemarie Mutton, went beyond the Carlton Association's burning of Ray Meagher in effigy,[50] exploiting middle-class Anglo-Australian unease with the presence of the migrant working class. They organised a mass demonstration of Richmond residents to assemble on the front lawn of the HCV's Chairman; he lived, conveniently, in a secluded street in Hawthorn, the salubrious adjacent suburb. Alarmed, he insisted instead on meeting the Association's members in his office, only to be faced by sixty or so ardent protestors. While it was almost certainly the North Fitzroy Brooks Crescent protests (detailed in Chapter 6) which finally broke the back of the Housing Commission's 'scorched earth' policies, the steady escalation of popular protest, culminating in the demonstration and confrontations of the early 1970s, had already sapped its resistance.

From the beginning, resident activists had sought to combine a desire to preserve the built fabric of their neighbourhoods with radical aspirations

---

[48] Graham Whitford, 'Historical – or Slum?' Melbourne *Age*, 26 May 1969, 14.

[49] 'Talk on Monash Riot Today' Melbourne *Age*, 8 May 1969, 1.

[50] See Chapter Three.

toward community self-determination and social progress. Each resident action group struck its own balance between these aims. In 1995 Ruth Crow contrasted the communitarian impulses of her own north Melbourne Community Development Association with the Carlton and Fitzroy associations in which, she believed, 'the main aim ... was to save the building stock'.[51] She overdrew the comparison. RAGs in all cities – even those of, for instance, Subiaco, which emphasised nineteenth century building retention[52] – were also concerned at very least with issues of scale and density and the resultant social implications. How each organisation struck the balance depended, not just on the social character of its membership or the ideological outlook of its leaders, but on the impact of external forces, including state bureaucracies and local government.

---

[51]   Crow, 'Early History of the NMA from the Mid 1960s to the Early 1970s', 1.
[52]   See Chapter Seven.

Chapter 5

THE RISE OF COMMUNITY POLITICS

In 1969 John Power, academic and founding president of Sydney's Balmain Association, wrote a prescient article entitled 'The New Politics in the Old Suburbs', identifying the recent development of a number of 'civic action groups' in the inner areas of Melbourne and Sydney where pressures for redevelopment from both public and private sources were intense. Power asked if the new style in metropolitan politics these groups represented, and which had emerged from the terrace houses in the last five years, was of wider significance or merely 'exotic flow overs from the Groves of Academe'? He found these new groups surprising. Why should 'cosmopolitans' – business executives in metropolitan and national firms and professionals employed by universities and newspapers – suddenly become so seriously involved in parochial affairs? Power thought the answer lay in the substantial numbers of middle-class home owners who in the 1960s had been experiencing some of the unpleasant effects of large-scale redevelopment, as low density areas were subject to more intensive development 'on a scale which is unprecedented in our history'. 'Large numbers of people in the middle classes', he wrote, 'are now experiencing assaults on the amenity of the areas in which they live'. This was compared with the acceptance of earlier HCV development, when lower income residents were moved from South Melbourne, North Melbourne and Collingwood and 'nobody except a few social workers cared much' – certainly not the local councils eager for development in their municipalities.[1]

What Was New in the New Politics?

The new politics was an outcome of social and economic changes in the inner suburbs. By the 1970s in Melbourne there were dense concentrations of tertiary educated professionals in Carlton, Parkville and East Melbourne and in Sydney in Paddington, Glebe and Balmain, resulting in the transformation of local politics, as Andrew Jakubowicz wrote in 1974:

---

[1]   John Power, 'The New Politics in the Old Suburbs' *Quadrant* (December 1969), 60–65.

Whereas for generations local government was that area of concern left to party hacks, real estate agents and the ambitious young politician, the move to the inner areas of the city by the returning professionals made it extremely important as a focus of their concerns.[2]

The expertise and political activism of resident action groups was a new phenomenon, creating a climate in which corporations, municipal councils and government departments were 'wide open to checking by expert and highly organised posses of private citizens'.[3] They brought new issues not only to the inner city but also (especially in Sydney) to suburban local councils previously controlled by the aforementioned real estate agents, developers and local businessmen with Liberal Party connections. The focus on active citizenship, environmental and planning issues and the commitment to open government and public participation was unprecedented in Australia.

Early residents' associations had not been focused on political involvement but emphasised civic participation and open government. Some groups explicitly disavowed party politics in their constitution. This led Power to predict that the number of independent members in state parliament and local government would increase. Such new developments threatened the established political parties, especially the ALP, given its traditional base in the inner working-class suburbs of Melbourne and Sydney. Britain's Labour Party was similarly scared by the challenges of new social movements that defied class analysis and which were seen as a threat to its control of local government in areas of the Greater London Council and northern manufacturing cities. Tony Benn was one of the few Labour leaders to see possibilities in the new social movements for the renewal of socialism and for grassroots dissidents to revitalise the party.

Also unprecedented in Australian politics was the extent and significance of women's leadership and involvement. Kate Nash argues in her analysis of the new politics that women's participation built on the interaction of personal, local and global that had characterised earlier movements such as the campaign for women's suffrage.[4] Women have always been active in Australian suburban communities but participation in RAGs involved younger women in a more political and influential leadership role. Meredith

---

2   Andrew Jakubowicz, 'The City Game: Urban Ideology and Social Conflict', in *Social Change in Australia*, ed. D. Edgar (Melbourne: Cheshire, 1974), 341.

3   Anne Latreille, 'They Fight for Their Suburbs' Melbourne *Age*, 1 June 1973, 8.

4   Kate Nash, *Universal Difference: Feminism and the Liberal Undecidability of "Women"* (Houndmills: Macmillan, 1998).

Burgmann in Glebe and Margaret Park in North Sydney were among talented leaders in Sydney while among Melbourne leaders were Ruth Crow in North Melbourne, Louise Elliott in Fitzroy and Barbara Niven in Emerald Hill.[5]

Women moving into Melbourne's inner suburbs were well educated, many with young families and anxious to escape the perceived isolation and lack of community spirit in the suburbs. When Anne Latreille left full-time work as a journalist at the *Age* she worried about the prospect of spending all her time at home: 'I thought I might become bored or worse neurotic'. There was no chance of that in South Yarra where she was drawn into community campaigns around traffic and the provision of services. She compared her experience with 'the limbo of the lonely women, the Valium takers of the Yarra Valley' identified in a contemporary study of outer suburban women. Latreille concluded that despite the disadvantages of inner-urban living, such as noise, traffic, rubbish and poor services, 'you won't find quite that empty hopelessness, that vacuum of despair in the inner suburbs'.[6] Jane Jacobs, the mother and housewife who had 'changed the world', was a role model and inspiration. Her Greenwich Village group was famously described by Robert Moses as 'only a bunch of, a bunch of mothers', but they had overturned his redevelopment plans for the area in the 1950s.[7] Latreille found Jacobs' 'concern for others – what she calls "the eyes on the street" – neighbours watching out and supporting others', as one of her most appealing aspects.

These were educated, confident, and politically aware women. Onella Stagoll, a member of the FRA, recalls that at the initial meeting between a group of mothers and the responsible minister, Walter Jona, about the future of the Isabel Henderson kindergarten marooned in Fitzroy by the proposed Eastern Freeway, he was surprised to discover that 'we were no longer the polite Clyde School Old Girls' who had previously managed the kindergarten and 'was thrown off balance by our levels of knowledge, directness and determination … He realised this community would not be a pushover, which was confirmed by subsequent events'.[8] It was as foolish to underestimate 'a bunch of mothers' in Melbourne as it was in New York.

---

5   Zula Nittim, 'The Coalition of Resident Action Groups' in *Twentieth Century Sydney, Studies in Urban and Social History*, ed. J. Roe (Sydney: Hale and Iremonger, 1980).

6   Anne Latreille, 'A Personal View' in *The Inner Suburbs*, 17.

7   Flint, *Wrestling with Moses*, 87.

8   Anne Coghlan and Onella Stagoll, 'Isabel Henderson Kindergarten Centre Re-location' in *Social Justice Walk of North Fitzroy*, ed. Brian Stagoll and Barry Pullen (June 2003).

Conflict with Old Labor in Melbourne

Political renewal was urgently needed in inner-city Sydney and Melbourne where ALP 'machines' dominated moribund and unrepresentative local councils.

The old locally-based inner-city labour movements were seen as inward looking, defending members' interests but 'showing very little concern with wider issues or more inclusive political participation' which characterised the 'new middle class social movements'.[9] The Labor split in 1955 and subsequent formation of the Democractic Labor Party had weakened the ALP's inner-city branches and it wasn't long before the new community groups had a much larger membership. However, given the dominance of the ALP in inner-city municipalities, cooperation was necessary if change was to be achieved and there was soon a 'crossover' membership between the RAGs and the ALP, especially in Melbourne. Local branches, many rumoured to have a membership that could fit in a telephone booth, found they had to dust off their minute books and arrange meetings.

Conflict between old and new Labor took different forms in Melbourne and Sydney. The huge redevelopment of inner-city Melbourne was all in ALP electorates and undertaken by the Liberal Party government of Henry Bolte with the support of the Country Party. Yet ALP councils in Collingwood, Fitzroy and Richmond welcomed slum abolition and the new high-rise housing estates. Hal Mackrell, one of the new breed elected to Fitzroy Council in 1971, identified the difference:

> There was the old Labor council which believed in high rise flats, getting people accommodation, having Labor people looked after in their own area, and new Labor which was looking after empowering the individual people and having them have a say in their own life and not making horizontal slums into vertical slums and looking at this sort of effort.

South Melbourne Council with its mixed membership of ALP, local industrialists and businessmen, also welcomed redevelopment. So did the conservative Melbourne City Council (MCC) which included Carlton, North Melbourne, Flemington, Kensington, East Melbourne and parts of South Yarra. It was described as a 'cosy boys' club' mainly representing commercial and development interests with even the few locally based MCC members supporting redevelopment of the inner city. The Bolte government's

---

[9]   Nash, *Universal Difference*, 105.

slum abolition policy was also supported in the Victorian Parliament by ALP members for inner-city electorates and by Clive Stoneham, the leader of the party until 1967.

Following the 1955 split in the Victorian ALP, the central executive was temporarily given control of all preselections for public office. Effectively this meant that Jack Tripovitch, ALP Victorian branch secretary and a member of the Legislative Council, along with a small group of trade unionists, determined preselection decisions. Most members of inner-city councils had a working-class background or were small businessmen or council employees. The few women members were usually widows of former councillors. Not only did the councillors lack expertise and experience, there were few professional staff employed by councils beyond the town clerk and the engineer who controlled roads, traffic and planning matters. Peter Hollingworth described the Fitzroy Council when he first came to the Brotherhood as 'absolutely shocking'.

Andrew McCutcheon was one of the first of the new breed to gain ALP preselection and election to Collingwood Council in 1965. Although the central executive was reluctant to pre-select a clergyman its members were impressed that he lived locally with his social worker wife Vivienne and their family in a HCV walk-up flat. McCutcheon recalls council meetings as a depressing scene: 'They were all sort of hopeless and had been giving jobs for the boys and featherbedding for years'. There was no involvement from those with an ethnic background, who were a large proportion of Collingwood's population and workers in the local industries. McCutcheon thought it 'absolutely woeful' that so little opportunity had been give to them for representation or encouragement to take part in the public decision-making process.

The new residents elected to Collingwood Council after 1970 were encouraged to join by McCutcheon and had ALP endorsement. McCutcheon recalls that there was only a small residents' association in Collingwood at the time, based on the middle-class enclave in Clifton Hill, so new members of council were not the outcome of a move by the professional middle class into the area. 'No, it was more the Labor Party branches getting their better people into council and that was just by networking and finding the activists in the Labor Party'. Greek-born Theo Sidiropoulos, elected to Collingwood Council in 1968, was the first migrant councillor and became mayor in 1977. Caroline Hogg, a teacher at Fitzroy High School, was the first woman of the new members to join Collingwood Council – 'under pressure' as she 'lived next door to the McCutcheons so there wasn't too much getting away from Andrew's persuasion. So I offered myself for pre-selection, which was a very Stalinist method in those days. There was no local component – the Victorian ALP did it … just 12 or 14 old blokes really, who asked me totally irrelevant questions'.

McCutcheon welcomed her support on the council; he was at least able to get a seconder for his motions. He recalls his opposition to the HCV proposal for high-rise flats in Collingwood and that other councillors 'were unwilling to resist' the HCV demand that the council forgo charging rates on the new developments for thirty years despite the large increase in population and demand for services. Although this arrangement had been accepted by the MCC, McCutcheon argued that it was a huge subsidy to the HCV and he was able through his membership of the influential Town and County Planning Association (TCPA) to generate opposition to the practice. This ability to mobilise support outside government was a well-used strategy of the new residents. McCutcheon was also concerned that the HCV provided no community services other than relying on open space around the Collingwood high-rise towers for play and passive recreational activities. Little help was offered in resettling residents whose homes would be demolished. McCutcheon remembers:

> There was absolutely no understanding of the fact that they had community networks and support systems and they might be scattered to the four winds and not be anywhere near the people they'd been neighbourly with before or shared family responsibilities or whatever. It was really disastrous. It was the absolute destruction of a basic sort of community resource.

The clash between old and new ALP members was different in Fitzroy where there were 'more university middle-class people' and a stronger and more active residents' association. The election of Brian Lennon to the council at first seemed to confirm John Power's prediction of the rise of independents. But there was a significant crossover of membership between the Fitzroy Residents' Association and the ALP and after Lennon's election association members elected to Council had ALP endorsement. Fitzroy mayors with FRA/ALP involvement included Paul Coghlan, Barry Pullen, Hal Mackrell, Carol Carney, Tom Merino and Bill Peterson. Their diverse backgrounds illustrate that not all residents' association political leaders came from the middle class.

Women were emboldened by their experiences in the residents' associations and Anne Polis observed that women activists became more political as 'the whole society was politicised'. This meant confronting the ALP's formidable inner-city 'Wren machine', a survival of the gambling empire of John Wren and still influential in Richmond, Collingwood and Carlton. Annemarie Mutton recalls that Richmond Council, a bastion of machine influence, 'was against us because we were all middle-class communists, and worse, intellectuals, academics, it was terrible'. A pioneer role model was Bev Genser whose 'tough Jewish background' helped her to confront Richmond's 'Tammany Hall' first as an activist and later as a member of the council.

Women activists were especially successful in election to the Fitzroy Council. Hal Mackrell recalls that in the 1970s the council was 'ridiculed in other suburbs for having five out of fifteen women councillors and other councils would say "couldn't you find any men?"' The women worked to make the council responsive to social issues such as childcare, community health and multicultural services. Carol Carney – the first of the new breed of women councillors elected in 1973 – Louise Elliot, Barbara Gayler and Helen Madden, worked to appoint Jenny Wills as the council's first social worker.[10] Wills established a pioneering Social Planning Office, a considerable achievement given that five years earlier Fitzroy was a 'roads and rubbish' council. Women elected to the Collingwood Council supported the appointment of Edith Morgan as that council's first social worker and another pioneer of local social services.

Because of opposition from the entrenched business and financial interests of the influential Civic Group and the voting gerrymander that favoured them, it was more difficult for members of residents' groups to be elected to the Melbourne City Council. It was the 1980s before major changes were made to the voting procedures enabling the election of resident association members and of Eddie Beacham of the CA as Lord Mayor in 1983. Lecki Ord became the first woman Lord Mayor of Melbourne in 1987, followed by Winsome McCaughey of the North Melbourne Association and Community Child Care the next year.

These councillors and mayors managed the strategic move from the RAGs to the more complex area of local government and were important contributors to the new style in metropolitan politics. Their involvement brought new life to moribund inner-city councils and transformed the limited agenda of local government.

---

[10]   Jenny Wills et al, *Local Government and Community Services. Fitzroy – A Case Study in Social Planning* (Melbourne: Hard Pressed Publications, 1985).

The Basket Weavers of Balmain

The conflict with old labour was different in Sydney where the ALP was in power in the City of Sydney Council and the right-wing Catholic faction dominated the party administration from the headquarters at Sussex Street. At the state level, the Liberal and Country Party coalition was in power from 1965 to 1976, led by Robert Askin for all but the last of those years. The Askin government was ruthlessly pro-development and soon at loggerheads with the SCC. Council boundaries were redrawn to eliminate some inner-suburban areas opposed to development and the SCC itself was sacked in 1968 to facilitate development in downtown Sydney. Soon there were giant redevelopment schemes for The Rocks, for Kings Cross, for all over the place'.[11]

The crucial battle between the residents' associations and old labour was in the inner suburb of Balmain, the birthplace of the first ALP branch. The Balmain Association (BA) had been formed as the middle class began to move in during the 1960s and had success in electing independent candidates to the Leichhardt Council. Conflict broke out over a permit application to build chemical tanks in the suburb, an application supported by the majority of ALP councillors. But two Labor members, Nick Origlass and Issy Wyner, broke ranks and joined residents' association councillors in voting against issuing the permit. Wyner's son Larrie recalls that Origlass, an ironworker, and Wyner, a former secretary of the Painters and Dockers Union and former Communist Party member, were not close to the dominant Right faction of the New South Wales ALP! They (and their families) were expelled from the ALP in 1967 for having voted against a caucus decision. Both were subsequently re-elected to Leichhardt Council as independents and each served as mayor, running open council meetings and encouraging participatory democracy.[12] The' battle for Balmain', between old labour and the new residents, was significant for its outcome in complex new political alignments. Jacubowicz wrote:

> The lesson of Leichhardt, presumably, has not been lost on the ALP
> and any broadening of the tendency on the electorate's part to link
> votes with issues and not with party platforms means that parties

---

[11] Terry Irving and Rowan Cahill, *Radical Sydney: Places, Portraits and Unruly Episodes* (Kensington: UNSW Press, 2010), 308.

[12] Unpublished Larry Wyner obituary 'Balmain Legend, 'Issy' Wyner' (1916–2008).

will have to adjust, quite radically in many platform areas, or suffer loss.[13]

The lesson was not totally learned by the New South Wales ALP during the conflicts in Balmain over the next twenty-five years. The fierce struggle between predominantly old working-class labour and a new more radicalised generation have been well documented in *Basket Weavers and True Believers*, Tony Harris's participant-observer account of the making and unmaking of the Labor Left in Leichhardt Municipality between 1970 and 1991. Paul Keating's famous taunt about the 'basket weavers of Balmain' reflected the New South Wales ALP's view that residents groups were trendies, obsessed with lifestyle rather than with substantial economic and social political issues. Eventually the council was taken over by independents and local swimming heroine Dawn Fraser was elected as an independent to the state parliament in 1988.[14]

Despite conflict between new and old labour in the inner city the new politics, as Tony Benn had predicted, did rejuvenate the ALP, bringing new issues and energetic, committed members into the party. More educated and experienced members were elected to local councils and to state parliaments. The reorganisation of the Victorian branch in 1973 led to the establishment of hard-working policy committees which developed comprehensive and sophisticated policies especially in urban affairs, education, women's affairs and health for implementation at local, state and federal levels. The clash between new and old labour should not detract from recognition that new labour drew on an inner-city radical labour tradition. Origlass and Wyner represented this in Balmain while the new members of ALP branches in Fitzroy and Richmond drew on and renewed the radical traditions of these suburbs.

The New Breed in North Sydney

In Sydney RAGs were formed not only in the inner city but also in middle-class suburbs, especially the harbour-side suburbs of the north shore affected by extensive private flat developments. In Melbourne, active RAGs were formed in the middle class suburbs of Hawthorn and Malvern. However, it

---

13   Andrew Jakubowitz, 'A New Politics of Suburbia' *Current Affairs Bulletin* 48 (11) (1972), 318.

14   Tim Bonyhady, 'The Battle for Balmain' *Urban Futures – Issues for Australian Cities*, 18 June 1995, Commonwealth Department of Housing and Regional Development, 25–34.

was not until the 1990s, under the Kennett Liberal government (1992–99), that more intensive redevelopment in Melbourne's middle ring suburbs prompted the formation of further residents' associations, which joined together in the 'Save our Suburbs' (SOS) movement.[15]

The first green bans imposed in Sydney by the NSW BLF were in the fashionable area of Hunters Hill in 1971. Jack Mundey responded to the pleas of a group of women residents committed to saving Kellys Bush, the last remaining bushland on the Parramatta River. The green bans successfully prevented development in the area and the Kellys Bush women, described by Mundey as 'very politically skilled', went on to endorse candidates on an environment and anti-flat policy, winning a majority of seats on Hunters Hill Council at the next election. Jack Mundey dismissed criticisms of the imposition of so-called 'bourgeois bans', arguing that the union should support new political alignments that were emerging in response to large-scale development:

> On the one hand you had the Askin government and sections of the union movement opposed to green bans and supporting development, while the bans attracted support from small l liberals and some Liberal Party members opposed to unfettered development.[16]

Such political alignments emerged as the pro development North Sydney Council, representing real estate agents, businessmen and developers, pushed ahead with large commercial and residential redevelopments in the 1970s. RAGs were formed to run independent community candidates for election to the council, who would oppose high-rise developments, increased traffic volumes and neglect of community services. Margaret Park writes that the 'new breed' of independent community councillors marked 'an important era in Sydney's planning and social history … not only related to the resident action movement but also part of the women's movement'.[17] Often women candidates 'had no prior interest in pursuing local government careers or even knew the location of the Council Chambers'. Yet Carole Baker, a North Sydney resident and ex-school teacher with strong networks, ran a successful

---

[15]   Miles Lewis, *Suburban Backlash: The Battle for the World's Most Liveable City* (Hawthorn: Blooming Books, 1999).

[16]   Meredith Burgmann and Verity Burgmann, *Green Bans, Red Union: Environmental Activism and the New South Wales Builders Labourers' Federation* (Sydney: UNSW Press, 1998), 73.

[17]   Margaret Park, *Designs on a Landscape: A History of Planning in North Sydney* (Rushcutters Bay: North Sydney Council/Halstead Press, 2002), 35.

'People before Profits' election campaign. Although new to political action, the North Sydney Society (its motto 'to enable individuals to influence the decisions that affect them') was able to win support from the local newspaper, the *North Sydney Post*. By 1972, after extensive community consultation, the residents' movement had developed a proposed new North Sydney Planning Scheme focused on community-based precinct areas.

The most high profile leader of the North Sydney Society was Ted Mack, who became mayor of North Sydney and was then elected to state and federal parliament as an independent, with the backing of the residents' action movement. Mack was one of the few independents elected to the Commonwealth parliament and was strongly identified with the residents' associations movement.

The RAGs struggled to influence the Melbourne and Sydney city councils, both bastions of commercial interests in the 1970s, although both included inner-city suburbs with strong residents' associations. Old-style MCC councillors were frustrated by these 'minority rate payer groups' which they believed undermined the basic principles of local government, while the residents' groups thought the MCC itself undermined these principles with its limited franchise and the making of decisions behind closed doors.[18] Despite these limits, the residents' groups were influential in bringing new social groups into politics and in challenging the entrenched party alignments. Their tactics and policies varied, but in the 1970s they achieved more open government, greater participation of women and more socially conscious policies.

Coalitions and Support

The inner suburbs in the small councils outside the MCC and SCC areas struggled with the impact of redevelopment as they had neither councillors nor staff able to articulate the social and physical impact of high-rise housing or freeways. The residents' associations were therefore important in their ability to provide the inner suburbs with 'the capacity to put their arguments and to make their case, to argue it publicly, and to start to develop support and political clout on issues which, in the past, have just been ridden over and ignored'.[19]

---

[18]   Renate Howe, 'Social and Political Realities' in *Melbourne Do or Die? Town Planning Seminar*, MCC, 28 April 1977.

[19]   Andrew McCutcheon, 'Management of the Inner Suburbs' in *The Inner Suburbs*, 24.

In Melbourne the associations were able to draw on the research of CURA and the growing research capacity of the BSL under the leadership of David Scott and Peter Hollingworth. Soon after its establishment in 1972 CURA studied the impact of proposed freeway routes for the Commonwealth Bureau of Roads as well as studies of housing displacement and new models for childcare services. In North Melbourne the knowledge and expertise of Ruth and Maurie Crow, aided by their extensive library (now the basis of the Crow Collection at Victoria University) were crucial to developing planning strategies and to campaigns for child care. Residents' associations became more sophisticated, developing subcommittees on matters such as planning, education, social welfare and heritage. The model was the Carlton Association, with its 2000 members able to divide into numerous sub-committees drawing on the expertise of professional members and academics.

There was a more coordinated approach between the associations, with the formation of coalitions in Sydney, Melbourne and Adelaide to achieve greater citizen participation in the planning process, the introduction of third party appeals against development consent and more cooperation with local residents and local government from state planning authorities. The largest and most active of the coalitions was the Coalition of Resident Action Groups (CRAG), formed in 1971, which gathered a membership of more than forty groups in Sydney and Newcastle. The North Sydney Association was important in the formation of CRAG. Its success between 1972 and 1975 was largely the work of Murray Geddes, a social worker and recently appointed tutor in social work at the University of New South Wales. He had moved from Melbourne where he had been involved with the resident action movement in Fitzroy and with CURA.[20]

CRAG was successful in negotiating satisfactory outcomes for local residents and the New South Wales Housing Commission tenants after the redevelopment of The Rocks area had been halted by BLF green bans. But CRAG came into conflict with residents when it opposed proposals for the redevelopment of 26 acres in Waterloo. Even more divisive was the redevelopment proposed for Victoria Street, Darlinghurst, by Frank Theeman, wealthy Sydney businessman turned property developer. A residents' association was soon formed to oppose the demolition of houses and displacement of residents, many of them low-income tenants. The

---

[20]   Murray Geddes, 'The Coalition of Resident Action Groups in New South Wales' *Ekstasis*, no. 4 (1972), 12–15.

residents had the support of *Now*, a Kings Cross newspaper founded by the Reverend Ted Noffs of the Wayside Chapel. The Victoria Street Residents' Association joined CRAG in 1973 following the eviction of squatters and tenants, but conflict soon emerged between the squatters and CRAG over tactics, following the disappearance and probable murder of Juanita Nielsen, the editor of *Now*.[21]

Despite these setbacks, Geddes continued to pursue a broad agenda for CRAG. In Melbourne he had been involved with his fellow social worker Colin Benjamin (son of the Parkville Association's Eric Benjamin) in establishing a regional organisation of councils in the western suburbs with the aim of achieving a more coordinated approach to social programs. In May 1972 CRAG coordinated a conference on 'Reforming government in Australia – New Federal and Regional Government Approaches Needed'. It called for more consultation and the 'recognition of the right of citizens to have a say in decisions which affect their living standards'.[22] CRAG split into regional groups in 1973 consistent with the regional strategy developed by the Department of Urban and Regional Development (DURD) following the election of the Whitlam government. The divisions in CRAG over strategy and the lukewarm response of residents' associations to a regional structure led to the group's influence waning, reinforced by the demise of the Whitlam government in 1975.

The Committee for Urban Action (CUA), formed in Melbourne in 1970, had different objectives from CRAG and did not aspire to be a comprehensive regional organisation. It was a coalition of 10 inner-city residents' associations, reflecting the different geography of the movement in Melbourne. It did not extend to the suburbs or regional cities. Geoff Baker of the NMA was a driving force in CUA, which met every six weeks, enabling association representatives to share and exchange information. A primary objective was 'to assist those working in residential associations and other amenity organisations who are anxious to control and improve flat developments in Melbourne'. CUA also contributed to the turnaround in the ALP position on urban renewal in state parliament. Miles Lewis from the Carlton Association led the negotiations on behalf of CUA with the state Labor leader Clyde Holding on the 1973 urban renewal bill then before parliament. Holding, the member for Richmond, had been elected as leader of the Parliamentary Labor Party in 1967, replacing Clive Stoneham.

---

[21] Nittim, 'The Coalition of Resident Action Groups', 270.

[22] Nittim, 'The Coalition of Resident Action Groups', 273.

Unlike Stoneham, Holding was in contact with the new members of local councils and inner-city ALP branches and if he could win caucus support was prepared to consider opposing the legislation.

Lewis was critical of the lack of support from CUA in the negotiations on the 1973 Urban Renewal Bill, describing it as 'moribund and ineffective', too informal, with a changing membership and badly in need of a constitution.[23] Nevertheless, Lewis prepared carefully for his meetings and followed up with detailed responses to the numerous written questions submitted by Holding in preparation for his submission to caucus. Lewis's responses reflected the residents' associations' political priorities and included opposition to inner-metropolitan freeways, overcoming secrecy in planning, ending the gerrymandered representation on Melbourne City Council, opposition to multi-unit flat development and the need to divest the HCV of responsibility for urban renewal. In his meetings with Holding, Lewis emphasised that CUA also wanted an undertaking that there would be no more high-rise flats should a state ALP government be elected.[24]

1973 – A Political Turning Point

The residents' associations in Victoria were becoming an important political force at local and increasingly at state government level. Confrontational demonstrations with protesters were politically damaging for the Bolte government. Carefully researched policy proposals prepared by the residents' associations on state and local government planning, housing, freeways and redevelopment proposals rivalled those of the government bureaucrats and received extensive publicity. The political influence of the residents' associations was strengthened by the support from the *Age* newspaper. At the local level the *Melbourne Times*, edited by Ann Polis and Tony Knox and circulating in the inner suburbs, gave an increasingly professional and effective coverage of residents' association issues. The paper 'didn't believe in impartiality' and pioneered investigative journalism in Melbourne, focusing on the corruption and incompetence associated with the state government infrastructure authorities.[25]

---

23   Miles Lewis, memo dated 26 February 1973, Urban Activists Collection, Deakin University.

24   Miles Lewis, letter dated 18 April 1973, Urban Activists Collection, Deakin University.

25   David Nichols, '"Activist" Local Newspapers and their Role in Protest Movements' *History Australia* 4 (2005), 233.

Both main parties were modernising. Gough Whitlam, elected as federal Labor leader in 1967, recognised that reform of the Victorian branch of the ALP was vital if the party was to win state and national elections and in 1971 the federal executive voted to intervene. The reforms of party structure which followed intervention paved the way for the election of a federal ALP government in December 1972. This win was in part due to the party's policy on modernising cities, and the establishment of DURD in 1973 was an important development for the urban reform movement in the states.

The Liberal Party in Victoria was also changing as a group of 'new liberals' struggled for power. This group recognised the value of working with the RAGs rather than confronting them. This changed view was evident with the accession of Rupert Hamer as Premier in late 1972, succeeding Henry Bolte. The contrast between the blunt farmer and urbane lawyer could not have been greater. Hamer recognised the political realities that the 'old school' Bolte had been unwilling to grasp and there were enough progressives in the Hamer cabinet – 'small-l Liberals compared with the old Tories' as Hunt put it – to make it possible for the party to take a new direction.

Hamer had been prepared to listen to the residents' associations as minister for local government under Bolte. He had opposed the first urban renewal bill introduced in 1970,[26] which took planning powers away from local government and the Town and Country Planning Board, part of Hamer's portfolio. Another Liberal prepared to listen to the RAGs was Alan Hunt, who claimed inner-city credentials as his father had been Methodist minister in Collingwood. Hunt was appointed minister for local government and promoted to cabinet under Hamer.

An indication of the changed political environment was Hunt's recognition of the importance of Britain's Skeffington Report of 1969 (*People and Planning. Report of the Committee on Public Participation in Planning*), an influential publication for the residents' associations as it recommended the overhaul of Britain's postwar planning legislation to include greater community participation. Hunt recalls that:

> it was the way to go, particularly in anything that had to do with community or planning. Consultation was essential. Without it there would never be community ownership of policies. If there was consultation and genuine participation and genuine listening, you got a result that people accepted, felt they owned it and so on.

---

[26]   John Messer, 'Point, counterpoint' Melbourne *Age*, 18 February 1970, 5.

Hamer had included a requirement for consultation with local government in amendments to the Town and Country Planning Act but there was no provision for public consultation in other legislation covering public authorities. Hunt recalled that his first speech on a planning matter as minister was:

> on the value of consultation and participation and its importance. I gave ten reasons. As you will see, I later developed this into a 60 point paper, 60 benefits. If you look at all the sub-points in it, it's probably more like 100, but there it is. In the early '70s, consultation started to take off.

Another of Hunt's important actions as minister was to stymie implementation of the 1973 Voumard *Report on Local Government* which recommended that a royal commission be established to examine the amalgamation of local government areas. This report (described in an *Age* editorial as generating 'new life for ... three poor sisters' – Fitzroy, Port Melbourne and South Melbourne)[27] was vigorously opposed by the inner-suburban RAGs on the grounds that it would erode the strong community identity of these suburbs and especially because they feared the subsuming of inner-suburban councils into an enlarged MCC. Amalgamation was a threat to the progressive political and social gains of the residents' associations. Peter Hollingworth thought Alan Hunt had been 'an enormously positive force', singling out his role in opposing amalgamation.

A spate of legislation followed the election of the Hamer government in 1973. Legislation was introduced to establish a Town Planning Appeals Tribunal to allow third party appeals against local government planning decisions. This was a historic step for Victoria. The Land and Environment Court of NSW established in the 1970s was more legalistic and did not provide the same access to community groups. In 1974 the Historic Buildings Act established a Historic Buildings Council and a register to list and protect heritage buildings. Significantly the 1973 urban renewal bill lapsed, as had its predecessor in 1971. According to Andrew McCutcheon 'they were the most elaborate procedures you had to go through to get an outcome. Practically nothing ever emerged because it was so complex'. The end of the high-rise building program also occurred on Hamer's watch; as Hunt points out, it was already clear these buildings had become ghettoes. HCV policy on inner-city housing was changed to encouraging infill housing sympathetic to the scale of surrounding development.

---

[27] Anon, 'Keeping Tabs on the "Third Tier"' Melbourne *Age*, 28 December 1976, 4.

More controversial was the decision by Hamer before the 1973 election to promise the abandonment of further freeway development in Melbourne, a response to fierce opposition especially to the Eastern Freeway which cut through the inner suburbs of Collingwood, Fitzroy and Carlton and to the proposed approaches to the Westgate Bridge through South Melbourne and Port Melbourne. Tom Hogg of the CBR is scathing of this decision and its implications for traffic dispersal. Hunt was also doubtful:

> I was very dubious about the abandonment of the freeways. They had been planned, and shown on the Planning Schemes, after a laborious process ... I thought any abandonment would foreclose opportunities. The decision was a political one. In a few places, not many, but in a few places it would go through existing communities and divide them. It would be like the Berlin Wall in a way. There was bitter opposition there.

These Hamer initiatives helped to block the rejuvenating ALP and deprived Holding of the opportunity to lead a state Labor government. It was 1982 before Hamer's successor Lindsay Thompson was defeated by the ALP under the leadership of John Cain. The Cain governments (1982–1990) included members and ministers with a RAG background including Barry Pullen, Caroline Hogg, Andrew McCutcheon, Giovanni Sgro and Theo Sideropoulos. Their experience in the urban movement informed reforms in many areas including planning, housing and ethnic affairs.

'Curiously Effective'

These words were used by a puzzled Andrew Jacubowicz in assessing the impact of the urban protest movement and the residents' associations. He concluded that 'in Australia, the groups and the issues differed from place to place and the measure of success varied. But what is important is the political climate being generated by this activity and its implications for the wider conduct of political affairs'. An essential element in this achievement was that 'their ability to use media and personal contacts within bureaucracies to talk the language of the experts and present cases with "all the homework" makes them in some cases more effective opponents than those presenting simply a demagogic face'.[28]

Alan Hunt briefly made the same point when asked about the influence of protests on the Hamer government. 'Yeah, well protest, or going to the

---

[28] Jakubowitz, 'A New Politics of Suburbia', 316.

barricades, is no substitute for sound argument. I preferred sound argument'.
Anne Latreille also identified the expertise of the residents' associations
as an explanation for their political influence, citing the architects and
town planning members of the Carlton Association's flat action subcom-
mittee who were 'reputed to be more familiar with the Uniform Building
Regulations than are the Melbourne city councillors'.[29] Given their lack
of resources, the development of detailed community-based plans by
the North Melbourne Association and the Carlton Association was an
exceptional achievement, as was that of the North Sydney Association's
comprehensive plan. Jim Holdsworth's work on assessing the impact on
residents of housing and freeway developments was later used as a model
by the Commonwealth Bureau of Roads. The research on social policy by
CURA and the BSL and on ethnicity by the Ecumenical Migration Centre
(EMC) were the basis for initiatives by local, state and federal government.
The expertise and studies of the residents' associations and associated
organisations, often resented by government bureaucracies, indicated a new
approach to political decision-making through what would now be called
evidence-based planning.

Nevertheless, John Power thought the associations were 'naïve' and put
too much faith in solving problems through community discussion and town
planning.[30] They were also criticised for failing to facilitate the political
participation of under-represented groups, especially migrants. William
Logan, author of *The Gentrification of Inner Melbourne*, and a member of the
Carlton Assocation in the early 1970s, was:

> not at all convinced that the reforming emphasis was a strong feature of
> all resident groups in the sense of empowering wider groups of residents.
> For example, there was never much effort as I remember it on the part
> of the Carlton Association to bring migrants into the organisation, to
> represent their views, or to help them develop their own muscle.[31]

As mentioned in the previous chapter, this lack of connection to migrant
residents was a concern from the earliest days of the Carlton Association.
However, while ethnic groups were not actively involved in the residents'
associations there was cooperation between FILEF (a Marxist-Italian organisation of migrant workers and their families), CURA and EMC around

---

29   Latreille, 'They Fight for Their Suburbs' Melbourne *Age*, 1 June 1973, 8.

30   Power, 'The New Politics in the Old Suburbs', 64.

31   William Logan, Research Committee Minutes, Urban Activists Collection, Deakin University.

ethnic rights,[32] and although ethnic groups did not officially participate in residents' associations, they were mobilised on particular campaigns. A brief study of the Greek newspaper *Neos Cosmos* found ten articles between May and August 1970 reporting concern over demolition of houses, evictions and reports of meetings in the Brooks Crescent area. The election of ALP ethnic councillors were important political breakthroughs despite the considerable language and cultural difficulties these councillors faced.

Another important political gain was the encouragement and opportunities the residents' associations gave for the political participation of women, with some women finding the residents' associations more challenging and involving than the emerging women's movement. In North Sydney, Robyn Read (Hamilton) didn't feel the need to get involved in the women's movement 'because I was doing that stuff with resident action'.[33] Ann Polis observed that activist women were learning on the job and had no direct connections with the Women's Electoral Lobby (WEL), which was getting off the ground at the same time: 'We were so passionate and tied up in what we were doing, whereas all around there was all that early feminist, all that stuff about women and I just didn't even feel it'. Caroline Hogg 'was aware of the consciousness-raising groups and the Women's Electoral Lobby during the 1970s', but did not join. She was 'too busy teaching, raising children and being a councillor and mayor of Collingwood'.

The most common criticism of the RAGs was that their achievements mainly benefited their middle-class membership. Anne Latreille resented 'smug condemnation' of those in the middle and outer suburbs: 'an attitude that inner suburban people are stirrers who want it all their own way'.[34] In their history of the green bans in Sydney, Verity Burgmann and Meredith Burgmann question the branding of activist movements as NIMBYs, especially interpretations of resident activism in Sydney in the 1970s that identify the middle class as benefiting the most from protests. The Burgmanns argue that this interpretation was inconsistent with BLF involvement, which 'gave previously powerless inner-city people power against big developers and government, an effective means of making their wishes known and altered the balance and transformed the process'.[35] Andrew McCutcheon

32   Lopez, *The Origins of Multiculturalism*, 148–52; Giovanni Sgro, *Mediterranean Son: Memoirs of a Calabrian Migrant* (Coburg: Scoprire il Sud, 2000).

33   Park, *Designs on a Landscape*, 44.

34   Latreille, 'A Personal View', 19.

35   Burgmann and Burgmann, *Green Bans, Red Union*, 97.

points to the danger of generalisation as the RAGs were 'an incredible pot-pourri of conflict, of values, of interests and concerns – some of them very much community-based and some of them very much self-interest-based'.[36]

Predictions that the residents' associations would lead to the election of more independents in the 1970s proved largely inaccurate in Melbourne. At the local level most urban activists worked within an existing party, usually the ALP, although some managed to build a strong independent base. Divisions over political strategies were to become more intense as the inner suburbs became attractive to more affluent residents and gentrification intensified. In the 1980s independents were elected to inner-city councils sometimes in opposition to leaders of the early residents' associations. Hal Mackrell recalls of Fitzroy Council that 'the change was instead of having Labor with perhaps one or two independents ... it got to when those who saw themselves as independents got control of the council'.

Although there are arguments over the motivation and impact of the urban protest movement it played a central role in transforming politics, especially in Australia's two largest cities. While the postwar politicians had focused on building a larger and more diverse population and a strong commercial and industrial economy, the new politics of the 1960s and 1970s had different objectives. The focus of the urban protest movement on active citizenship, the importance of environmental and planning issues and the commitment to open and participatory government set a new direction for Australian politics. The groups that emerged from the terrace houses in the 1960s had not been 'merely exotic flow overs from the Groves of Academe' but a significant new movement in metropolitan politics.

---

[36] McCutcheon, 'Management of the Inner Suburbs', 24–25.

Chapter 6

BIG BRAWLS

The first half of the 1970s in Australia will be remembered not only for the political impact of the federal Labor government; it will also be recalled as a period in which a diverse number of social movements forcefully opposed the imposition of planned technological change. Protests were made against airport extensions, against the siting of certain industries and business, in opposition to the intrusion of buildings into parklands, against urban renewal, and against freeway construction.[1]

This prediction of sociologist Patrick Mullins in 1977 was prescient. The early 70s was a period of intense political and social activity as urban protest movements became a strong extra-parliamentary force demanding more participatory and open government. Community-based approaches to opposing inappropriate development in Australia in the late 1960s and early 1970s included an extraordinary range of differing tactics, from violent clashes with authorities to adjusting policy from within formalised democratic forums. This chapter and the next explore two sides of the activist coin – taking the issues 'to the streets' and taking them to the backrooms and civil institutions. Brawls over freeway plans, demolition and redevelopment and the location of industrial sites brought together diverse groups from outside the residents' associations, such as the National Trust, professional associations and trade unions.

Radical action was spurred by frustration and anger at the unreasonable intransigence of bureaucracy, business, planners and government. Union bans on demolition and construction work in Sydney and Melbourne were a distinguishing feature of Australian urban protests and a crucial factor in the outcome of many big brawls. One Victorian BLF flyer produced

---

[1]   Patrick Mullins, 'Social Implications of the Brisbane Northern Freeway' in *Planning in Turbulent Environments*, ed. John S. Western and Paul R. Wilson (St Lucia: University of Queensland Press, 1977), 140–162.

during its battle for survival in the mid-1980s claimed that the union had first used bans for conservation purposes in 1947; Norm Gallagher claimed that the first use of bans was even earlier, in 1940, when the BLF prevented construction of a factory close to the Royal Melbourne Hospital. More famously, unions – and particularly the BLF – were prominent in Melbourne in 1970 in the battle over railway land in North Carlton, where 'black bans' long predated the imposition of what came to be known as 'green bans' in the Kelly's Bush campaign in Sydney. Jack Mundey was to argue that while union bans had been used first in Melbourne, they had been confined to a series of isolated events, whereas the New South Wales BLF 'could see them all tied together' as part of a coordinated urban environment strategy.[2] It is true that the 26 rebel unions led by Ken Carr in Melbourne were not as strongly focused on environmental issues as their New South Wales counterparts. Carr's strategy was to broaden the agenda of the union movement from wages and conditions to putting the 'social' back into socialism. The NSW BLF bans on demolition and construction work were more numerous and involved using severe and extensive ministrations to oppose large developments, including multi-million dollar renewal projects in The Rocks and Woolloomooloo. In Sydney the BLF came to be regarded as 'the most powerful town planning agency operating in NSW'.[3]

The big brawls in Sydney were bitterly contested; the battle for Woolloomooloo was perhaps the most fervent. Pat Fiske and Denise White's *Woolloomooloo*, an hour-long documentary released in 1977, combines commentary and interviews with residents of the inner-city Sydney 'human community' with footage of evictions and protest. This film is a valuable social document: the final scenes show Victoria Street's last resident, Mick Fowler, evacuated, and the burial of a coffin bearing the words 'The Right of Low Income Earners to Live in Victoria St'. At the centre of this dispute was a proposal by developer and underworld figure Frank Theeman to demolish housing in Victoria Street near King's Cross and build three 45 storey towers of luxury flats. The BLF placed a green ban on the area, which remained in place for two years, until October 1974. Violence erupted following a protracted court case and police evictions of tenants and squatters – individuals who had formed a cooperative so radical that CRAG had split

---

2   'Green Bans Art Walk: Green Bans Bibliography' *Green Bans*, accessed 1 August 2012, greenbans.net.au/biblio.php.

3   Burgmann and Burgmann, *Green Bans, Red Union*, 50.

over its application for membership. The siege of Victoria Street culminated in the disappearance in mid-1975 of local newspaper proprietor and editor, Juanita Neilsen. Neilsen was almost certainly murdered, although her body has yet to be found.[4] The thuggery associated with the battle and Mundey's subsequent removal from leadership of the NSW BLF had a devastating effect on Sydney's urban protest movement. Delayed and altered, the luxury apartment towers were nevertheless built; they opened in 1979.

Brooks Crescent and the Boa Constrictor

The Brooks Crescent struggle in North Fitzroy was the climactic Melbourne brawl with the HCV over an urban renewal site: it was, though the parlance is unlikely to have been used at the time, the 'game changer' in the fight against the HCV in Melbourne as an unaccountable and underhand urban renewal authority. Along with the Carlton Association's Lee Street campaign, the Brooks Crescent protests effectively ended the HCV policy of reclaiming inner-city land for bulldozing to build high-rise housing as well as walk-up flats. By February 1974 when a joint planning committee was set up to oversee a new approach to development in Brooks Crescent – restoring a modest streetscape and repairing where possible – the HCV had already had a significant impact on inner Melbourne, proclaiming over 300 acres of inner-city land to be slums and constructing 47 high-rise towers.[5]

Pete Steedman recalls the Brooks Crescent 'brawl' as an event 'where, I think, a lot of people got blooded'. Perhaps strangely, those involved in the Brooks Crescent struggle felt no sense of victory at the end. 'In these struggles', Barry Pullen remembers,

> sometimes it is difficult knowing when you've won … everybody felt the same exhaustion and some were very sad at the loss of particular houses. But it did mark the end of block clearance and the end of high rise policy by the housing authority in Melbourne.[6]

It was not just a street that was at stake: the name of Brooks (since changed to 'Brookes') Crescent came to represent not just one picturesque street, but the 15½ acre (6.3 hectare) area surrounding it, bounded by Church, Reid,

---

[4]   Irving and Cahill, *Radical Sydney*, 308.

[5]   Fitzroy Residents' Association, *Brooks Crescent: A Study of Current Slum Reclamation Procedures of the Housing Commission of Victoria* (Fitzroy: FRA, 1972), 4.

[6]   Barry Pullen, Paul Madden and Andrew Burbidge, 'Brooks Crescent and the Fight with the Housing Commission' *North Fitzroy Social Justice Walk*, June 2003, 3.

Rae and Nicholson streets in North Fitzroy. It was a mixture of housing and light industry, mostly shoe and clothing factories; it was meticulously mapped and surveyed by the Fitzroy Residents' Association (FRA) in *Brooks Crescent: A Study of the Current Slum Reclamation Procedures of the Housing Commission of Victoria*,[7] an example of the comprehensive studies that underpinned many such battles. The survey found that seventy-five percent of the 176 Brooks Crescent dwellings were owner-occupied. Residents were fifty percent Australian-born and fifty percent recent migrants, mainly of Greek and Italian origin. Many locals worked in factories close to their homes; most had lived in the area for more than five years and were not interested in moving.

In the Brooks Crescent battle, the HCV's cat-and-mouse tactics were carried to extremes. Although Brooks Crescent was officially declared a slum reclamation area in July 1970, the HCV had begun acquisition of houses half-way through the previous decade, creating an atmosphere of rumour and uncertainty. By the time of the declaration, the HCV had demolished fifty of the eighty homes it owned – without a demolition order. Approaches made by residents to the rebel unions, which included most of the building unions, resulted in a black ban being placed on demolition of the remaining HCV owned houses. Rebel union leader, Ken Carr, justified the action by suggesting that unions such as his were 'perhaps the only force in the community at the present time that can help people get on top of the Government'.[8]

However, the Brooks Crescent ban was largely unsuccessful as the Commission, which by this time had three sites banned by unions, responded by hiring 'fly-by-night' private contractors, so-called because they undertook demolitions secretly, under cover of darkness. Elsewhere, the HCV simply left homes to deteriorate, thus 'white anting' streets to create scenes of decay and decline in the area.

A public meeting held in the local Methodist church in May 1970 was attended by 250 people and a North Fitzroy Residents' Association (NFRA) was formed. It was clear at this meeting that many residents were uncertain whether they would be better off selling their homes to the HCV or staying and fighting to remain in the area. Migrant families struggled to understand their rights. Although the HCV had sent notice of the declaration to householders in five languages, due to a mistake in translation, Italian

---

7   Fitzroy Residents' Association, *Brooks Crescent*.

8   John Stevens, 'Fitzroy versus Trendies' Melbourne *Age*, 14 November 1974, 17.

readers were told 'to smile in face of adversity', a mistake seized upon by local panel beater and mechanic Giacomo (Jack) Strocchi who told a *Herald* reporter that 'while our houses and businesses are being torn down we have to smile at our bad luck'.[9] Residents were terrified that their houses would be declared slums, fearing this would mean they would not receive adequate compensation.

The Brooks Crescent campaign was notable for the support it received from the Victorian branch of the Royal Australian Institute of Architects (RAIA), which had previously been reluctant to oppose the HCV's urban renewal program. In April 1970 the executive discussed whether it was appropriate for the RAIA, as a professional organisation, to act as a pressure group. A compromise was reached whereby the institute supported community movements by acting as a clearing house for information and research and a library for local reports. Pressure from younger architects resulted in the RAIA declaring its public opposition to the Brooks Crescent redevelopment and sponsoring a comprehensive study of housing conditions and street character in the area that convincingly demonstrated it could not so easily be dismissed as a slum. The study found that housing was in reasonable condition largely due to renovations by migrant families and that the layout of the area, including the Crescent itself, contributed to a pleasant urban environment. The RAIA also endorsed an alternative plan developed by local architect Maggie Edmond that envisaged preservation of most of the area, rehabilitation of houses, some demolition and the building of 30 new dwellings. The alternative plan included community facilities such as a kindergarten and crèche and demonstrated that satisfactory densities could be achieved by infill housing, the retention and renovation of existing housing, medium-density developments and well located open space. Maggie Edmond constructed a model of the revitalised Brooks Crescent plan on her kitchen table; it was to become important not only for Brooks Crescent but also for later HCV developments. The architect and TCPA member Neil Clerehan thought the plan 'a wonderful alternative to the concrete towers'.[10]

Brooks Crescent was also significant for the initiation of a legal challenge to prevent the declaration of the area as a 'slum', made possible by financial support from local factory owners. Norman Yarr was secretary of the company which owned Paddle Shoes, a factory that had been in the area for

---

9   Sam Leone, 'Italians Are Furious over Flats' Melbourne *Herald*, 4 August 1970.

10   Fitzroy Residents' Association, *Brooks Crescent*, 8.

close to sixty years. He believed the HCV had 'ruined the area. They should clear out …'[11] Yarr helped prepare and arranged finance from factories in the area for the court case. At the preliminary hearing in February 1971, Mr Justice Newton decided the residents had a substantial case and granted an interlocutory restraining injunction on the HCV, preventing further acquisition and demolition of properties. The matter was listed for a full Supreme Court hearing where evidence as to the 'slum' status of the Brooks Crescent area could be tested. During the three year wait for the Supreme Court hearing, the HCV left the resumed houses to deteriorate further. The FRA commented:

> The general approach of the Housing Commission can be compared only to the slowly strangling effect of attack by a boa-constrictor. The Commission grips an area, applies steady but intermittent pressure, withdraws, attacks at a different point, uncoils and tightens its grasp: … The only end for the household is in the belly of the Housing Commission.[12]

Local support held firm despite continued pressure from the HCV to purchase homes. Daisy Crofts, a worker at a local factory, became a symbol of resistance when the *Age* published a photograph of her on the verandah of her home holding a shotgun with a sign proclaiming 'This House Not for Sale to the Housing Commission' prominently displayed in the background. The photograph was also used on the cover of a CURA publication edited by Kay Hargreaves, *This House Not for Sale*. It traced the HCV offers to purchase that Crofts had received and refused.

As is clear from the above – and as noted by Ruth and Maurie Crow's Town Planning Research Group in 1970 – few of the Brooks Crescent residents could be described as 'trendies'.[13] Many migrant families resisted; some took the opportunity to sell and move. The leadership of Jack Strocchi was important for communication with Italian families. Harold Mackrell recalls that Strocchi, who had been involved in the Italian resistance movement during the war, thought the ruthless tactics of the HCV closely resembled those of Mussolini and Italian fascism. The NFRA relied on support from the FRA. Local resident and teacher Martin Jansen was appointed

---

11   Henry Rosenbloom, 'Slumming it in North Fitzroy' *Nation Review* (19–25 August 1972), 1269.

12   Fitzroy Residents' Association, *Brooks Crescent*, 15.

13   See Anon, 'Fitzroy Feels Its Way Forward' *Irregular* 33 (June 1970), 3, Crow Collection, Victoria University.

spokesperson for the Brooks Crescent residents and became responsible for liaison with the FRA and the new FRA members on Fitzroy Council.

Two stories on one page in the *Nation Review* in August 1972 perhaps said everything there was to say about 'problems' like Brooks Crescent, and potential solutions. The title 'The way of the octopus' covered two stories; one on state of play in North Fitzroy, and a story about new consultative planning measures in the Adelaide suburb of Hackney, where Premier Don Dunstan had responded to bitter resistance to the clearing of an urban area with a 'drastic reversal' of top-down policy.[14] Hackney was potentially a good news story, highlighting a 'participation revolution' and the Dunstan government's proactive and progressive approach to development.[15] It made the HCV's activities in Brooks Crescent seem even more tragic. 'Today the whole Brooks crescent area ...' wrote Henry Rosenbloom, 'is a slum. Nearly five years ago, when the HCV first started buying and demolishing houses, an area of approximately only one acre was substandard'. Rosenbloom reported that court action had required the HCV to 'announce – for the first time – its plans for the area', through an unpublicised three-day display indicating 'an estate of low rise flats with an estimated population density of 159 per acre ... No provision for community facilities are included in the plan – apart from a school site which the education department knows nothing about.'[16]

After a three year hiatus, the moment of decision came as to whether to procede with the Supreme Court case. The long wait had taken its toll and due to HCV tactics the area had further deteriorated. Residents had raised money for the court case but news that the HCV, with access to government funding, was approaching QCs for representation, made them nervous. Though the residents thought they could win the case, they were unsure about their resources. At a final dramatic meeting it was decided the financial risk was too great, and the case was abandoned.

However, the resistance was not in vain. In 1973, after the election of the Hamer government, a joint planning committee was formed with representatives from the City of Fitzroy and the HCV to plan and rebuild the Brooks Crescent area.[17] Hamer also announced the end of the HCV program of slum reclamation, including the building of high-rise towers.

---

[14]   Stuart Hart interviewed by Alan Hutchings 11 July 2007, *Don Dunstan Foundation Oral History Project* (Adelaide: Flinders University, 2011), 5.

[15]   John Richards, 'Having a Go in Hackney Housing' *Nation Review* (19–25 August 1972), 1269.

[16]   Rosenbloom, 'Slumming It in North Fitzroy', 1269.

[17]   Anon, 'Commission Us As a Developer' Melbourne *Age*, 14 November 1973, 2.

Seven years had passed since the HCV first started acquiring properties in the Brooks Crescent area. Only seventy of the original houses remained and few of the residents who had attended the initial meeting of the NFRA still lived there. During a Social Justice Walk to Brooks Crescent thirty years later, doubts were expressed as to whether the outcome of the battle was a success for the residents. Paul Madden thought it was a moral, local and statewide victory:

> Were they successful? I think the answer is yes. In all social conflicts there is a clash between the social values and interests on both sides of the table. Through the fifties and sixties the support for a particular housing policy was enormous, from business, from the churches, from bureaucrats and particularly from the planners [yet] the whole policy was stopped right on this spot by the Brooks Crescent residents.[18]

Kids not Kleenex

One of Melbourne's most celebrated 'big brawls' of the early 1970s did not involve the HCV with its redevelopment plans, or the planners and builders of freeways. Instead, it was a conflict between local residents and private enterprise on a small section of land surrounding a railway line in North Carlton. Ultimately the strength of community support, combined with a union black ban, was able to save the railway land from development and it was turned into a park.

The site was part of a railway reservation for the Inner Circle line – a passenger route until 1948 and in 1970 still used irregularly as a goods line. Developer (and one time Broadmeadows councillor) Reg Rayner, of Glenroy, leased land in North Carlton, in the area known locally as Princes Hill, from Victorian Railways, for the purpose of building a large warehouse. Rayner had already signed an agreement with the paper goods manufacturer Kimberly-Clark, which intended to use the warehouse as a distribution point for its Kleenex brand paper products. When work started on the site local residents, who had not been notified of the development, became concerned at the loss of open space, the size of the proposed distribution warehouse and the impact of heavy truck traffic on their residential streets.

The newly formed Carlton Association took up the issue. It ran an energetic community campaign organising deputations to Hamer, then the minister for local government, and the MMBW, the body responsible for

---

18   Fitzroy Residents' Association, *Brooks Crescent*.

planning. Its lack of success brought home the difficulty of influencing the intransigent Bolte government. The MCC, for which Princes Hill marked a northern border, gave only token support to the residents' concerns. An attempt by the CA to obtain an injunction that would prevent construction of the building proceeding before a permit was issued had to be abandoned; as was the case at Brooks Crescent a few years later, the CA was unable to continue due to the heavy legal costs involved.[19]

Despite these setbacks, the Princes Hill community continued to oppose the development. In June 1970 over 200 people attending a public protest meeting heard rousing speeches from representatives of the CA and 'many more such protest meetings, often combined with a barbecue, were to follow on the railway land generating a sense of community support and solidarity'.[20] The loss of potential parkland and the likely impact of such a large development motivated women with families to join the campaign. Although these women are not prominent in the written record, Dale Masterson and Peter Baroutis's short film *Struggle*, made with union support, records the importance of their involvement, with numerous kaftan-clad young mothers with children and prams at public meetings on the railway land. Local women organised rosters to ensure constant surveillance of the Rayner site. Such vigilance, and the women's extensive community networks, enabling the rapid mobilisation of residents at times of crisis, were crucial in this big battle.

Opposition to the railway land development also came from the *Melbourne Times*, a paper with a large local circulation recently taken over by Tony Knox and Ann Polis. An *Age* journalist sent to investigate the new *Melbourne Times* found Polis working in her tiny office above Knox's Poppyshop on Lygon Street. The former schoolteacher with a BA was the epitome of the activist women in the inner city: 'a freckled face 31 year old, with a quick smile and adequate hips to carry her ten month old baby girl Mary and married to a university lecturer'.[21] The battle over the Railway Land was one of the first issues taken up by the paper, which saw the protection of the local community as its mission.

As work continued on the site the CA supported MCC councillor Fred Hardy in his approach, in mid-1970, to the rebel unions for a black ban. This was a route particularly favoured by Norm Gallagher, state secretary of

---

[19] Jeff Atkinson, *North Carlton Railway House: A History of the North Carlton Railway Neighbourhood House* (North Carlton: The Author, 2010), 21.

[20] Atkinson, *North Carlton Railway House*, 21.

[21] Anon, 'Commission Us As a Developer' Melbourne *Age*, 14 November 1973, 2.

the BLF, the main rebel union involved in construction work. The BLF were already actively supporting the retention of the Lee Street block in South Carlton through similar means.[22] The black ban at Princes Hill stopped work but it started again in November when Rayner employed non-union labour. Residents attempted to halt construction and police were called on several occasions. In *Struggle*, the Malones relate an incident in which they were nearly run down in a neighbourhood street by a car registered to Rayner's business. These confrontations came to a head on 14 November when work started on the site at 5am. Residents immediately alerted Gallagher who on arrival confronted members of the Rayner family. The police were called and arrested Gallagher for assault. An urgent community meeting of angry residents and supporters was called for the following day, where it was announced that the Trades Hall Council, representing the rest of the union movement, was now also supporting the black ban. Two days later, a petrol bomb was lobbed at one of Rayner's firm's trucks at his Glenroy base. 'Threats of violence against my wife and family are not going to force me to give in', he told the *Age*.[23]

Rayner's resolve may have been firm, but the adverse publicity over violence at the site and Gallagher's arrest had its impact. The negative attention generated by the union ban was perturbing; a meeting at the BLF office between the residents and the company, at which the Association threatened to hand out 'Kids before Kleenex' posters at supermarkets, was additionally worrying. Malone later recalled:

> We had all these big piles of paper. On top of each, the first ten sheets, were posters 'Kids Before Kleenex', and we announced that these would be handed out at supermarkets all round Melbourne.
>
> We hadn't really printed all of them. Most of them were all blank paper but the Managing Director wasn't to know that. We threatened we would have people handing them out and you can imagine what that would have done to their product. Kimberly Clark climbed down immediately. That was a decisive factor, frightening the Manager Director of Kleenex the Storemen and Packers' Union pulling the rug from under them and so forth.[24]

---

22 Anne Latreille, 'Council May Enter Carlton Land Battle', Melbourne *Age*, 28 June 1973, 11.

23 Anon, 'Carlton Row: Truck Bombed' Melbourne *Age*, 16 November 1970, 6.

24 Interview with Richard Malone, http://www.unimelb.edu.au/infoserv/lee/htm/richard_malone.htm.

The company withdrew from the lease contract in early December 1970. Three months later Gallagher and another unionist, Mick Lewis, attended a hearing at the crowded Carlton Courthouse and were sentenced to a jail term. CA members and students rallied in support of Gallagher both on his arrival and on his release from Pentridge prison, as the demonstrations captured in *Struggle* show.

After further confrontations and arrests on the Princes Hill site, Rayner's withdrawal was finally negotiated in July 1971. Although the black ban had been a vital factor in preventing the construction of the warehouse there were divided opinions around Gallagher's intervention from both the union movement and the residents. While the NSW BLF had supported the Victorian branch intervention, Mundey thought Gallagher was 'grandstanding' and had little commitment to environmental issues.[25] Gallagher himself came to feel ambivalent about his involvement, believing that he had been used by the CA and that the residents' groups' ongoing opposition to development had cost union members jobs.[26] Some CA leaders, such as David Beauchamp, president at the time of the battle against Rayner, also had mixed feelings. While acknowledging that 'Gallagher did help', he felt that the union leader 'was out for the main chance', wanting to attract positive publicity for the unions. Others in the CA believed Gallagher was a hero who went to gaol for pioneering union bans.[27]

The objective of the 26 Rebel Unions had been to give unions a wider appeal, especially to young people. Despite the publicity around Gallagher's arrest Ken Carr, the organising secretary, felt the unions had emerged with a more positive image.[28] Carr himself is depicted in the film *Struggle* insisting that the only building the unions would allow on the railway site would be a community centre. The battle over the railway land, which had demonstrated the power of the combined action of unions and residents, can be seen, as it is by Terry Irving and Rowan Cahill, as 'a bridge between new middle-class activism and older working class militancy'.[29] Gallagher reflected in a 1987 interview, 'it just wasn't the Builders Labourers' Union that saved the park, it was people's actions that saved it in the end'. In truth,

25   Burgmann and Burgmann, *Green Bans, Red Union*, 50.
26   Atkinson, *North Carlton Railway House*, 25.
27   Tyson, *Activism, Conservation and Residents' Associations*, 12.
28   Neil Sutherland, 'Union Rebel Lays Down Terms' Melbourne *Age*, 8 August 1970, 6.
29   Irving and Cahill, *Radical Sydney*, 305.

it was the combination of both that had prevailed.[30] Gallagher and Hardy were shown in the *Age* in June 1974 toasting their success in preserving the land; the space is now known as Hardy Gallagher Reserve.[31]

Anti-freeway Protests in Brisbane

Bronwyn Barwell, Garry Lane and Peter Gray began producing the short documentary *The Battle for Bowen Hills* in 1973 by filming protests and discussion with a view to use in propaganda. It was finished in 1982 – long after the abandonment of the first Brisbane freeway plan, but in the same year the iconic Cloudland Ballroom in Bowen Hills was illegally demolished overnight, with the blessing of the Bjelke-Petersen government and Brisbane City Council.[32]

Perhaps this was a rearguard action from governments who'd learnt about the kind of tenacity people might show in Bowen Hills. *The Battle for Bowen Hills* was concerned with another joint project between Brisbane City Council and the Queensland government plan, which treated the working-class suburb with contempt. It was a 'coal face' study of the local impact of a freeway plan, conceived by Wilbur Smith and Associates in the mid-1960s and begun in earnest at the end of that decade. *The Battle for Bowen Hills* is similar, in many ways, to *Struggle*, although Gray, who was involved over a ten year period, had not seen the earlier film. Common elements include scenes of police violence against demonstrators; an invitation to the viewer to observe and perhaps identify workers defying union bans; an interview with a hostile central figure (Reg Rayner in *Struggle*; Russ Hinze in *Bowen Hills*); and a concluding rallying speech from an anti-development leader, the unionist Jack Masterson or the coordinator of the Brisbane anti-freeway campaign, Betty Hounslow.

In the early 1970s both Queensland and Victoria were presided over by cunning and paternalistic conservative premiers who preached what they styled as 'rural values', and 'common sense', and who sought to set these virtues apart in the public mind from the execution of slick, sophisticated politics. There was only a brief four year period during which their reigns coincided: Henry Bolte ruled Victoria between 1955 and 1972;

---

30   Atkinson, *North Carlton Railway House*, 25–26.

31   Vincent Basile, 'Corks Pop at Carlton Park' Melbourne *Age*, 13 June 1974, 26.

32   Diana Hacker, ed. *Booroodabin: A Sesquicentenary History of Breakfast Creek, Bowen Hills, Newstead and Teneriffe, 1823–2009* (Bowen Hills: Queensland Women's Historical Association, 2009), 212.

Joh Bjelke-Petersen was Queensland premier between 1968 and 1988. Bjelke-Petersen's government was to become infamous for its corruption, lack of accountability, brutal legal and police tactics, particularly but not exclusively to control public demonstrations, and of course its manipulation of the electoral system. Queenslanders who were not fervent supporters of Bjelke-Petersen gained a reputation for responding to his government's excesses with apathy to the point of inertia. But a rump of politically motivated activists raged against the government and its activities. As Matt Foley wrote in 2008, 'Brisbane in the 1970s was alive with the politics of social protest and government repression'.[33] In many instances, such as the protests against the Springbok tour in 1971, the government successfully turned unrest to its political advantage.

Perhaps for this reason the anti-freeway campaign in Brisbane in the early 1970s was fought not on the grounds of destruction of a marginalised inner-city community, or in expectation that Queenslanders would empathise with campaigners per se, but as a battle for fair compensation. Between November 1972 and September 1974 Patrick Mullins took part in and observed Brisbane Freeway Protest and Compensation Committee meetings. The papers he produced from his research in this field provide some of the best reportage and analysis of the BFPCC's (and, indeed, any similar group's) activities, and the communities affected, at this time.

The policy of the Department of Main Roads in the 1960s had been to 'not provide, on the ground, visible evidence of possible or probable routes ... until the precise alignment was fixed; thus avoiding needless worry to residents', but also to 'keep the affected public as fully informed as possible' and to 'maintain a sympathetic and helpful attitude' to residents. The department's knowledge of the residential population was apparently based on inspections done on foot, and from cars and helicopters, building a 'mental picture' of the area.[34] Despite the multi-pronged investigation, it might not have been much more sophisticated than a windscreen survey. 'Housing along the route was generally of low standard', wrote Erik Finger and Nelson English in 1972, 'which indicated the existence of low income groups. Some evidence of the existence of ethnic groups was available, principally in the form of

---

33   John Birmingham, Matt Foley, Stuart Glover, Phil Brown and Craig Munro 'The Olden Days' in *Griffith Review* 21 (Spring 2008), 46; see also Carole Ferrier and Ken Mansell, 'Student Revolt, 1960s and 1970s' in *Radical Brisbane*, ed. Raymond Evans and Carole Ferrier (Carlton: Vulgar Press, 2004), 266–272.

34   Erik Finger and Nelson English, 'Freeway Design' Symposium Design and Construction of the South-East Freeway, 20 July 1972, 1.9.

special public buildings ...'[35] In the final analysis, it may not have mattered much who lived in freeway-affected areas, as the decision to demolish for the freeway had been made.

The responsible authorities consistently undervalued the homes in the path of the new roads, and it was evident that displaced residents would be unlikely to find affordable replacements in comparable areas. *The Battle for Bowen Hills* highlights this issue with the case of Mary Tisdall, an elderly woman who had been offered a minimal amount ($8000) for her house: 'I knew I could barely buy ground for that'. The film explores Tisdall's quandary largely in terms of the lack of respect and courtesy accorded her by the 'Main Roads', a ministry presided over by Ron Camm, also (and more famously) minister for mines. However, Tisdall relates, 'I met this wonderful group of people, the freeway group. They've helped me, they've bolstered me when I felt very low indeed, not knowing where I'd go'.

Mullins details a course of protests against the freeways that was unusual compared with other cities. He notes Queensland's rapid development in the 1960s, with mineral resources as the prime impetus, which perhaps explains the early readiness to embrace planning, primarily on behalf of the car. This wealth, in Mullins' view, allowed Brisbane to emerge from a 'squalid' condition, inadequate in both sewerage and road development.[36] Through the ministrations of Labor mayor Clem Jones, the American firm Wilbur Smith and Associates was invited to report on Brisbane's transport needs. In 1965 Wilbur Smith (which also worked on a freeway plan for Melbourne in collaboration with Len T Frazer) advocated a freeway network for Brisbane which resembled a drawing of a pinwheel, with a ring-road around the city's CBD at the centre, and a roughly triangular arrangement of northwest, southwest and southeast roads.

Campaigning began in 1966 against the plan, purely on the basis that a fair price should be given for resumed land, an approach that predated a left-leaning anti-freeway movement. Mullins discusses the Stage One Southside Citizens Advisory Association (SOSCAA) initiated by conservative locals in Kangaroo Point, Buranda and Woolloongabba: 'its stated purpose', Mullins writes, 'was to act solely as an agent for helping residents get the best possible compensation'.[37] In doing so, it shaped the nature of collective

---

[35]   Finger and English, 'Freeway Design', 1.6.

[36]   Patrick Mullins, 'The Struggle Against Brisbane's Freeways: 1966–74' *International Journal of Urban and Regional Research* 3 (4) (December 1979), 543.

[37]   Mullins, 'The Struggle Against Brisbane's Freeways', 545.

protest, limiting it largely to the compensation argument and isolating any household that wished to argue around or outside such terms. However, following this initial false start, a grassroots campaign began, with a local Catholic priest as a crystallising figure. It united local Bowen Hills people from a multitude of backgrounds – indigenous, recent migrant, working-class Anglo-Australian; Tisdall, who belonged to this last group, had been born in the house she was being forced from.

Fourteen kilometres of freeway opened between 1966 and 1974, including the Story Bridge Expressway (opened 1970) and the Southeastern Freeway (now Pacific Motorway, opened 1973); and part of the Western Freeway, which was completed by 1979.[38]

The anti-freeway movement employed a coordinator. Tom O'Brien, a University of Queensland-educated social worker was the first, replaced by Betty Hounslow, also a UQ graduate. Hounslow was given a wage of $30 a week from a $1 weekly contribution made by thirty residents. Guilo Cerasani, a member of the protest committee, allowed the group to use a house he owned as its headquarters, and Hounslow also lived in it. Members of a prominent Brisbane Aboriginal family, the Watsons, were her neighbours and also became involved in the anti-freeway campaign. She recalls meetings held in the partially-demolished street, with residents placing chairs on the road, but memories of a neighbourhood brought together in adversity are tempered by the genuinely sinister activities of the authorities, such as the special branch police parking in the street outside the house for purposes of intimidation. On one occasion, they knocked on Hounslow's door and, laughing, informed her they had been told the neo-nazi Ross 'The Skull' May was at that moment travelling on a train to Brisbane with the intention of killing her.

Both *The Battle for Bowen Hills* and an associated publication, *Go Back You Are Going the Wrong Way*, suggested that one reason the freeway was planned through Bowen Hills was the wish by the state government to avoid a route across the site of Queensland Newspapers' premises. Queensland Newspapers was the publisher of the *Courier-Mail* and, until 1988, its evening sister publication, the *Telegraph*. Certainly there was little coverage in the press of resistance to compulsory acquisition, demolition and 'white-anting' of areas such as Bowen Hills. Gray remembers that the mainstream press response was 'very much in line with the official government position, and the

---

[38] Brisbane Freeway Protest and Compensation Committee, *Go Back You Are Going the Wrong Way* (Brisbane: BFPACC, 1974), 5.

protesters were [represented as] basically dolebludgers and ratbags'. Finger and English observed in 1972 that 'no adverse publicity was encountered' in the resumption process.[39] Indeed, the freeway protests are largely forgotten amongst the cavalcade of moratoriums, protests and marches staged in Brisbane, often on state or international issues. A recent history (avowedly 'A history, not THE history') of Bowen Hills and surrounding areas does not mention issues surrounding the freeway in the early 1970s or even the fact of its construction.[40] More ingenuous is the recollection by Allan Krosch of anti-freeway protest in his 2009 series of articles 'A History of Brisbane's Major Arterial Roads'. Krosch minimises both the anti-freeway movement and Brisbane protest movements in general, declaring them culturally derivative and ignoring the extensive range of forerunners to the local campaign.[41]

The Markwell Street conflict, given little attention by Krosch, is also discussed in the protestors' *Go Back …* in terms of a longer campaign of occupation of vacant houses:

> When it became clear that the occupiers of Hurworth St and a second house at 5 Markwell St were working successfully against the freeway and galvanizing the residents into an effective vocal group, the Main Roads Dept. sought to divert the issue by having the protestors violently evicted and demolishing both houses. The Anti-freeway movement soon found a new centre at 15 Markwell St. However when they tried to repair two vacant houses at no. 11 and 13 Markwell St, for families who lost their homes in the flood, the MRD repeated their tactics and had the houses demolished under a heavy police guard on 5th June 1974.[42]

Krosch opines that the election of the Whitlam government in 1972 led to the demise of the first Brisbane freeway plan: Whitlam 'had a policy that was anti-urban freeways'.[43] If federal funds would no longer be available for freeway construction, it was likely throughout 1973 – as the Main Roads proceeded on moneys already apportioned – that freeway development

---

[39] Finger and English, 'Freeway Design', 1.14.

[40] Hacker, ed., *Booroodabin*, 1.

[41] Allan Krosch 'History of Brisbane's Major Arterial Roads – A Main Roads Perspective' *Queensland Roads* 7 (March 2009), 16.

[42] Brisbane Freeway Protest and Compensation Committee, *Go Back You Are Going the Wrong Way*, 48.

[43] Krosch, 'History of Brisbane's Major Arterial Roads', 14.

would be curtailed. This fact did not prevent the ministry's bureaucracy from continuing to leave purchased properties vacant through 1973 and '74, even in a time of housing shortage in Brisbane exacerbated by the housing and infrastructure stress following the January 1974 flood. *The Battle for Bowen Hills* explores one particularly stressful incident during which an inexpert non-union demolition crew partially destroys a house placing the adjoining home – owned and occupied by the Cerasani family – in peril.

Krosch writes of the 'soul-destroying' nature of working on freeway designs at Main Roads during this period, 'that had little hope of being funded'.[44] The Wilbur Smith freeway plan was abandoned, in its detail at least, for some years, and for many in Bowen Hills and the anti-freeway protestors in general, it appeared to be a rare instance of a people-power victory. Main Roads may have lost a battle, but chose to fight its war in similar conflicts in other Brisbane suburbs over subsequent years.[45]

'Freeway – Who's Free?' The Battle over the F19 in Melbourne

Bowen Hills residents protested against the impact a freeway would have on their working-class suburb in 1973 with exceptional bravery in the face of a partisan, brutal police force. Four years later, a similar conflict erupted in Melbourne, when a mixture of old and new residents of Collingwood and Fitzroy barricaded Alexandra Parade – the intended gateway to the F19 freeway – against the road builders. The intersection of Alexandra Parade and Wellington Street, four kilometres from Hardy Gallagher Reserve and two kilometres from Brooks Crescent, would be the site of one of the most visceral urban battles of the 1970s.

An extensive (and, many would say today, ill-considered) freeway net-work had been proposed in 1969, but its finer details had remained secret.[46] The CA had been made aware of the section that would affect Carlton when, in 1971, Labor's MP for Brunswick East David Bornstein came across a map on a table in the Parliamentary Library showing a freeway steamrollering through Carlton from Nicholson Street to Sydney Road. 'It was a little unfortunate for the C.R.B.', Richard Malone has said, 'that practically half of Melbourne University's Town Planning Department lived

---

44   Krosch, 'History of Brisbane's Major Arterial Roads', 14.
45   See Nathalie Haymann, *Resumed in Protest* (Grays Pt: Bungoona, 1994).
46   Davison with Yelland, *Car Wars*.

in this area and they were well motivated to fight'.[47] The plans for freeways through Melbourne's immediate north were argued down. Within two years, in March 1973, Rupert Hamer 'slashed' a large part (approximately half) of the planned freeway network, a move which was assumed by many commentators to be an election-winning strategy.[48] If this is true, it is in itself a sign of an exceptional turnaround in public opinion in a relatively short time. Thirty years later, Hamer mused on this major alteration to the plan:

> After all, none of them were there so it was all future and where they were going to do a lot of damage to areas which needed looking after, that was a main principle involved and trying to provide them in areas not fully developed was part of the future plan, very important. I don't know whether we slashed too many. No one knows.

The mayor of Fitzroy, Bill Petersen, told the *Age* reporter Ron Holdsworth of his relief that the F19, later known as the Eastern Freeway, would not 'rip through' his suburb. But the F19 – which would take commuters to and from Doncaster and Templestowe, through the vast bushland of Studley Park – was well under way in 1971. Its Fitzroy section was part of Hamer's cull, but there would still be major traffic problems at its eastern end. The debate about an east-west link, current at the time of writing, is a long term legacy of that decision.

In late 1976, visitors driving or walking along Alexandra Parade would encounter a small tent accompanied by two portable toilets and a Christmas tree on the road's central nature strip. Occupied by a group of 'urban gypsies', the tent also contained, journalist John Larkin found, mattresses, 'a few flagons, one apple juice ... a folding table, and a few balloons on their way down'. A rostered staff of protestors maintained a vigil as the freeway building came further west. The city of Collingwood provided electricity, and the toilets.[49]

By the late 1970s Collingwood Council, like Fitzroy's, was typical of the new breed of inner-city council concerned with amenity and environment; the two adjoining local government areas funded a group known as Citizens

---

47   Interview with Richard Malone, http://www.unimelb.edu.au/infoserv/lee/htm/ richard_malone.htm.

48   Ron Holdsworth, 'He'll Look at Other Plans for the City' Melbourne *Age*, 29 March 1973, 2.

49   John Larkin, 'Tent holds back the freeway tide in Collingwood' Melbourne *Age*, 28 December 1976, 4.

Against Freeways. When the people of Collingwood were anticipating the approach of the F19 into their territory 'with mingled anger, resentment and dismay',[50] their elected representatives' response was to re-make Alexandra Parade, the intended approach to the new freeway, into a narrow two-lane road with nature strips. The newly reduced 'Parade' lasted three days, between 7 and 9 October, 1977 when the Country Roads Board declared it a State Highway.

Just over two weeks later, Collingwood residents were preventing CRB workers from building works by occupying the site – usually, merely 'sitting down'. One witness, Julie New, told the radical historians' Question Mark Collective in 1999:

> There was a good mixture of people. A cross section of those who had lived there forever and the nouveau riche, the people who started the gentrification. It was really interesting to see that mix of people. It unified people. The spirit of people working together, even though they didn't know each other, was inspiring.[51]

Testimony related in the anonymous account of the F19 protests, *Barricade*, suggests that the early weeks were good-natured and equanimous, with police, CRB employees and protesters behaving sociably – even engaging in a Melbourne Cup day sweep. But early civilities gave way to demonstrations of police force which led to thousands more residents assembling on the site. *Barricade*'s authors detail a dynamic in which a minority of participants (described as 'some of the official leaders') proposed a meeting at Fitzroy Town Hall. The majority rejected this suggestion in favour of building a barricade – a resolution made all the more potent by the approach of the police 'inching further up the parade'. Accounts suggest the two-metre high wall of detritus began with some car bodies towed into place by protesters. They were soon joined by more refuse. An unnamed 'Clifton Hill resident' recalled:

> It was a very spontaneous effort that started off with a few little bits and pieces of timber and chairs, and when they were put there without any action on the police's behalf, everybody got enthusiastic about it and everybody was busting their britches to show what they thought of the

---

50 Davison with Yelland, *Car Wars*, 207.

51 Interview with Julie New, *Radical Tradition*, 1999, accessed 2 December 2012, http://www.takver.com/history/julienew.htm.

freeway and this was a physical way that people could get themselves involved and vent their feelings ...[52]

The barricade was added to over the second week of November, 1977. Perhaps even more impressive than its bulk was the way it was protected and even inhabited, with locals playing guitars and continued monitoring of bonfires, particularly useful at night. Ongoing objections to the barricade's perceived contents (it was described as containing household refuse and attracting vermin and members of Citizens Against Freeways sprayed it with 'chemicals and antiseptics')[53] were deflected by protestors mindful of the mainstream media which, in most cases, did not support the barricade or its intention: the freeway was a fait accompli, and its completion seen as a necessity. Meanwhile, graffiti on the car bodies of the barricade declared 'CRB + COPS TO WRECK KIDS PLAYGROUND', 'TRAINS + TRAMS NOT TRAFFIC JAMS' and 'FREEWAY ... WHO'S FREE?'

On 24 November, when there were ostensibly discussions under way in a working party established with the Hamer government, the police descended on the barricade without warning and demolished it. Fifteen arrests were made, with considerable brutality. Trevor Huggard, a Carlton Association member (and later Lord Mayor of Melbourne) 'didn't believe until then that the police would use that kind of show of force and, without provocation, such violent action'. Julie New said in 1999:

> I wasn't there for the final eviction. As I recall it happened early in the morning and we went down afterwards to see what had happened. The feeling was one of being empty, that the campaign had been lost. Feelings of hopelessness and helplessness, of desolation. People did realise that they had won something though.

The sensation, similar to that reported by Brooks Crescent campaigners, is common after a battle. In both these cases, however, the gains and losses were hard to assess. Traffic flowed through Alexandra Parade to and from the F19 from December, 1977. It was nonetheless the dying gasp of Melbourne's already fractured 1960s freeway program, and the point had been decisively made. Soon afterwards, Fitzroy Council instituted a major scheme of road blockages and roundabouts in side streets adjoining Alexandra Parade, to ensure its own residential streets were not porous to freeway users seeking

---

[52]   *Barricade*, 9.

[53]   Ross Warneke, 'Clean Bill of Health for Road Barricade' Melbourne *Age*, 23 November 1977, 3.

short-cuts. The residents on the Parade itself nonetheless bore the brunt of noxious traffic fumes, noise and danger from this point. Less than a year after its opening, Anne Latreille was describing the Eastern Freeway thus:

> The rumble of heavy trucks wakes some locals from 4 a.m. onwards, when fumes mean constant heaviness in the air, where people have had to move their bedrooms to get away from the hum of the traffic, where the tail lights on the freeway are there flashing at you all night, where would-be freeway travellers hare down side-streets to find they do not take them to the freeway and either do a screeching U-turn or reverse at high speed all the way back up the street.[54]

Blockade protests and occupations like the F19 barricade were symbolic and, to the organised state, easily swept aside. Their imagery, however, continues to resonate, and the photographs and other ephemera from November 1977 paint a picture of organised action based not only on NIMBYism but on a genuine concern for both the environment and for the future of the city, particularly but not exclusively amongst the new left-leaning inner-city residents.

For many casual observers in 1970s Australia, disruptive and aggressive protests were not the appropriate way to address disputes over planning decisions. Taking to the streets was associated in many minds with student protests, the Vietnam moratorium, union or other political action; the associations for many were not positive. Politicians and bureaucrats were able to dismiss campaigners as unrepresentative or uncivilised, and images of 'mob' protest, while visceral, were far from genteel – a particular issue for resident groups who wished to distance themselves from conventional associations with 'slum' areas. Many activists found themselves most effective with a combination of public protest and private negotiation; some, as the next chapter shows, operated under the radar, in the corridors of power, and with recourse to tradition, history and, indeed, reason.

---

[54] Latreille, 'A Personal View', 18.

Chapter 7

QUIET REVOLUTIONS

NORH ADELAIDE AND SUBIACO

As we have seen, resident action in the 1960s and 70s was often a by-product of the process known internationally as 'gentrification', the occupation of old inner-city working-class neighbourhoods by the university-educated middle class. Australians sometimes preferred the term 'trendification', on the grounds that Australia had no gentry. But there was at least one significant exception to this rule: South Australia's most influential resident action group appeared, not in response to the middle-classing of an old working-class suburb, but as Australia's most self-conscious urban gentry defended a territory that had been theirs for almost one hundred and fifty years.

North Adelaide: 'A Way of Life Distinct from Suburban Life'

When Surveyor-General Colonel William Light laid out Adelaide in the late 1830s, he surrounded the city with a belt of parkland – the first urban greenbelt in the world, its citizens liked to boast. Adelaide was a product of systematic colonisation and ideals of planning and civic improvement ran deep in its culture. Along North Terrace, overlooking the parkland, there gradually appeared the city's most important civic institutions: Parliament House, the Supreme Court, the University of Adelaide, the South Australian Museum and Art Gallery, and the Adelaide Club. Nearby, across the river Torrens on gently rising land, Light laid out a residential annex, North Adelaide. The wide streets and squares of Upper North Adelaide, modelled on the fashionable residential quarters of Regency London, became the home of Adelaide's leading families, descendants of the philosophic radicals and religious dissenters who had founded the colony. Nearby were the Adelaide Cricket Ground, St Peter's Cathedral and College, and Brougham Place Congregational Church, once the spiritual centre of the 'Paradise of Dissent'. Nearer the Torrens, on narrower streets and smaller allotments, was

Lower North Adelaide, designed for the residences of servants, tradesmen and other humbler classes. Nowhere in Australia, perhaps, were gentility, civility and urbanity so perfectly combined. Surrounded by parkland, and within easy walking distance of the city, North Adelaide was a world of its own, an enclave rather than a suburb. By the 1960s, some old families had moved out, to be replaced by a more diverse population of lawyers, medical practitioners (Royal Adelaide Hospital was close by), academics, businessmen and shopkeepers. As restaurants and art galleries began to appear along O'Connell Street, its main shopping centre, North Adelaide became a little trendier, but without ever quite ceasing to be genteel.[1] It combined the traditionalism of Melbourne's Parkville and East Melbourne with the radical chic of North Carlton.

Left alone, as it preferred, North Adelaide may never have stirred itself to political action. Gradually, however, pressures of modernisation and development were encroaching. The first rumblings came in 1968 when locals opposed the demolition of the picturesque German baronial mansion and local landmark, 'Carclew', the former residence of Adelaide newspaper baron Sir Langdon Bonython.[2] But it was the state government's 1968 Metropolitan Adelaide Transportation Scheme (MATS), and its proposal to turn North Adelaide's peaceful Margaret Street into a six-lane northbound freeway, that roused them to collective action. Like Melbourne's Metropolitan Transportation Plan, MATS was the work of technocratic state planners advised by American consultants. It applied the standard American recipe for urban growth – a network of radial freeways linking the city to its far-flung suburbs.[3] In a manufacturing city-state where cars provided jobs as well as transport, the plan won support, as well as opposition, from both businessman and trade unions. It split both Liberal and Labor parties. Liberal Premier Steele Hall backed it, in spite of backbench opposition. Gentleman-banker, Legislative Councillor and resident of Brougham Place, Sir Arthur Rymill, questioned 'the attitude that no one counts except traffic engineers and no considerations count except traffic engineering'. The trouble with freeways, he insisted, echoing

---

[1]   Dirk van Dissel, 'The Adelaide Gentry, 1850–1920' in *The Flinders History of South Australia: Social History*, ed. Eric Richards (Adelaide: Wakefield Press, 1992), 333–368; Paula Nagel, *A Social History of North Adelaide* (Adelaide: Paula Nagel and T.J. Strehlow, 1971); Graeme Davison, *'Capital Cities' in Australians 1888*, eds. G. Davison, J.W. McCarty and Ailsa McLeary (Sydney: Fairfax, Syme and Weldon, 1987), 213–214.

[2]   Sharon Mosler, *Heritage Politics in Adelaide* (Adelaide: University of Adelaide Press, 2011), 59.

[3]   Hugh Stretton, *Ideas for Australian Cities* (Adelaide: The Author, 1970), 183–188.

his North Adelaide neighbours, was that they only generated more traffic. 'When we make them we are only building up fresh trouble for ourselves'.[4]

The North Adelaide Society – note 'society' not 'association', much less 'action group' – was formed in 1970 to oppose the plan, but soon applied its energies to a wider range of local issues. In formulating its objectives, the Society's members had consciously sought to balance the desire to 'protect' and 'preserve' their neighbourhood, with an acceptance of the inevitability of change. 'Improvement' rather than 'development' was their aim.[5] They opposed the demolition of buildings that gave 'character' to the area and the construction of 'unsightly' new ones, especially high-rise offices and apartments, kept watch for tree-lopping and 'vandalous' incursions into the parkland. Their efforts drew strength from the conviction that 'North Adelaide is an area of unique character' with a 'way of life quite distinct from suburban life'.[6] Anxious to avoid accusations of snobbery and exclusiveness, they sought to build 'a powerful membership from all walks of life'. 'A small cottage in a side street is just as important as a mansion', Chairman Peter Stephens declared in 1971.[7] Some of the houses lying in the path of the projected freeway were such small cottages inhabited by longstanding working-class residents. The upper-middle-class leaders of the Society took pains to cultivate, or at least not to alienate, the suburb's working and lower-middle-class residents, preferring, for example, to refer to 'the Melbourne Street area' rather than to the traditional, but possibly invidious, 'Lower North Adelaide'.[8]

Despite these efforts to build cross-class support, the leaders and members of the North Adelaide Society remained overwhelmingly upper-middle-class. Its 350 members included representatives of old Adelaide families like the Angases, Bagots, Bonythons, Duttons, Elders, Magareys, Morgans and the Rymills, half a dozen knights and ladies, a handful of judges, company directors and stockbrokers and a phalanx of doctors and doctors' wives. One of the reasons for choosing the name 'society' rather than 'association' had been to avoid the implication that it represented the interests only of residents; but it secured only token support from shopkeepers and other commercial interests and few working people. Anglo-Saxon and German

---

4   As quoted in Leonie Sandercock, *Cities for Sale: Property, Politics and Urban Planning in Australia* (Carlton: Melbourne University Press, 1975), 131–135.

5   Objects of the North Adelaide Society, SRG 807/1, State Library of South Australia.

6   Chairman's Address, North Adelaide Society, 15 July 1970, SRG 807/3.

7   Chairman's Address, North Adelaide Society, 12 July 1971, SRG 807/3.

8   Chairman's Address, North Adelaide Society, 18 November 1970, SRG 807/3.

names, with scarcely a single Greek, Italian or Serb, predominated. Most members joined as couples, joint custodians of the homes that the Society was sworn to defend, and, as in Melbourne, women, both wives and singles, provided much of its volunteer workforce.[9] Its office-holders were mainly professionals and academics, such as lawyer Roy Grubb, engineer Peter Stephens, and architects Jack McConnell and Dudley Campbell-Smith.[10]

A key role as advocates and strategists of the Society was played by academics, including historians Hugh Stretton, Robert Dare and Norman Etherington. Stretton, a resident of Tynte Street, addressed its first annual meeting and offered a shrewd analysis of the potential of resident action:

> Since I think that Residents' Associations are a good thing and that all sorts of good flows from having them, strong and vigorous, I have often thought it would be a good policy for a city to have a portable six lane highway and point it, as a threat, at neighbourhood after neighbourhood. You only have to point it at them for 6 months and the neighbourhood is politically organised, socially aware; they know each other like they never did before; they have taken control of their local government and all good things are in store for them. Then you can take the highway away because they have had their first victory.[11]

Only a few months earlier Stretton had published his seminal book *Ideas for Australian Cities*, a guide to national urban issues, that drew lessons from his own neighbourhood. A patrician with social democratic inclinations, Stretton was the natural spokesperson for a suburb with elements of both. Cities were best, he argued, taking a page from Jane Jacobs as well as his own experience, when they were socially and functionally mixed. 'My own residential street', he explained, 'includes a scatter of shops and offices, a school, fire station, pub, church, library, post office, a builders' yard, a couple of broadcasting stations, and a few ruins'.[12] The North Adelaide Society, he now argued, should be similarly inclusive and encouraging of diversity. It should resist any tendency to defend its own territory to the exclusion of the public good. 'If you are composed of mainly rich people,

---

9   North Adelaide Society Membership List, 29 March 1984, SRG 807 Adelaide Electoral Roll 1981.

10   North Adelaide Society, First Committee Meeting, 28 May 1970, SRG 807/4.

11   Amalgam of Extracts from Hugh Stretton's Talks to the First General Meetings of the Adelaide Residents' Society [sic] and the Residents' Association of Dulwich Rose Park & Toorak Gardens, n.d. State Library of South Australia, 1.

12   Stretton, *Ideas for Australian Cities*, 74.

there is a danger that they will assume a rather frozen conservatism that says nothing must change in this neighbourhood – every vacant lot is sacred and every decaying house that we have grown up with we should like to keep there'. Social diversity, he suggested, was the best guarantee of political strength and credibility.[13] Stretton's was an idealised image of North Adelaide, where in reality the few remaining working-class residents were rapidly selling out to young professionals, but it was a useful fiction to a reformer eager to promote as much social democracy as he could. For Stretton activism was a social good that transcended the immediate cause that generated it.

From the beginning, the North Adelaide Society had been, as its first chairman explained, 'vigorous in remaining non-political at all times'. While everyone agreed with this aspiration, it was harder to say what it meant. It certainly didn't mean that politicians were excluded: its members included a number of state and federal politicians, such as Labor's Neal Blewett, Chris Hurford and John Kerin. Nor did it mean that the Society could not support its own political candidates, as it did, successfully, in City of Adelaide elections. But in a state where urban issues divided parties internally, and traditions of liberal reform were strong, it was prudent not to become strongly aligned with either side. 'It is almost essential', Stretton argued, 'if you want to be politically effective ... to see that you don't become a Labor captive or a Liberal captive or become suspected of being the voice of just one party rather than the other'. Being non-political was a matter of style as well as ideological alignment. As 'the *responsible* voice of North Adelaide', the Society was jealous of its reputation for moderation.[14] Quiet persuasion through its members' many avenues of influence was preferable to rowdy demonstrations: 'It is always worth beginning with pleasant, civil approaches because you find out from those what proportion of the public authorities are willing to be on your side and to disclose to listen and to inform on all the things you may want them to do'. It sought always to back its contentions with expert evidence, and to offer reasonable alternatives to every policy it opposed. In the year of the Vietnam Moratorium, when 100,000 marched in Melbourne, Adelaide drew only 5000 to a march described as 'quiet' by its main newspaper. While street protests were not to be ruled out, they needed to be employed with care and only when supported by large numbers. 'Demonstrations are successful in proportion to the

---

13   Amalgam of Extracts, 2.
14   North Adelaide Society, Constitution and Rules, 28 May 1970, SRG 807/1.

number of middle aged and mothers with small children in conservative dress who can be put up the front of the demonstration', Stretton shrewdly suggested.[15]

In an era of big brawls, when inner-city Sydney and Melbourne witnessed deep and protracted struggles over urban renewal and urban transport, and residents' groups resorted to militant tactics of protest and civil disobedience, Adelaide remained seemingly immune. Geoffrey Dutton, North Adelaidian, scion of the gentry, and biographer of William Light, credited the abandonment of the MATS plan to the 'popular rebellions of citizens'.[16] If it was a rebellion it was a quiet one. Hundreds of citizens attended protest meetings, but their mood was indignant rather than rebellious. By the time of the election, an Adelaide University survey found scarcely one in five people supported the MATS plan. As soon as it was abandoned, their militancy largely evaporated.

In his policy speech, Dunstan pledged to reverse the Plan. Hall did nothing to defend it. Even before election day it was doomed. As Stretton recognised, the pressures for redevelopment in Adelaide, a middle-sized city with room still to grow, were never as urgent as in the eastern capitals. Perhaps, too, Stretton's 'pleasant civil approaches' more easily bore fruit in a city and state where political and bureaucratic power structures were more permeable than in Melbourne. No sooner had the Dunstan government been installed than Stretton was appointed a member of the South Australian Housing Trust, the state's principal provider of public housing and a significant planning authority in its own right. He later became deputy-chairman. Probably no other resident activist of the era achieved such influence so quickly, but it was most likely his recent emergence as a planning guru with a national reputation, rather than his local activism, that got him the job.

Stretton had hoped that the civic consciousness generated by the threatened six-lane freeway would survive to bring 'all good things' in its train. A decade after its foundation, the North Adelaide Society could congratulate itself on having 'earned the respect of both Government and Council'. They were not 'just a bunch of rabble-rousers who would last 3 months'. They had remained vigilant watchdogs on local planning issues and a lively debating forum on environmental issues, ranging from housing densities to

---

15   Amalgam of Extracts, 3.

16   Geoffrey Dutton, 'Adelaide' in *Seven Cities of Australia*, ed. Ian Moffitt et al (Sydney: John Ferguson, 1978), 155.

pollution. Like other residents' associations, they agonised about whether to emphasise historical preservation or social activism. 'They were generally concerned about the environment, but not sufficiently interested in people', a committee member admitted.[17] It was a common refrain in a movement that aimed to include liberals, conservatives and radicals. 'Because you have come together as residents bound together by that common interest, it is a great mistake to suppose that you agree about everything', Hugh Stretton had warned in 1970. The further they strayed from their common interest – the defence of home and neighbourhood – the more disagreement they risked. Considering the diversity of their base, it is perhaps surprising that the North Adelaidians were as united as they were.

Subiaco: 'Concerted Campaigns All the Time'

The Perth suburb of Subiaco – named for a settlement founded by Benedictine monks in 1851 – also saw ongoing and purposeful resistance to densifying new development and renewal, and the concurrent and successful creation of a planning regime and process in the 1970s. Like North Adelaide, emphasis was placed on negotiation; it was, in the main, a peaceful resistance. Additionally – perhaps in part due to awareness of the wider national issues and what had gone before in inner suburbs in eastern Australia – conservation practices were instituted through far less confrontational means, an approach often typified as diligent rather than provocative. Yet, as Richard Diggins, leader of a conservation-themed resistance movement that begain in the early 1970s, and Mayor of Subiaco between 1978 and 1989, puts it: 'there were concerted campaigns all the time. Discussions around dinner tables, public meetings, discussions in the street, in fact most social occasions at that time, the main topic of discussion was the future of our city'. Notably, both Diggins and local member Tom Dadour were Liberals at loggerheads with their own party on local issues. The Subiaco 'battle' maintained many of the same essential qualities that formed the grounding for the eastern suburban 'battles'. Unlike North Adelaide, however, it was not led by entrenched residents but a new influx of 'young professional people, nearly all of whom had been overseas'.[18]

The conflicts in Subiaco in the 1970s take place in the context of a city which had surprised itself less than a decade before with its own vehement

---

17 North Adelaide Committee Minutes, 9 October 1974, SRG 807/4.

18 Eileen Dean quoted in Ken Spillman, *Identity Prized* (Nedlands: UWA Press/City of Subiaco, 1985), 339.

reaction to plans to demolish one iconic building. Though residents of other Australian cities had previously massed to call for the retention of fine 19th century buildings – for instance, the 10,000 Melburnians who gathered in April 1963 to protest the ABC's plan to take over and build on a portion of the grounds of the Rippon Lea estate in Elsternwick[19] – the Barracks Arch controversy was a remarkable example of the recording and encouragement of popular support for conservation, by media.

'The careful retention of old buildings is not a sentimental matter', wrote recently arrived City of Perth Planner Paul Ritter; 'even when history is only 150 years long. It is a matter of richness of life, education and environment'.[20]

Ritter, an eccentric and impressive figure of Czech-English background, found himself leading a 'disturbing ... ring freeway system' he saw as unworkable, restrictive and undemocratic. He also noted that the 'freeway tragedy of Perth is paralleled in almost every other city'.[21] Ritter's plan for Perth – including the now well-established Hay Street and Forrest Place malls – was publicised and discussed in the very midst of the Barracks debate.[22]

The route of the proposed Mitchell Freeway, the northern section of the 'ring', required demolition of the hundred-year-old Barracks, built to house convict guards. Some members of the Main Roads Department may have felt hostility towards the building: the authority had been 'squeezed into the Barracks building ... along with the Public Works Department and the Water Supply Department' since 1930.[23] The 1955 Stephenson plan for Perth required its demise.[24] When matters came to a head in 1966, there had already been a Barracks Defence Council, campaigning for the Barracks' preservation, in existence for five years; it was led by former Bishop of Bendigo Charles Riley, a keen and effective user of the print media to put the case.

---

[19]   '10,000 in "Save Rippon Lea" call' Melbourne *Sun*, 22 April 1963, 1.

[20]   Paul Ritter, *City Planning Perth 1965–1967* (Kelmscott: Ritter Press, 1968), 57.

[21]   Ritter, *City Planning Perth*, 41.

[22]   'PCC Sees Plan' Perth *Daily News*, 22 March 1966, 4.

[23]   Leigh Edmonds, *The Vital Link: A History of Main Roads Western Australia* (Nedlands: University of WA Press, 1997), 198; see also Malcolm J. L. Uren and F. Parrick, *Servant of the State: The History of the Main Roads Department 1926–1976* (Western Australia: Commissioner of Main Roads, 1976), 3.

[24]   Andrea Whitcomb, 'The Past in the Present' in *Heritage and Identity: Engagement and Demission in the Contemporary World*, eds. Marta Anico and Elsa Peralta (Hoboken: Taylor and Francis 2008), 171.

Polls roundly condemned the demolition. One held on radio station 6IX involving 2747 people found that 2688 favoured retaining the Barracks.[25] No Perth resident could pretend they did not know the building: 'The Old Barracks' was on the cover of the *Western Australian Telephone Directory* for 1966.[26] M. Dawkins of Cottesloe wrote to the *News*:

> We are told that places like the Barracks must go to make way for progress. But there is always more than one way to implement progress especially progress involving new roads ... We entrust to Premier Brand and his fellow administrators and civil servants the management of the public utilities ... There is nobody else to turn to when we want protection for things we value and wish to preserve. These things may be beautiful, or quaint, or strange, but they are things that make each town or city unique and not just a collection of buildings.[27]

Premier David Brand, while unwilling to consider retention of the bulk of the building, consented in late March to leave the archway at the centre of the building standing for an indeterminate period of time.[28] It remains to this day.

Bret Christian and his wife Bettye moved to Subiaco, four kilometres west of the city's CBD, in 1975. Christian recalls:

> It was a slum, near enough ... an old working-class suburb that had run right down and it was regarded as ripe for redevelopment because it was zoned for high density development and there were lots of old houses. About 40% of them were owned by developers and rented out. So there were bikies and students and it was a pretty vibrant place but in terms of gentrification, it was probably ten years behind South Melbourne and, I suppose, Centennial Park in Sydney.

Ken Spillman's history of the suburb, *Identity Prized*, presents a history of a small, high-density suburb valued by both residents and visitors alike. As Spillman shows in the final part of his book, entitled 'Change', the postwar history of Subiaco mirrored similar turns in attitude in the inner suburbia of the eastern states. It began with the postwar enthusiasm for modernity, which in Subiaco's case came to be identified particularly with

---

25   'Brand Talks on Barracks' Perth *Daily News*, 21 March 1966, 6.

26   Australian Post Office, *Western Australia Telephone Directory 1966*, cover and 1.

27   M. Dawkins, letter, 'In the Name of Progress', Cottesloe *Daily News*, 25 May 1966, 10.

28   Max Beattie, 'Brand: We'll Share Arch Cost, if ...' Perth *Daily News*, 23 March 1966, 1.

an enthusiasm for residential renewal through the building of multistorey apartments:

> The emerging pattern of post-war metropolitan development seemed to decree that older, inner suburbs – not only within Perth but all around Australia – would inevitably be given over to business and high density housing, and there were few within Subiaco inclined to interfere with such a 'natural' course of events. To do so would have seemed incompatible with 'progressive' ideals … While aesthetic considerations were at best secondary, these too seemed to support the demolition of 'the old Subiaco', for in the view of most at the time, 'old' was generally ugly while 'modern' was invariably attractive.[29]

A major landmark, and a symbol of the progress intended to revive this rundown and poor area, was the 10 storey Wandana flat development, opened in 1955 as public housing. Spillman portrays a typical pro-development inner-city council of the period, tirelessly working to facilitate private development in the belief that such 'natural' change would bolster a declining population figure while replenishing housing stock.

The Subiaco Historical Society was formed in late 1973, with the Bank of New South Wales' public relations manager for WA, Richard Diggins, as president. It 'aimed from the outset to crusade for preservation and restoration'[30] and soon became 'a fierce and tireless watchdog on all planning matters'.[31] Its objectives were stated as:

> The study of the history of Subiaco.
>
> The preservation of artifacts in our museum.
>
> The encouragement of public interest in the appropriate conservation and re-use of the many interesting older buildings in Subiaco
>
> The maintaining of an interest in current developments in the City and how they affect the residential qualities and the residents of Subiaco.

With peculiar logic, this Historical Society justified its concern for 'town planning' on the basis that 'events of today will be history in years to come':

---

[29]   Spillman, *Identity Prized*, 281–3.
[30]   Spillman, *Identity Prized*, 339.
[31]   Spillman, *Identity Prized*, 341.

The Society is therefore actively concerned with present and future developments in Subiaco as these still affect the fabric and the residents of the City. The Society's Town Planning Committee is actively studying various aspects of planning in Subiaco, including a review of the Town Planning Schemes and the implementation of new traffic and transportation policies.[32]

The Society was by no means a mere front for activism. The Local History Seminar, conducted in Subiaco's public buildings in August 1974, demonstrates a large number (170) of dedicated amateurs (and some professionals) arguing the case for local history, inspired by what Geoffrey Bolton typified as an 'upsurge of nationalism' but also a fascination with a type of history imbued with the familiar and 'a greater sense of reality'. This came in part, Bolton felt, from the fact that in Perth:

[I]n the last ten years there has been what, for using a neutral term I will call an 'architectural revolution' in the main city centre, and people become quickly aware of the transience of the past, of the ease with which a sense of contact with the familiar can be lost …[33]

Diggins recalled the Society aiming to 'slow down the mad push by developers who were only interested in demolishing substantial old houses, putting up one and two bedroom units, taking their profits and vanishing into the night, leaving the Council with problems – eg. traffic, carparking, loss of privacy for neighbours etc. – to sort out'. In Diggins' words the society 'virtually pioneered the first local government Municipal Inventory of Heritage Places in Western Australia':

Initially the Society members were seen to be radicals, upstarts, troublemakers and left wingers by the Council who were not prepared to accept change was on its way. It was becoming apparent that the Council was coming under greater pressure as a result of the Historical Society's existence and closed ranks and minds regarding change particularly when recommendations were made by the Society. It was then that the Society decided we would recruit potential local government representatives and were successful in subsequent elections to change personnel with our members. At one time there

---

32   Subiaco Historical Society (Inc): 'Who We Are What We Do and Why', pamphlet in Subiaco collection Battye Library, PR 8679/SUB.

33   Geoffrey Bolton, *Local History in Western Australia, A Guide to Research, Local History Seminar*, Subiaco, 1974, 6.

were eight Historical Society members elected to Council out of a total of twelve.

Bret Christian, as founder, editor and publisher of the Subiaco *Post*, had an impact as least as forceful as Diggins on Subiaco's renewal, and his *Post* can be seen as the West Australian equivalent of the *Melbourne Times*. Christian had worked as a reporter for the Perth *Daily News* for eleven years and lived for three years in Sydney and one in Melbourne. He moved to Subiaco aware of the 'yuppified' inner-city areas of Sydney and Melbourne but at a time when it was still the case that 'no one in their right mind who wasn't poor, would live in Subi'. He began the *Post* in 1977 with 'the idea of doing suburban journalism really well but using the principles of a major metropolitan paper, like the *Sydney Morning Herald*', eschewing advertorial and the nepotism of conventional local newspaper practice. The first issue commented on demolition practices, asking 'how much history will the unit boom leave?' Christian recalls of his days on the *Daily News* that it 'took up small issues, they'd send out a reporter to write about a stop sign needed on a corner because there were too many crashes ... next thing, the Main Roads Dept would put a stop sign in'. The *Daily News* had also, of course, been the key paper in the fight to retain the Barracks Arch. Christian took the *Daily News'* approach to his own paper, a rare example of a citywide newspaper's approach as an influence on an activist press.

Importantly, however, while the demolition and increasing density in the area were causes for concern, Subiaco also became host to new, more sympathetic structures, such as early forays by architect/developers Gare and Klopper, noted for their environmentally responsive, open plan vernacular homes.[34]

Diggins' Subiaco council was a Liberal-dominated organisation. On Brand's departure from the Premier's office, Western Australia's next government was led by John Tonkin for the ALP, followed by another Liberal administration under Premier Charles Court. Subiaco was often at loggerheads with Court's government. Conflict with the state government was heightened when the railway line from Perth to Fremantle – Subiaco is a station on the line – was closed to passenger traffic in 1979. The history of the Fremantle Society (which, along with the Mount Lawley Society, was a sister group to the Subiaco Historical Society) suggests this was a manifestation of 'a strange blind spot' Court had when it came to Fremantle.

---

[34] Marcus Collins, 'Brian Klopper: Improbable Architecture' *Architecture Australia* 101 (5) (September 2012).

The transport minister ostentatiously ignored 99,480 signatures collected in protest against the closure and, according to Subiaco councillor Malcolm Morgan, those opposing the closure 'were facing a rock of Gibraltar in the person of the Premier'.[35] The *Post* reported that the State government had refused to release reports on the rail closure to councils on the basis that they were 'too technical for the councils to understand'.[36] As had been the case in the east a decade earlier, unions took a socially progressive view: supporting the disadvantaged locals dependent on public transport, the railways union refused to pull up the track.[37]

Bret Christian recalls of the closure:

> First of all, it severed a historic link because the whole suburb had grown up on the railway line, all the best houses were built along the railway line and the main road tram routes, the closer you were to the transport, the higher the value. It also threatened to change the suburb hugely, it would have become totally dependent on cars. Of course, the concept was to change the rail reserve into a freeway ... We campaigned quite strongly on that ... We used to feed stories to some mates we had on the daily papers as well, to put the pressure on.

Diggins acknowledges the work of a dedicated local Liberal member, Dr Gabriel 'Tom' Dadour. Dadour 'spearheaded the revolt against his own party's decision to close the railway but in the end he won the day'.

> The closure of the railway was a totally disastrous decision and caused a lot of heartache to a lot of people. Sir Charles Court's government claimed that the economics didn't stand up and that this State couldn't afford to have a railway line between its capital city and its port. The Government's case wasn't believed by the wider community and there were numerous public meetings held along the western suburbs once served by the railway. The public meetings without exception all condemned the government's decision but try as hard as they did to reverse the government's decision the Western Regions Councils failed.

When Brian Bourke's Labor government reopened the line, Dadour drove the first train; Subiaco railway station is now a key component of a

---

35   'Supporters of Railway Face a "Rock of Gibralter" [sic]' Subiaco *Post*, 30 May 1979, 4.

36   '"Deceptions and False Statements": Claremont Takes up the Fight to Save Railway' Subiaco *Post*, 27 June 1979, 16.

37   Ron Davidson and Dianne Davidson, *Fighting for Fremantle: The Fremantle Society Story* (Fremantle: Fremantle Press, 2010), 74.

major renewal project, Subi Centro, under the Metropolitan Redevelopment Authority. Dadour himself is now commemorated in the name of the local Community Centre; a kilometre to its east lies Richard Diggins Park.

All of the scenarios described in this chapter and the one which preceded it have unique elements, yet similar underlying issues and criteria persist. In each case, community ministrations were brought to bear on bureaucratic decisions which had been made outside the community itself and which impacted decisively on community daily life. In each instance, we see action taken by established authority figures to use extant networks for new purposes, in some instances purposes unlikely to have been considered possible even years before. In each case, too, while activists emphasise the historic value of the built environment, this is accompanied by a vital new vision of the possibilities of the inner city. Campaigners were reacting to what in Weberian terms might be described as self-interested bureaucratic intransigence, or to what others – such as Jane Jacobs – might have labelled modernist planning, gone awry.

Such cases can now be seen as expressions of a major shift, in the last third of the twentieth century, in perceptions of how the the inner city was formulated (in terms of an 'urban village') and organised (via 'community' and cultural and class variety) and in perceptions of how its nineteenth century landscape looked, aesthetically.

Chapter 8

GRASSROOTS PARTICIPATION

The urban activists of the 1960s and 70s were a new type of Australian public intellectual leading debates on issues of planning and communities. There was a commitment to strengthen civil society, especially through participatory 'grassroots' planning. This was an important achievement given that state and local government planning regulation was slow to respond to postwar urban expansion. Tony Dalton, one of the new appointments to DURD after the election of the Whitlam government in 1972, described planning legislation at that time as anti-democratic, giving as examples the proposed Urban Renewal Act in Victoria and the strategic plan prepared for the Sydney City Council by consultant planners. In both cases citizens and associations were asked only for opinions or comments and 'at no point [were] there any statutory provisions requiring the renewal authority or the council to give any information to those it consults'.[1] This lack of consultation can be compared with the 1969 Skeffington Report in Britain, which recommended public participation in planning decisions through such means as questionnaires, public meetings, advisory groups and the presentation of alternative plans. In the same year Sherry Arnstein published 'A Ladder of Participation' in the *Journal of the American Planning Association*, based on her experience of participation in Lyndon Johnson's War on Poverty.[2] 'Arnstein's Ladder' was a typology of citizen participation, the eighth rung of the ladder being 'Citizen Control'.

The lack of any statutory requirement for consultation in Victoria was the focus of the Committee of Urban Action's detailed response, prepared by Miles Lewis, to the draft Urban Renewal Bill of 1969. In a letter to Ray Meagher, the Minister for Housing, he compared the lack of consultative mechanisms in the draft Bill with the British Town and Country Planning

---

[1]   Tony Dalton, 'Citizen Participation: A Review of Political Form and of Participation in Planning', *Archetype*, New Zealand, 3 (May 1973), 20.

[2]   Sherry Arnstein, 'A Ladder of Citizen Participation' *Journal of the American Planning Association* 35 (4) (July 1969), 216–224.

Act of 1968, 'which gives the citizen a statutory guarantee that he will be kept informed of all stages of planning and will have the chance to make constructive suggestions, not merely to object after the proposal has been worked out'.[3]

Anger and frustration at this lack of participation loomed large in Melbourne where the powerful state infrastructure authorities had few processes if any in place for consultation on the massive urban renewal and freeway programs, and indeed were themselves not subject to planning and zoning controls. In his analysis of housing policy in Melbourne, sociologist Michael Jones deplored the 'social insensitivity of the 1960s in policy'.[4] Although the MMBW had overriding responsibility for the planning of Melbourne there had been little commitment to participatory planning. Consultation was usually confined to displays of plans at the board's offices, at the Town and Country Planning Board, and in the offices of affected municipalities.[5]

The response of RAGs in Sydney and Melbourne to the lack of consultation was to develop their own plans. Citizens' plans were prepared by residents in North Sydney, Paddington and Leichhardt, and in Melbourne for the North Fitzroy Brooks Crescent area, Carlton, North Melbourne and West Melbourne. These were sophisticated plans, drawing on local expertise and produced by community groups with little or no administrative support. The main residents' associations in the City of Melbourne – the Carlton Association and the North Melbourne Association – were able to utilise members with considerable skills in strategic planning, developing plans that were to have a lasting impact on the city. The Carlton Association had the planning expertise of experienced architects Peter Saunders, George Tibbits and Miles Lewis, engineers David Beauchamp and Trevor Huggard and geographer William Logan. The North Melbourne Association drew on its links to TCPA members, especially Ruth and Maurie Crow. In 1967 the Crows established the Town Planning Research Group (TRG) a small informal 'ginger' group' which met monthly and produced *Irregular* (later *Ecoso Exchange*), a roneod newsletter that promoted participatory, grassroots alternative planning and popularised the process of creating local community plans. TRG members included Ewan Ogilvy, a lecturer

---

3   Miles Lewis to Ray Meagher, 17 February 1970, Urban Activists Collection, Deakin University.

4   Michael Jones, 'Economic Patterns and Alternatives in the Inner Suburbs' in *The Inner Suburbs*, 37.

5   *Living City* 8 (Spring–Summer 1970), 5.

in town planning at the University of Melbourne, and Sheila Byard who taught planning at Footscray Institute of Technology and was a founder of the Kensington Social Action Group. The TRG was formed to assist community groups scrutinise official plans and emphasised the importance of collectively working out value judgements before preparing alternative plans. The group 'aimed to break down the immensity of planning issues to human scale. It sought common ground for planners, trade unionists municipal councillors and activists in community and urban organisations'.[6]

As noted in earlier chapters, community planning opened up opportunities for women to take part in urban decison-making. Women's participation in residents' associations is often interpreted in terms of women seeking distraction from boring child rearing and domestic responsibilities, an interpretation that dimishes their significant contribution to strategic planning and community building. Their ideas for communities were in stark contrast to Melbourne's urban renewal proposals developed by Victoria's public authorities. Kaye Oddie of the NMA thought the battle for urban communities by Melbourne women was similar to the opposition of Jane Jacobs and the Greenwich Village residents to the urban renewal plans of Robert Moses. In Melbourne the CRB, HCV and MMBW were all dominated by male engineers and 'you can imagine what the result was – isolating high-rise towers of public housing and destructive urban freeways'. In contrast, women emphasised community building as the basis for urban renewal. Oddie especially paid tribute to the influence of Ruth Crow in community planning. 'Ruth was the greatest facilitator I have known. She took our fledging interest, involved that interest by way of a particular project, nurtured it and watched it grow into a fully blown commitment and involvement in community issues and organisations'.

The Melbourne RAGs were well placed to take advantage of community consultation opportunities as they emerged in the 1970s. In 1971 the MCC acknowledged the need for strategic planning with the appointment of architect Peter McIntyre as principal planner for the city. The following year the MCC appointed the Interplan group, an Australian-American consortium with Gordon Jacoby as executive planning officer, to assist with the development of a draft strategy plan. Interplan was committed to community consultation and the consortium included American planners

---

6   Sheila Byard, 'The Citizen's Action Plan for North and West Melbourne 1973' in
     The Public and the City Plan, Seminar Papers, March 1998, Crow Collection, Victoria
     University.

with experience in the area. It soon called for input from residents groups in planning special areas within the framework of the strategy plan.[7]

The MMBW under chief planner Alistair Hepburn was more sensitive to the demand for consultation. The board maintained that the *Planning Policies for the Melbourne Metropolitan Region*, completed in 1971, was 'not an arbitrary zoning arrangement whereby people are pushed this way and that. It is not a whimsy of power happy planners. It is a democratic scheme aiming at the greatest good for the greatest number'.[8] Objections to the report were invited and the 4000 responses received were dealt with in a further *Report on General Concept Objections* in 1974.

Community consultation improved markedly when Rupert Hamer replaced Henry Bolte as premier, with Alan Hunt as minister for local government. By today's standards, where ministers are surrounded by media consultants and minders, Hamer and Hunt were amazingly accessible. Ann Polis, editor of the *Melbourne Times* in the early 1970s, recalls that to her 'utter surprise, here I was still with a child on my hip and looking very scruffy ... but people like Rupert Hamer and Alan Hunt gave us interviews'. Barbara Niven of the Emerald Hill Association thought that 'it was not worth the tram fare' to attempt a meeting with Bolte but was astonished at the access to Hunt and Hamer, recalling when one of the association's members

> got fed up with the whole thing to do with the freeway stuff and she said 'this is nonsense. I am going to see Dick Hamer'. She got on a tram, went in and said she wanted to see him and confronted him and had a few things to say about the planning of the freeway.

Hamer recalled that he was prepared to urge consultation on the planning bureaucracies 'as a new wave of thought was sweeping the State'.

> I did insist that as far as possible the Board of Works should consult with each of the parties ... it was fundamental to proper planning I thought to let people know what was proposed and to get their opinion and also to take into account their representations.

Residents' associations were not just reactive but proactive, employing a range of techniques and tactics. In response to Interplan, the Carlton Association rebutted plans for urban renewal in *Urban Renewal, Carlton*

---

7   *Polis, University of Melbourne Planning and Architecture School* (August 1974), 28.

8   'Design for a Great City' *Living City* 9 (Autumn-Winter 1971), 5.

(1972) and in *Carlton Plan a Strategic Policy*, an alternative plan for the entire suburb. The CA also produced *The Freeway Crisis* in 1972, which examined alternatives to freeways. An assessment of Melbourne's residents' associations judged 'this practice of producing substantial scholarly and well-argued reports and submissions – often devastating in their effects', and the Carlton Association the most professional and effective of the associations.[9] The FRA also developed a critique of high-rise and urban renewal, evident in the 1971 alternative plan for Brooks Crescent which envisaged the preservation of most of the area and showed that there was an alternative to block clearance: renovating existing housing and building well-designed and affordable terrace housing.

As has been discussed earlier, the most comprehensive of the Melbourne resident association plans was the *Citizens Action Plan for North and West Melbourne* (CAN) 1973. CAN was a response to the request by the City of Melbourne and Interplan for public participation in the preparation of the Strategy Plan. A core of fifty members of the North Melbourne Association worked on preparing the plan, a great voluntary achievement in the time available. This achievement was largely due to the expertise of Ruth and Maurie Crow and the time they committed to the project. The first section of CAN set out the value judgements regarded as fundamental to planning. The prime objective was to place social values before economic ones to achieve 'a mixed and participatory city' for people who lived and worked in the area. This would be achieved partly through centres which would make people feel they belonged to a community, and which would provide accessible services. Two Neighbourhood Focal Centres were recommended in CAN, one in North Melbourne and one in West Melbourne and the possibility of a third district level community service and resource centre was also considered. These centres would be coordinated with community resources such as children's centres, neighbourhood parks and schools.

The CAN report recommended three grades of environmental areas – street, local and district – where through traffic was discouraged and a system of walkways, bicycle tracks and improved public transport would encourage community interaction and accessibility. Freeways and heavy traffic routes, regarded as barriers that would fragment communities and neighbourhood centres, were kept to the perimeter. Rather than high-rise housing developments, the report recommended maintaining and rehabilitating the existing scale and character of residential areas. The retention of building

9   Tyson, *Activism, Conservation and Residents' Associations*, 8.

stock was recommended for the preservation of community, which would also be assisted by building infill housing. As an alternative to high-density public housing, low-income housing could be provided on vacant sites.

These environmental and mixed-use areas recognised the ecology of urban communities which Jacobs had emphasised – the importance of street patterns, the opportunities for interaction to ensure neighbourhood safety. The plan identified opportunities for new mixed development on under-used land, especially the Newmarket stock saleyards and abattoirs in Kensington, and the moving of associated noxious trades to more appropriate locations. The retention of Victoria Market – at this point still under threat of redevelopment as an office block, the 'Victoria Centre' – was recommended and sites for new industrial uses compatible within mixed-use areas were identified.

Annemarie Mutton of the Richmond Association, who had attended CAN meetings, thought that with the leadership of Ruth and Maurie Crow the group had developed a well thought-out 'brilliant plan for beautiful Melbourne'. Kaye Oddie recalls that interest in the report extended to residents' groups in other cities 'looking for an alternative to the development of car based suburbs on the American model as the CAN Report looked at issues such as neighbourhood focuses, facilities, heritage, traffic, various open space measures'.

> It was hailed in its day as being an incredible work from a group of residents and I can remember even when I joined the North Melbourne Association as secretary that people were writing from all around Australia still wanting copies. So it was hailed as the work of a group of concerned people who just put this together as what they wanted for their community.

For Sheila Byard of the KSAG, and a member of the CAN planning committee, the process demonstrated 'the promise that people in the street could assist to bring improvements about and to dissolve notions of planning as a mystery performed by experts'.[10]

All residents groups in the MCC area responded to the Interplan report. Gordon Jacoby had ensured that one of the most fundamental parts of the Strategy Plan was public participation and that 'large sections of the community [were] in the position of being well informed on all recommendations'. He thought the residents' groups were 'fairly important

---

[10]   Byard, 'The Citizens Action Plan for North and West Melbourne 1973'.

in determining our planning. They play a very positive part'. Nevertheless, when the Interplan report *Final Goals and Action Plans* was released in 1973 it received a cautious response from the residents' groups.

The report recommended that the City of Melbourne move from a planning system based on industrial, commercial and residential zoning to strategic planning. Implementation of the main objectives of the Strategic Plan would be through flexible action plans within the overall framework. This recommendation was welcomed by Miles Lewis in an assessment of the Interplan report undertaken for the Carlton Association. The zoning system was no longer adequate and 'it has been an open scandal under the present system that public authorities have been able and willing to ignore both the spirit and the letter of zoning controls'.[11] He concluded that the move might require new legislation and a transfer of some planning powers from the MCC, as well as clarification about consultation over the action plans. The Carlton Association and the CAN group welcomed proposals to contain the expansion of the CBD and to prevent the building of high-rise office towers along arterial roads, although they were sceptical that the recommended policies could achieve these objectives.

Both groups also questioned the suggestion that an action plan on historic preservation would eliminate the need for separate heritage legislation. Although Interplan proposed that new buildings be on the scale and character of existing residential areas, it did not place emphasis on retaining existing building stock. The CAN response noted that 'the Interplan report does not accept that the historic character of the inner areas should be maintained and that the retention of heritage areas would depend on the market rather than planning policies.[12] While the CAN group was strongly against a 'precious' preservation policy, heritage protection was important for fostering community identity and protecting 'the whole historic flavour and character of the suburbs' beyond the limited areas such as Parkville and parts of East Melbourne identified in the Interplan report. Lewis thought that too much had been left to the action plans which included vital areas suitable for intensive new development, housing improvement and renewal, renewal of older industrial sites and historic preservation. These areas should not be left to action plans and separate state government legislation was needed for urban renewal and historic preservation.

---

[11]   Miles Lewis, 'Response to the Interplan Report', November 1973, Urban Activists Collection, Deakin University.

[12]   'CAN's Counter Proposals to Interplan' Supplement to the CAN Report, 1973, 6–7.

CAN was highly critical of the Interplan report for its 'lack of understanding of the nature of a participatory community, of its lack of concern for neighbourhood focal centres or environment areas'.[13] The CAN proposals for participatory neighbourhood focal centres had been ignored, along with the proposals for environmental areas that discouraged through-traffic.

Integrating the Melbourne Strategy Plan into metropolitan and state planning was a fundamental problem. The recently established State Planning Council, a coordinating body representing relevant ministers and the large infrastructure authorities, gave a lukewarm response to the Interplan report, reiterating the primacy of their own Statement of Planning Policy. The Planning Council especially opposed separate legislation for historic preservation and affirmed that public authorities should remain responsible for planning legislation. The Interplan recommendation for a joint coordinating body was ignored and there was no acknowledgement of the need for consultation.

Nevertheless a change in attitudes to consultation had taken place, compared with the paternalism of the past. The Interplan process had been the first substantial consultation on future planning for the city and the proposed Strategy Plan specifically recommended that public participation should continue in monitoring of the plan. Although participation in the Interplan process had been by invitation only, the CAN report concluded that despite their differences 'one significant contribution that the Interplan team has made to planning in general, has been the persistent way in which they have encouraged participation in planning by the public at different levels ... a somewhat novel experience in Melbourne'.[14]

Although public participation in Melbourne had made its debut via Interplan, it had been promoted not by planning professionals but by activists in the residents' associations. 'Among the actionists, the feeling was that the authorities and the professionals running them could not be trusted to do the right thing. They were insensitive to aesthetic and ecological values and to the sensitivities of social and community structures'.[15] Andrew McCutcheon recalled that 'we did work very hard at trying to develop consultative processes ... So there was a whole inner-city thing of trying to help people participate more and understand that they could

---

13   'CAN's Counter Proposals to Interplan', 15.

14   'CAN's Counter Proposals to Interplan', 20.

15   Bruce Hartnett and John Handfield, 'Planning and Social Change: Restructuring Planning Education' *Polis* 2 (23) (August 1975), 6.

have an influence on their own environment'. The urban sociologist Manuel Castells has written that a major question for the 1970s urban protest movements was 'how to advance grassroots democracy when the state [had] become an overwhelming, centralized and insulated bureaucracy?'[16] An answer in Melbourne was the development of comprehensive plans by the residents' associations in Carlton, North Melbourne and Fitzroy that not only demonstrated the value of public participation and created alternative, community-sensitive models for the renewal of Melbourne's inner suburbs, but also challenged the influence of business and development interests in local government decision-making.

How Grassroots Was Grassroots Planning?

Even as public participation in planning was winning acceptance questions were raised as to how representative the residents' associations were of inner-suburban communities. In an article on the Interplan report, Latreille described the associations as having 'inflated egos at the top, general apathy from round about and a lack of consistently hard workers ... generally the pattern seems to be a well-attended annual general meeting at which people vent their spleens then disappear for a year, expecting immediate action to miraculously follow these outbursts'. Although the activists claimed to work on behalf of inner-suburban communities, membership of the residents' associations was largely middle class, although Latreille conceded that 'they worried about this'.[17]

That the membership of residents' associations only marginally rep-resented the diverse population of the inner city raised questions about the validity of their claims for grassroots planning. Although the process of preparing the Brooks Crescent plan had included consultation with those who lived in the area there had been little involvement of migrants or workers in the preparation of the Carlton Association plan or of CAN. The fundamental principle of citizen participation – that all could participate as equal citizens – did not take into account the complexity of inner-city communities and differences in socio-economic power relations. By 1975 it was realised in the USA that the aspirations of President Lyndon Johnson's War on Poverty for 'the maximum feasible involvement of the poor' in the development of programs had not been achieved among the

---

16   Manuel Castells, *The City and the Grassroots: A Cross-Cultural Theory of Urban Social Movements* (London: Edward Arnold, 1983), 329.

17   Latreille, 'They Fight for their Suburbs' Melbourne *Age*, 1 June 1973, 8.

black and Hispanic populations living in inner-city areas with the greatest deprivation and needs. Sherry Arnstein, who had optimistically developed the 'Ladder of Participation' as a guide to implementing the 'maximum feasible participation' of minority groups in War on Poverty programs, concluded that 'participation without redistribution of power is an empty and frustrating process for the powerless. It allows the power holders to claim that all sides were considered, but makes it possible for only some of those sides to benefit. It maintains the status quo'.[18]

In a seminar held in 1997 to reflect on the effectiveness of CAN, Angela Munro, who had been involved in the planning group, acknowledged that 'there are sections of the local community which have been insufficiently represented in community planning to date – including indigenous people, those of diverse, non-English speaking backgrounds and low-income residents. Reconciliation must be fundamental to the participatory planning of the North and West Melbourne community as it faces the new millennium'.[19]

Following the consultation on the Interplan report there were calls for a new approach to community planning. An early edition of the journal *Polis*, founded by faculty and students in architecture and planning at the University of Melbourne, called for a revamp of current planning courses to reflect 'modern' planning – to move beyond public participation in planning to involving community leaders in the planning process.

> By and large, the motivation for becoming involved in public participation normally stems from desires to oppose rather than support projects. No one has ever screamed for its application to permit them to put up constructive ideas ... [P]ublic meetings and seminars do not necessarily provide a range of views and can simply reflect the attitudes of activists.[20]

The article concluded with a cartoon showing 'Public Participation Tonic – it won't cure you but it'll make you feel better'.

Manuel Castells identified the emphasis on local communities as characteristic of the urban movement of the 1960s and 1970s. Jane Jacobs built her campaigns against Robert Moses and urban renewal around the vital importance of urban neighbourhood communities. If for many of the new

---

18 Arnstein, 'A Ladder of Citizen Participation', 220.
19 *The Public and the City Plan*, 2.
20 Hartnett and Handfield, 'Planning and Social Change', 5–8.

residents in inner-city Melbourne the push factor had been the 'suburban ethos' of the 1950s and 1960s, a pull factor was the attraction of the traditional Australian working-class culture and the diversity of the inner suburbs. This was especially true for women activists. Kaye Oddie thought 'that you suddenly do realise that you are part of a community ... and that's what has attracted people and what's probably been the base of all these associations'. Asked what were the disadvantages of inner-city living, Anne Polis 'couldn't see a single one'. Appointments to inner-suburban churches were sought by young clergy wanting to serve diverse disadvantaged inner-suburban communities rather than complacent suburban congregations, while Carlton Association activists George Tibbits and Trevor Huggard had settled in Carlton because the strong community ethos reminded them of the country towns where they had grown up.

The working-class culture of the inner suburbs was seen as authentically Australian, based on a tradition of mutual support that had been strengthened during the tragedies of the depression and war years. Kaye Oddie observed that for the older inner suburbs 'this community feeling seems to come naturally, and they are particularly desperate to maintain it'. As older residents 'did not have the knowledge about how to go out and fight these battles' they supported the professionals in the residents' associations. Danny Keating was a North Melbourne 'old timer' who:

> felt the sense of community at a neighbourhood and personal level and was active in opposing clearing for the HCV Hotham estate. He felt that people had their sense of personal identity, their security and the important features that comprise each neighbourhood were being taken away such as the shopping centres and he was fighting on that fact.

Male working-class culture, rough but fair with a strong sense of mateship, was seen to be represented by the inner-suburban Australian Rules football teams. The FRA chose the Fitzroy Football Club's jumper as the background for a poster opposing the MCC proposal for inner-suburban amalgamations. 'Whacker on the Wing', a weekly report of the Carlton Football Club's game, written by the University of Melbourne archivist and Carlton Association leader Frank Strahan, was a popular article in the *Melbourne Times* – in the religion section! Strahan's presentation of the 'Downlow Medal' at the end of the season, held in a local pub, was widely attended and reported.

The new residents were avidly interested in the history of inner suburbs, long neglected in Australian historiography, and they supported local history societies and research. The FRA sponsored research on Fitzroy's history, resulting in a photographic exhibition and later a book on the suburb. Barbara Niven and the Emerald Hill Association undertook a detailed study of South Melbourne housing in response to threats of the demolition of Lanark Terrace and redevelopment of the Melbourne Orphanage site, which was the basis of later local government heritage studies. Members of the associations worked tirelessly on recording inner-city historic buildings and houses for the National Trust enabling the Trust to expand its list of classified buildings beyond the eastern suburbs.

However, Peter Hall's analysis of the gentrification of working-class areas of London is sceptical of the recall by the new residents of a rich community life in the past 'preserving the area as it was and ceased to be'.[21] Melbourne's inner-city residents' associations have also been identified as having a romantic idea of community that meant more to middle class professionals than it did to locals and which glossed over the reality that most of the 'old' residents were taking the opportunity to leave the inner-suburban areas behind and move to new suburbs.

Idealisation of earlier inner-city communities ignored the reality of tensions between new and old residents. Annemarie Mutton of the Richmond Association:

> would have liked to draw into it a few of the trade union men who lived in Richmond but they didn't come to our meetings because they considered us bourgeois. You see this mania to be working class. I understand the differences and I understand why, but you know in the end we need each other. We need the people who have studied architecture, we need the people who can give us their expertise in law and as doctors and all the rest you know?

Dilapidated and overcrowded inner-city schools were often sites of conflict. There were tensions on school councils and mothers' clubs at primary schools over the direction of education, with new residents wanting to improve buildings and playing spaces, raise the standard of teaching and provide more space in the curriculum for self expression. There was also conflict over the Greek and Italian after-school programs organised by ethnic groups. Choice of school was a test of the commitment of new residents to inner-city diversity and the working-class past. Many of the new families opted out of the inner-city schools, sending their children to

---

21   Peter Hall, *London 2001* (London: Boston Unwin Hyman, 1989), 87.

private schools in the suburbs or selecting more suitable nearby local schools. Parents whose children did attend the local school faced very real challenges as the children of recent migrants enrolled in already overcrowded schools with poor facilities. North Fitzroy Primary School in Alfred Crescent was the largest in the state with nearly a thousand pupils taught in old school buildings and twelve temporary classrooms crammed on the school's half acre site. Demonstrations coordinated by the new parents drew attention to the shameful state of the school as did Alan Jordan's extensive photographic study. Inner-city schools later benefited from increased state government funding and the Whitlam government's Disadvantaged Schools Programme but they were an initial reality test for new residents.

There were also tensions between the alternative communities and the residents' associations as the inner suburbs increasingly attracted those seeking new urban lifestyles. Shared student houses, group houses and communes mushroomed in the 1970s. One of the most well known was the Rathdowne Street Commune, a large house with a core of longer term residents that included Helen Garner, whose book *Monkey Grip* is a famous literary record of inner-city alternative communities and their cultural links to Carlton's Pram Factory and La Mama.[22] The Trotskyist political views of some commune residents brought them into conflict with the residents' associations, especially over strategies in the campaign against the Eastern Freeway. When the Rathdowne Street collective was disbanded in 1973 and the house demolished, residents Helen Garner and Ruth Madison wrote articles for the alternative newspaper *Digger*, reflecting that while there was support for particular battles, most group houses were inward looking, with a revolving population not directly involved in urban protest movements.[23]

For Pete Steedman (briefly a resident of Rathdowne Street), residents' associations put too much weight on community as place. 'Carlton was not a community in the sense of all doing things together. I think Carlton was a melting pot and a transient place'. Tony Birch emphasises the spiritual value of community for the indigenous population brutally evicted from homes in Fitzroy to make way for the HCV Atherton Gardens Estate redevelopment and subsequently resettled in surrounding suburbs.[24] Despite this uprooting, indigenous groups maintained a close association

---

22   See Chapters Two and Three.

23   Helen Garner, 'The End of a Collective', *Digger* (Nov 10–8 Dec 1973), 4.

24   Tony Birch, *Shadowboxing* (Carlton North: Scribe, 2006), 75–87.

with Fitzroy and the suburb continues to be an important indigenous spiritual and spatial community.

In his analysis of the opposition to freeways in *Car Wars*, Graeme Davison asks the following fundamental questions: Did community mean more to middle-class professionals than it did to the locals? Was 'community' the watchword of collective self-interest? To what extent did protection of the community drive the activists and influence their planning initiatives and how much were they driven by self interest?'[25]

Tom Hogg, then an officer with the Commonwealth Bureau of Roads, felt strongly that the answer to the last question was 'Quite a lot', in relation to the opposition of resident action groups to the building of freeways.

> Our view was that this was a piece of self-serving nonsense by well-heeled middle class people who had chosen to live in the most accessible parts of Melbourne and just wanted to preserve that for their own rights and reserves and the rest of Melbourne could go to hell.

While the background of most residents' association members was pre-dominantly middle class there was a range of backgrounds.[26] Although William Logan cannot remember any interest in ethnic involvement in the Carlton Association, there was extensive interaction in the Richmond Association with the Greek population over opposition to HCV develop-ments, the provision of childcare services, and the establishment of the North Richmond Community Health Centre. Annemarie Mutton recalls that the Richmond Association was important in giving a voice to migrant residents demanding compensation for displacement by the HCV for redevelopments in Highett Street and Elizabeth Street.

> They were battling for what they felt, their pay, they worked hard, the women went to work, the men went to work, the kids helped you know? And here they had a house, a home and they were going to take that away, it was unbelievable.

There was often broad cooperation between a wide variety of community groups and residents' associations on particular issues and battles. The Brooks Crescent Residents' Association represented most residents in the area proclaimed for redevelopment by the HCV, including students, migrants, older Australian factory workers, and new residents.

---

25   Davison with Yelland, *Car Wars*, 220–221.
26   See Chapter Four.

Davison concludes that 'Community' was above all 'the product of the activists' shared struggle against the powerful and impersonal forces that threatened to "divide" or erase it'.[27] What does emerge from this study is that no suburb was a monolithic community but a collection of communities and networks that residents' associations mobilised over issues and battles. Castells' observation that community associations were responding to paternalistic, bureaucratic and powerful state bureaucracies applies especially to Melbourne where the residents' associations were vital catalysts for community based movements opposing the imposition of extensive redevelopment by Melbourne's undemocratic and powerful state authorities. However, the citizens' plans were not negative responses and addressed the need to accommodate change and demonstrate that a mix of uses and sympathetic redevelopment could foster the community traditions and vitality of the inner suburbs.

The MCC Strategy Plan did not in the end lead to an approved planning scheme. In 1974 the Council adopted the Strategy Plan in principle but efforts to implement it through a planning scheme failed. Key recommendations were opposed by the influential CBD lobby group the Building Owners and Managers Association (BOMA) which was increasingly concerned at the impact of planning restrictions on office developments, especially as the Save Collins Street movement gained momentum. Piecemeal implementation through amendments to the existing planning scheme diverted time and energy from implementation of the Strategy Plan as a whole, although some of the social planning recommendations were implemented following MCC consultations on children's services, employment services and services for the elderly. Despite the failure to fully implement the Strategy Plan, Sheila Byard thought the CAN process of bringing planning to the people was to have 'far reaching consequences for the practice of planning not just in the central municipality of Australia's second largest metropolitan region, but in the State as a whole and beyond'.[28]

The Crows continued to work for value based planning. Ruth worked on community-based child care producing a comprehensive history of child care services in the City of Melbourne while Maurie drew on his extensive networks to produce the book *Seeds for Change: Creatively Confronting the Energy Crisis*[29] as 'a first step towards widespread discussion of the technical,

---

27   Davison with Yelland, *Car Wars*, 220–221.

28   Sheila Byard, 'The Citizens Action Plan for North and West Melbourne 1973'.

29   Deborah White et al, *Seeds for Change: Creatively Confronting the Energy Crisis* (North Melbourne: Patchwork Press, 1978).

social and economic issues related to energy'. While focused on the energy crisis and its implications the book was also about people and lifestyles, government, and decision making. It further developed 'The Model' proposed in CAN of neighbourhood communities and an appropriate city structure for conserving energy through the integration of transport and land use planning, anticipating policies now being promoted as an integral response to global warming.

Research and Action

As well as community participation in decision making there was also a commitment to community empowerment and a major contribution of Melbourne's urban movement was the development of evidence based social policy, experimental social programs and the encouragement of rights organisations. 'Once upon a time protests were mainly a matter of petitions meetings and processions. Now they can also be backed by research'. So observed an article in the *Bulletin* commenting on Melbourne's urban protest movement against

> invasions by the Commission's demolition contractors of the charming Victorian terrace houses of Carlton and Fitzroy which were being ripped up and replaced by the Stalinesque structures of Moscow or East Berlin. The Carlton Association had started the research with an open day of one block slated for demolition to show that they were perfectly good houses or at least repairable. This see-for-yourself research was now being augmented by professional studies.[30]

The strength of urban and social research that emerged in response to Melbourne's urban protest movements was exceptional and had extraordinary influence on Australian social policy. When in 1999 Brian Stagoll of the North Yarra Community Health Centre and Pauline Spencer of the Fitzroy Legal Service organised a 'Social Justice Walk' around a block in Fitzroy (Brunswick, Johnston, Gertrude and Napier streets) they were able to include forty-two sites and former sites, including the Brotherhood of St Laurence, the Centre for Urban Research and Action, the Hanover Centre, the Open House foundation, the Aboriginal Health Centre, the Fitzroy Legal Centre, the North Yarra Community Health Centre, the Family Day Care Centre and the Fitzroy Council Social Planning Office. All had

---

[30]   Anon, *The Bulletin*, 17 January 1970, 16.

contributed to major reforms in Australian social policy through leadership, research and lobbying. In explaining the concentration in Fitzroy, Pete Steedman observed that a large number of these bodies had their roots in church related organisations in that suburb:

> That community thing I think was probably just starting to develop in the late 1960s when you did get the bourgeoisie and the socially committed priests like Hollingworth and Howe ... [T]hey were galvanising communities to work for their own interests – and fight the bureaucracy.

The two influential church related organisations in Fitzroy were CURA (until 1975 the Fitzroy Ecumenical Centre, or FEC) which was located in offices behind the Presbyterian church in Napier Street. The director, Brian Howe, had been the minister of the large bluestone Methodist Church in Brunswick Street, demolished in 1970 as part of the HCV Atherton Estate redevelopment. Howe had fought demolition of the church, especially the rear bluestone chapel that dated from the early settlement of Melbourne. The Fitzroy Residents' Association, of which Howe was a founding member, joined in resisting demolition of the chapel after the main church was demolished. FRA members organised to keep watch on the chapel building which had been hastily classified by the National Trust. Jane Lennon recalls her involvement and the tense confrontations with demolition workers during this vigil. However, in a dawn swoop, the Commission bulldozers demolished the chapel, a significant building from pre-goldrush Melbourne, later using the site for a carpark.

There was a positive outcome from this devastating defeat, so symbolic of the Commission's obduracy and refusal to negotiate with communities. With the assistance of a modest grant from the Methodist Church Home Mission Department, Brian Howe was able to develop the FEC as an urban research and action centre to confront the complex social issues of the inner suburbs. In an interview with John Larkin of the *Age*, Howe envisaged that the Centre would provide supportive services for community organisations and overcome social fragmentation by bringing people together as 'the inter-dependency of the city is much more than in the suburbs'.[31] Larkin described the Centre as a 'social workshop for the inner city'. The slogan of the Centre – Research, Training and Action – reflected the ideas Howe brought back from Chicago where, as noted in Chapter 3, he had studied theology in the

---

[31]   John Larkin, 'Social Workshop for the Inner City' Melbourne *Age*, 2 April 1970, 2.

mid-1960s. The Centre also built on the experience of the Hanover Centre, an experimental program for homeless men developed by Alan Jordan from the former soup kitchen at the Brunswick Street Methodist church. Jordan was undertaking a study of homelessness for a PhD at Latrobe University and worked as both social worker and researcher. The Hanover Centre became a cooperative venture involving the BSL, Wesley Church and other providers of services for the large number of homeless in the city and Fitzroy area. Jordan's research was later the basis for the Homeless Persons Assistance Act (1974) passed by the Whitlam government, which introduced a system of income support for the homeless and provided grants for services.

On the other side of the HCV's Atherton Gardens housing estate was the Brunswick Street headquarters of the Brotherhood of St Laurence. Established in Fitzroy by Father Tucker in the aftermath of the 1930s depression, the Brotherhood had developed as a social agency with a national reputation for its progressive social work and research. The Brotherhood had a long involvement with the proposed HCV redevelopment site opposite their premises on Brunswick Street. The area included 'The Narrows', a notorious area of derelict housing, prostitution and crime. In the 1940s the BSL had produced a film, *Beautiful Melbourne*, which exposed the appalling state of housing and living conditions in the Fitzroy area. The BSL had long pressed for redevelopment of the area and initially welcomed HCV plans for the Atherton Gardens estate.

However, as the Atherton estate redevelopment proceeded, BSL Director David Scott was increasingly concerned at density on the site after Fitzroy Council agreed to the building of a fourth 20 storey tower despite the lack of support services for residents. It was a mantra of the HCV that as a housing authority it built houses and planned estates but did not provide community facilities for its developments. There was little effort to coordinate either with other state government departments or with local government to provide services that would obviously be needed on these large estates. The Commission had no prior experience of large estate development and, as already noted, seemed not to be aware of the social problems emerging in high-rise estates in other countries. Over 3000 low income and disadvantaged residents, the size of a country town, were housed on the Fitzroy site located in a suburb already poorly supplied with services such as schools and health centres. Andrew McCutcheon had already confronted this problem in Collingwood and 'had warned Fitzroy (Council) that there was no community services and no infrastructure other than housing and that something needed to be done and they should resist. Unfortunately they didn't resist'.

David Scott with Marie Coleman, head of the welfare umbrella group the Victorian Council of Social Services (VCOSS), called a meeting at the Fitzroy Town Hall in 1969 to address the need for more coordinated and effective welfare provision. Bruce Hanford recalls the meeting as rowdy and chaotic with tempers running high as attention turned to the likely influence of HCV redevelopments on Fitzroy. 'The Housing Commission served a kind of symbolic function. I mean, let's face it, it was hard to like'. Paul Coglan, later to be a councillor and Mayor of Fitzroy, recalled the meeting as one of the most famous in Fitzroy 'but also, as most of the meetings that were held then, it collapsed in disarray', ending with the Mayor of Fitzroy forced from the chair.[32] A Fitzroy Social Services Committee was eventually formed, representing local organisations but with a community-building rather than a VCOSS style coordinating role.

Interaction with the FRA and CURA was to influence the future direction of the Brotherhood. Peter Hollingworth recalled that the BSL was always socially aware 'but we hadn't developed the notion of participation, grassroots participation':

> I felt that we had to do whatever we could by putting our energies into empowering local communities. Funding initiatives for people with good ideas and commitment. So in the 70s and 80s a lot of money went towards the kind of empowering of new initiatives rather than by agencies going it alone.

As social change in the inner suburbs gathered pace, the BSL began a creative and empowering period, contributing to major new directions in Australian social policy and the delivery of welfare services. The Brotherhood funded Michael Salvaris, based at CURA, to organise a Tenants' Union. The BSL also funded a pilot Family Day Care program under the leadership of social worker Barbara Spalding. A grant was given to assist the founding of the Fitzroy Legal Centre. Land was given in Brunswick Street for a Community Health Centre with a policy of outreach into the community, a joint initiative with the Victorian Health Department. It was not only the financial support that was important but the BSL also gave respectability to these new organisations, providing an umbrella under which young activists could operate. The BSL also provided important backup. David Scott's background in public relations ensured the effective communication

---

[32] Brian Stagoll, ed., *Social Justice Walk Around Fitzroy, 18 April 1999* (Fitzroy: Fitzroy Historical Society/Fitzroy Legal Service, 1999), 10.

of policies and programs and the Brotherhood staff were insistent lobbyists of state and federal governments.

BSL research capacity was expanded from the mid-1960s following on from the research projects of Judith O'Neill and Anne Stephenson on housing and poverty. The BSL also had a close relationship with the Poverty Commission under the leadership of Professor Ronald Henderson, undertaking Australia's first major national study of the causes and nature of poverty. The Commission assisted with the funding of a number of BSL projects including the Family Centre, a BSL experimental project on income support led by Connie Benn.[33] This step towards evidence based social policy was very important given the limited research capacities of state and local government and the limited social remit of federal departments. The combined social research capacity of the BSL and FEC/CURA, which also increased research staff in this period, provided opportunities for young graduates from social work and social science courses to undertake significant projects on a wide range of economic and social issues.

Across the road at the All Saints Roman Catholic Church in King William Street, which immediately abutted the HCV estate, there was a different approach to sharing and empowerment. The priests, concerned at the implications of the HCV development, made a terrace house available to social workers Brian Noone, who was working at the Hanover Centre, and Mary Doyle, to set up a community house. They were joined by Brian's brother and former priest Val Noone along with others in establishing the Open House foundation. The Open House foundation was influenced by the American anarchist-pacifist and founder of the Catholic worker movement Dorothy Day, who ran a house for homeless people in New York and campaigned tirelessly for peace. Dorothy Day's visit to Melbourne in 1970 included a shared meal at King William Street that the residents found inspiring.

Mary Doyle recalls that for the next seven years 'an amazing number of people came in our door, including homeless men and draft resisters'. The Open House Diary records an extraordinary range of activities and visitors, theological and political discussions, meetings of the Vietnam Moratorium Group and the constant and demanding requests for care and food. At a gathering on the fortieth anniversary of Dorothy Day's visit Mary Doyle

---

[33]   Colin Holden and Richard Trembath with Judith Brett, *Divine Discontent: The Brotherhood of St Laurence; A History* (North Melbourne: Australian Scholarly Publishing, 2008).

thought the Open House marked 'our attempts to live by the general principle "an injury to one is an injury to all". We had a go, and it's not over yet'.[34] For Val Noone the Open House was part of 'a period of big changes. Not only was society at large changing, but one of the more massive institutions of western society, namely the Roman Catholic Church was going through a period of change'.[35]

The Young Christian Workers (YCW) was another offshoot of the Catholic workers' movement active in Fitzroy. John Finlayson was one of the outreach youth workers with the YCW and a catalyst for the establishment of a Fitzroy Legal Service in the basement of the Town Hall. For Finlayson 'they were very exciting days' with long queues forming outside the centre as soon as it opened, despite the resistance of the Victorian Law Institute. 'That's how the demand was: people came from all over the place. Obviously we hit a nerve of need and not just a need of Fitzroy'.[36]

One of the stops on the Social Justice Walk was the Fitzroy Town Hall, where the new residents had achieved considerable success in council elections, leading the revolution in Melbourne's inner-city local government. Among the achievements of the Council was the establishment of a 'social' shop front in Brunswick Street. Few inner-city councils had dedicated staff to work on social issues although their municipalities included high proportions of residents living in poverty. South Melbourne and the City of Melbourne were large enough to employ a range of 'social' staff but the smaller councils still relied on voluntary groups such as the Ladies Benevolent Societies to hand out 'material aid' to residents. There was little oversight of these voluntary groups and at the time of the chaotic 1969 VCOSS meeting it was estimated there were a total of 51 welfare organisations operating in Fitzroy.

Fitzroy Council's decision to appoint Jenny Wills as the council's social worker reflected the priorities of the new resident councillors. Jenny Wills had the backing of women councillors especially Barbara Gaylor and Helen Madden, in planning for a Social Planning Office (SPO) which would integrate social issues into planning decision-making, be easily accessible to residents, provide a coordinated service and focus on community building rather than welfare handouts and service delivery. When the controversial SPO opened in Brunswick Street it was opposed by some existing welfare agencies, Council members and staff. An important development was the

---

34   Mary Doyle, *Backgrounder for Open House Reunion*, newsletter, 14 August 2010.
35   Stagoll, ed., *Social Justice Walk Around Fitzroy*, 6–7.
36   Stagoll, ed., *Social Justice Walk Around Fitzroy*, 12.

move to the SPO of the Fitzroy Advisory Service headed by Anna Fratta who had worked for the YCW. The Advisory Service 'sought not to take on a social worker type of role'. It provided information, established a community newspaper and directory for non-English speaking residents and brought together the major services that people needed.[37]

One of the most important contributions to grassroots empowerment was the role of CURA in supporting the move from integrationist policies to an ethnic rights movement between 1969–1972. In his study of the ethnic rights movement that developed in inner-city Melbourne around the Ecumenical Migration Centre (EMC) in Richmond and around FEC/CURA, Mark Lopez identifies their national influence on developing a policy of multiculturalism.[38] If the CURA objective of grassroots community mobilisation and empowerment was to be taken seriously then the cultures, values and needs of migrant residents had to be confronted. *Ekstasis*, the journal begun in 1972, announced in the June 1973 issue that 'the continuing work of the Centre will primarily be concerned with raising issues related to the central theme of the rights of ethnic minorities'. The Centre's resources would be directed towards 'the development of the capacity of ethnic groups and communities to take action on fundamental and urgent issues affecting the status of migrant and ethnic people in Australia', and that as a result of this decision 'the Centre's activity necessarily became less centred at Fitzroy, or any geographic area'.[39]

Although CURA continued to be involved in local community issues, the focus on ethnic rights and multiculturalism was a major change of direction. The emphasis of the new ethnic rights activism was on political activity, organising local residents and fighting campaigns.[40] Activists soon established links with those involved in Greek community politics, especially George Papadopoulos and Spiro Moraitis of the Australian Greek Welfare Society, while involvement with the Italian community was mainly through FILEF and its leaders Anne and Giovanni Sgro.[41] CURA staff members Des Storer and Arthur Faulkner organised seminars on multiculturalism, which had been adopted as a policy of the Whitlam Government. The publication

---

37   Jenny Wills et al, *Local Government and Community Services. Fitzroy – A Case Study in Social Planning* (Melbourne: Hard Pressed Publications, 1985).

38   Mark Lopez, *The Origins of Multiculturalism*, Chapter 4.

39   *Ekstasis*, no. 6 (June 1973), 1–2.

40   Lopez, *The Origins of Multiculturalism*, 140.

41   Giovanni Sgro, *Mediterranean Son: Memoirs of a Calabrian Migrant* (Coburg: Scoprire il Sud, 2000).

of *Ethnic Rights, Power and Participation*[42] spelt out the fundamental requirements for achieving a multicultural Australia and was a result of
consultation and the cooperation of a range of ethnic organisations.

Lopez questions the influence of the CURA campaign on multiculturalism, as most migrants were focused on the interests of their own community and did not exhibit concern for the broader community or interest in
building a pluralist society.[43] However, he concedes that the focus of CURA
research on migrant workers, especially *But I Wouldn't Want My Wife to Work
Here*,[44] a study of migrant women workers in Melbourne's manufacturing
industry, along with other Centre activities and publications, did focus public
attention on the appalling working conditions and exploitation of migrant
workers. The Centre also assisted the political representation of migrant
groups in the ALP through the integration of ethnic branches and the pre-
selection of ethnic leaders. Theo Sideropoulos and Giovanni Sgro were later
elected as members of the Victorian parliament and ethnic representation
increased on local inner-city councils and inner-northern suburbs.

CURA's focus on migrant workers marked a move away from the
community focus of the RAGs. This was evident in conflict over a major
recommendation of the survey of migrant working women, mostly young
married women with families working in inner-city factories. The CURA
survey found women wanted the provision of work-based child care and
this was one of the recommendations of the report. Such a recommendation
was fiercely opposed by the Community Child Care movement and the
Working Women's Centre who were committed to the location and
management of child care centres in local communities rather than places
of work. The argument for community-based child care had been central
to Ruth Crow's meticulously researched *History of Children's Services in
Melbourne Municipality 1910–1980*[45] and integral to the recommendations
of the CAN report.

In his study of community conflict in the Mission District of San Fran-
cisco, Mauel Castells has written that 'Alinsky-style community movements

---

42   Des Storer, ed., *Ethnic Rights, Power and Participation Toward a Multi-Cultural
      Australia* (Melbourne: Clearing House on Migration Issues, Ecumenical Migration
      Centre and CURA, 1975).

43   Lopez, *The Origins of Multiculturalism*, 144.

44   Centre for Urban Research and Action, *But I Wouldn't Want My Wife to Work Here:
      A Study of Migrant Women in Melbourne Industry; Research Report for International
      Women's Year* (Fitzroy: CURA, 1975).

45   Ruth Crow, *History of Children's Services in Melbourne Municipality, 1910 to 1980*
      (North Melbourne, Crow Collection Association, 1983).

showed a remarkable capacity to combine grassroots organisations with institutional social reform'.[46] The overall contribution of the work by the community based residents' associations, and by CURA and the BSL in Fitzroy in the 1970s was a major contribution to creative thinking in the area of social planning and policy. There was recognition that new institutions and new forms of community were needed to respond to the social and economic changes of the period, and an urgent need for the development of political and social power at a 'grassroots' level.

[46]   Castells, *The City and the Grassroots*, 109.

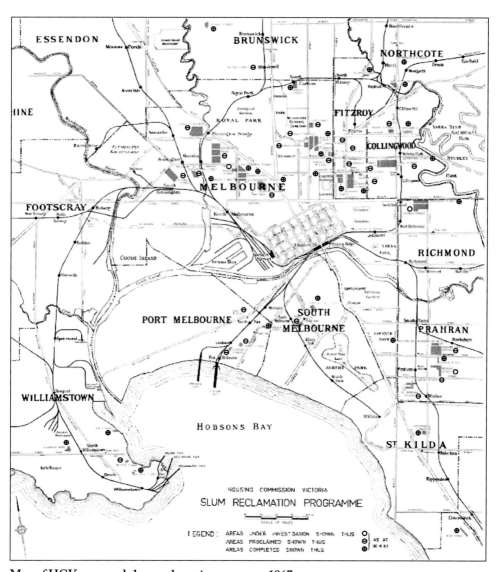

Map of HCV proposed slum reclamation program, 1967.

From the authors' collection.

Above: McCutcheon
family in front of HCV
flats, Collingwood, c1969.

Courtesy of Vivienne
McCutcheon.

Left: University of
Melbourne expansion plan.

Courtesy of the Carlton
Association.

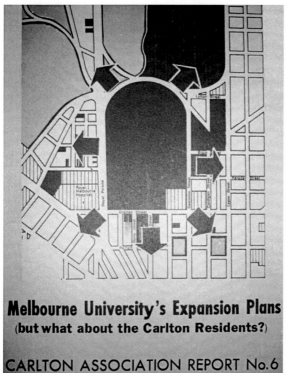

Melbourne University's Expansion Plans
(but what about the Carlton Residents?)

CARLTON ASSOCIATION REPORT No.6

Above: Ruth and Maurie Crow.

Courtesy of Crow Collection, Victoria University.

Above, right: Brian Lennon poster for Fitzroy City Council election.

Courtesy of Jane Lennon.

Below: George Tibbits.

Courtesy of Di Tibbits.

Opposite page,
clockwise from top left:

Anne Polis with Mary
working on 'The
Melbourne Times', the
Age, 14 November 1970.

Courtesy of Fairfax Media
Publications.

Brian Howe.

Courtesy of Alan K. Jordan
photographic collection,
State Library of Victoria.
Image H2010.105/200c

Carol Carney; Paul
Coghlan; and Bruce and
Annie Hanford.

Photos courtesy of the
Jordan Family.

This page, from top:

Richmond Assocation
poster.

Urban Activists Collection,
Deakin University.

Norm Gallagher
escorted from the
Carlton Courthouse, the
Age, 5 February 1971.

Courtesy of Fairfax Media
Publications.

Top left: Hugh Stretton.

Courtesy of Hugh Stretton.

Top right: Alfred Crescent Primary School demonstration, 1962.

Courtesy of Alan K. Jordan photographic collection, State Library of Victoria. Image H2010.105/162c.

Above: Peter Hollingworth and David Scott with poster of Father Tucker, the founder of the Brotherhood of St Laurence.

Courtesy of the Brotherhood of St Laurence.

Left: Jack Strocchi's bumper bar cross, Brooks Crescent demonstration, 1970.

Courtesy of Alan K. Jordan photographic collection, State Library of Victoria. Image H2010.105/573d.

Below: Brooks Crescent model, 1970.

Courtesy of Alan K. Jordan photographic collection, State Library of Victoria. Image H2010.105/431f.

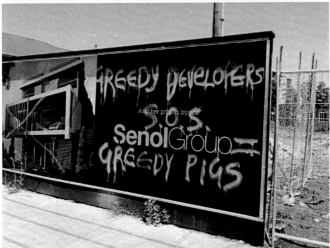

From top:

Poster produced by the Citizens Against the Freeway Action Centre, c.1977.

Courtesy of the Ralph McLean collection, 19880.0034, item 74, University of Melbourne Archives.

Gentrification in Brunswick, 2013.

Courtesy of David Nichols.

Poster opposing East West Link, 2013.

Courtesy of David Nichols.

Chapter 9

GENTRIFICATION AND TRENDIFICATION

Bret Christian, founder and editor of the Subiaco *Post*, remembers Subiaco in the mid-1970s as an area rich in conflict and colour:

> When we moved into 52 Churchill Avenue, that first little terrace where we started the paper, my son was born and all these old ladies came up with presents, he'd been the first born in the street for 20 years. The woman over the road was 99 and she was being looked after by her young spinister daughter who was 75, who had looked after her all her life. She said "When Mum dies I'm going to get married," and she did. There was a lot of that, loads and loads of old people, fantastic characters. There were two boarding houses just up the road full of old drunks, you know, they'd sit outside on the steps of their houses at night and get pissed and throw bottles at each other. On one side of us was the truck driver who fostered homeless children and beat his wife for sport and on the other old Mrs Kelly who had alienated her entire family and lived entirely on VB ... There were bikies two doors up from us, seven bikies, and they used to ride their motorbikes into the house and keep them in the lounge room. Loads and loads of overcrowded student houses, all paying a couple of bucks each a week, because the university was here, down the road, and there were three big teaching hospitals in Subiaco as well.

He recalls Subiaco as 'a party suburb and I miss that as well'. His regret tallies with one of Ken Spillman's interviewees, Irene Greenwood, who commented in the 1990s that 'now young people with families are coming in and building brick walls and swimming pools, and it's now a trendy suburb'.[1] Reflecting on the Subi Centro development – a brownfields 'new urbanist' residential and retail precinct which involved the sinking of the railway and station – Christian adds:

---

[1]   Irene Greenwood quoted in Ken Spillman, *Identity Prized*, 339.

I think the dormitory part of Subi is a lot less vibrant now than it was ...
It's a lot cleaner and people mow their verges and they don't burn their
leaves in the gutter and there are no rusting cars out the front and it's
sort of not as interesting.

There are a lot of old people, mostly women living alone in single
houses. There are a lot of people of my vintage, baby boomers, who
moved here in the 70s and 80s ... Then there's the new wave and some
of those people, strangely enough they've sold their lovely old federation
houses and moved into what I call sea container houses in Subi Centro.
It's sort of lego land.

It's going to be hell on earth one day, it probably is already, the
architecture is two sea containers stacked up ... Yet, people have
changed ... They don't want the upkeep, they don't want to fiddle
around the garden on weekends, they want to stay up all night and
sleep all day in their leisure time, if they haven't got kids.

Here, Christian puts his finger on the 'slippery and contested nature' of
an area's character, which can for some local residents in Subiaco be 'seen as
separate to Subiaco's built form, and yet ... still be destroyed by certain types
of development'.[2]

This chapter discusses the early twenty-first century gentrification of the
Australian inner city in the context of the widespread urban activism of the
1960s and 70s, with particular reference to Carlton, the Melbourne inner
suburb at the heart of so many battles, even now. It is argued that to typify
inner cities as gentrified, and the urban activists as self-interested gentrifiers,
is too simplistic an assessment. It also suggests that the creation of gentrified
pockets of the inner city is only a negative outcome for these areas insofar
as income and advantage inequality between neighbourhoods is itself a
negative outcome. Indeed, it is short sighted to see this as an *outcome*, that
is, a permanent 'end game' state of affairs. Rather, as Andrew McCutcheon
suggests, it seems likely that 'in the end something else will happen and
it will all run down again. There might be a 50-year cycle where it's not
popular again, hopefully'. As he goes on to say:

It's very hard to foresee how the cycle goes because they were very
fashionable houses in Fitzroy and Carlton 100 years ago, 80 years ago.

---

2   Gethin Davison and Emma Rowden, '"There's Something About Subi": Defending
and Creating Neighbourhood Character in Perth, Australia' *Journal of Urban Design*
17 (2) (2012), 191.

Then they became very unfashionable and people looked down their noses at Victorian houses and rushed to the suburbs and passed through the inner suburbs with their noses in the air.

The Gentrification of Inner Melbourne

Population change in the inner cities was a global phenomenon and the interpretative concept of gentrification was especially embraced by British urban geographers and sociologists.[3] Neil Smith was a leader in this interpretation, linking gentrification with the emergence of late capitalist economy and employment associated with finance capital and information technology in world cities. Melbourne's inner-city residents' associations were also identified as gentrifiers, displacing working-class renters and home owners, protecting the value of their inner-city properties and enjoying all the amenity and accessability of the inner suburbs. Is this the pattern that gentrification followed in Melbourne and can it be traced? Or is 'trendification', which emphasises the importance of social and cultural factors, a more appropriate description of Melbourne's inner-city change?[4]

In 1985 William Stewart Logan published *The Gentrification of Inner Melbourne: A Political Geography of Inner City Housing*, based primarily on (but updating) his 1980 PhD thesis *Gentrification in Inner Melbourne: Pattern, Process and Meaning*. Logan – who it should be acknowledged was a chief investigator on the research project from which much of this book takes its source material – was seeking to contribute to a 'new political geography' in which a 'major aim' was 'to accurately record the unfolding of the gentrification process especially during the critical period of the early 1970s'.[5] In so doing he similarly hoped to track 'the nature and distribution of power and conflict in society'.[6] Like Patrick Mullins,[7] Logan was a participant observer – he was a member of the Carlton Association and served as its historical group convenor – though (unlike Mullins) he also went so far as to describe himself as 'an early member of the so-called "gentry"'.[8]

---

[3] Neil Smith and Peter Williams, ed. *Gentrification of the City* (Boston: Unwin Hyman, 1986).

[4] Tanya Lukins, 'Gentrification and Cosmopolitan Leisure in Inner-Urban Melbourne, Australia, 1960s-1970s' *Urban Policy and Research* 27 (3) (September 2009), 265–276.

[5] William Stewart Logan, *The Gentrification of Inner Melbourne: The Political Geography of Inner City Housing* (St Lucia: University of Queensland Press, 1985), xxxi.

[6] Logan, *The Gentrification of Inner Melbourne*, 287.

[7] See Chapter Six.

[8] Logan, *The Gentrification of Inner Melbourne*, xxxii.

Logan's definition of gentrification was based on rising numbers of Australian born and rising occupancy status indicated by increased proportions of owner-occupied houses. It included renovation of older buildings as 'the translation of different aesthetic standards into physical environmental terms', leading to sharpening of 'social-spatial contrasts'.[9] Examining the data from the four censuses between 1961 and 1976, Logan found that while there was evidence of change in ethnic makeup in inner suburbs over this period (moving, and indeed returning, towards a greater proportion of Anglo-Australians), there was little indication that housing had shifted from rental-to owner-occupation in that fifteen year period.[10] Using Melbourne City Council rate cards and concentrating only on three sample areas – East Melbourne, Kensington and North Carlton – Logan found that 'the evidence for an active gentrification process based on middle-class property purchase is unconvincing, even at the detailed street and precinct level of analysis'.[11] Indeed, he considers at one point that what was occurring was perhaps less a matter of 'gentrification', as recognised at an international level, and more a case of 'trendification', a phenomenon 'related to the new and young renting population and its day-to-day spending habits and styles in household decoration'.[12]

Nonetheless, Logan describes the multiple facets of the inner-city changes in the 1960s and 70s, to the extent possible, in terms of international understandings of 'gentrification'. He raises the class issues inherent in (for instance) the Carlton Association's objection to Reg Rayner's use of the railway land for the Kleenex warehouse, and discusses with acuity the motives beneath the campaign to save the Lee Street block from classification as a 'slum' by the HCV:

> In Lee Street, the CA was *ostensibly* protecting the traditional residents, but was it perhaps primarily motivated by the desire to protect the value of middle-class investments in the more general area …?[13]

Such questions cast doubt on the motives of the 'gentry' as Logan defines them, and the activities of new middle-class residents in the inner city as a whole. Logan concluded that although new residents were attracted by low

---

9   Logan, *The Gentrification of Inner Melbourne*, 3–5.
10   Logan, *The Gentrification of Inner Melbourne*, 18.
11   Logan, *The Gentrification of Inner Melbourne*, 51.
12   Logan, *The Gentrification of Inner Melbourne*, 52.
13   Logan, *The Gentrification of Inner Melbourne*, 197.

housing prices, few had bought for investment purposes or had chosen to locate in the inner city expecting to benefit from rising house prices, and there was little evidence of large-scale speculative investment.[14] There was no evidence of a trendies invasion.

The value of a study such as Logan's – much like Mullins' in Brisbane the previous decade – is not inherently in its predictive qualities. However, Logan did foresee that, after the 'environmental up-grading' of north and east inner Melbourne, 'the more industrialized western parts' would become the focus of gentrifiers' attentions. Indeed, he writes, houses 'thought a decade ago to be unfit for human habitation according to statutory definitions are now emerging as desirable residential locations', and 'there is considerable support for the contention that the entire inner-suburban area may be transformed into a middle-class residential zone'.[15] An analysis of current statistics using Logan's criteria to measure gentrification, especially home ownership, reveals a complex picture. In East Melbourne in 1976, 65.4% of houses were owner-occupied; in 2012, the figure was 66.8%. This minimal increase is not a surprising statistic – the real contrast would probably be found in the comparison of apartment dwellings, but unfortunately this does not feature in the earlier figures. However, in Kensington, to the west of the city and within the MCC boundaries, home ownership accounts for 59.06% of housing stock, a significant fall from the 1976 figure of 70.7% and more than ten percent below the state average. Logan saw the beginnings of this decline in the late 1970s when 'high owner-occupancy areas had contracted to a number of scattered cores' in the area. Overall, Logan noted in 1977 that that analysis of property purchases had limitations in identifying cultural issues, such as the attraction of the diversity of people and lifestyles, in explaining inner city change.

The question then might ultimately be what direct connection remains between the gentry – or the activists, who may or may not constitute a 'gentry' – of the 1970s, and the inner-urban residents of today. The Carlton area, for instance, has seen a rapid increase in apartment development in the twenty-first century, either for students (336 were created in 2008–9 alone) or other residents (102).[16] Those who anticipated the trend and moved to Melbourne's inner city before 1975 are now predominantly in their 60s

[14] Logan, *The Gentrification of Inner Melbourne*, 140.
[15] Logan, *The Gentrification of Inner Melbourne*, 5–6.
[16] Nick Casey, *Melbourne City Research: Analysis of Population and Housing in Melbourne Local Government Area 2001 to 2009* (Melbourne: City of Melbourne, 2010), 5.

and 70s. Almost by definition, as discussed below, they are only a subset of 'the original inhabitants' of the inner city. Yet those who remained a quarter of a century after the peak of the turmoil in Melbourne were still reflective. Had their actions been entirely self-serving and discriminatory? And had the primary outcome of their actions been the alienation of low-waged communities from cheap, accessible housing? To what extent had they paved the way for a later wave of property purchasers driven by the commercial advantages of inner-city location?

Clouds in My Coffee: The Activists Reflect

In 2004, Mayne and Zygmuntowicz noted, 'The residents of Carlton's historic homes are now more likely to be professionals, usually singles or childless couples, than working-class families'.[17] Brendan Gleeson also notes the contribution of the gay community to what is generally considered gentrification.[18] In 2014, we are at a moment in McCutcheon's cycle where living in the inner city takes a financial toll – one which many still feel is eminently worth paying.

In 2008, the international coffee chain Starbucks announced its seven year tenure in Lygon Street, Carlton, was coming to an end. 'Carlton traders were up in arms in 2001 when the Melbourne Council allowed the chain to open on Lygon Street, heartland of Melbourne's coffee culture', wrote the *Age*'s Max Cooper.[19] The rejection of an American chain store – whose insertion into Lygon Street was seen by many as cheeky, if not insulting – can be seen as a gauge of the inner city's continued defence of its own 'terrain', now on relatively petty terms. Yet it is pertinent to compare the sterile, serviceable, generic interior of a Starbucks with the ambience of a café/bar such as North Carlton's Residential Kitchen.

It is just after 9 am in late winter. Residential Kitchen, a café/bar filling two shopfronts opposite what was once the Rising Sun Hotel, now Enoteca – is rapidly filling. Solitary older men read papers, while middle-aged women, men and children under ten occupy other tables. One woman in her early twenties sits smoking alone in the cold outside.

---

[17] Alan Mayne and Kasia Zygmuntowicz, 'Changing Fortunes' in *Carlton: A History*, 38.

[18] Brendan Gleeson, *Australian Heartlands: Making Space for Hope in the Suburbs* (Crows Nest: Allen and Unwin, 2006), 58.

[19] Max Cooper, 'Starbucks Goes Cold on Lygon Street' Melbourne *Age*, 31 July 2008, http://www.theage.com.au; see also Daniella Miletic, Tom Arup and Daniel Emerson, 'Hundreds of Jobs Lost As Starbucks Shuts 61 Shops' Melbourne *Age*, 30 July 2008, 3.

Décor within the establishment is a curious blend. An inner-city 'trendy' of forty years ago would instantly recognise some of these elements: the hessian coffee bags which line the outside of the counter (one even covers the shade of the oversize lamp which sits atop it), and the alcohol and soft-drink bottles, pragmatic storage and colourful cheer, queued on the shelves. Of all things, a spring mattress from what must have been a child's bed is hung, askew, from one surface. Photographs of 'café society' are arranged elsewhere, and painted on the southern wall names in a typewriter font: 'Araglin', 'Hassal Green', 'Villa Aurora', 'Pen-y-Bryn'. Talk – which might even be 'chatter' – is voluble, fuelled by the fine coffee and the omnipresent awareness that we are inside, while the bleak and rainy street is without. There, new cars, many of them large, are parked on Lygon's east side in front of a jagged row of mainly single-storey brick terraces. Around the corner, inner-city whimsy is displayed in the woollen covers painstakingly crocheted for the stainless-steel bicycle stands. In the early twenty-first century, the clichés about Melbourne, its coffee, its Italian influences, its laneways and Victorian-era streets abound, and are known and commented on not just nationally but internationally. An 'urban activist' of the early 1970s might ponder such a scene and wonder whether this was what was being fought for: in a way, and not to diminish the importance of those fights, it was: a quiet, attractive, functional, dense community close to amenities and the central city.

It is a cliché to state that victors write history, but the underlying assumption – that those who have triumphed in a battle are those who participated in the battle – is often misguided. The critique of the 'urban activists' prevalent even in the late 1960s, that they were 'trendies', seeking a boutique 'lifestyle' at the expense of progress, low-income housing residents, or migrant communities was, as we have seen, an oversimplification. Nonetheless it is true that (as Gleeson points out) what were once low-income areas have 'been transformed by decades of gentrification and by generous public investments in cultural and physical infrastructure that have greatly enhanced their ability to capture and hold social wealth'.[20]

An inner-city activism seminar held at inner-Melbourne's Richmond Town Hall in 2001 to reflect on the achievements of the residents' associations was sponsored by the City of Yarra, an amalgamation of the Fitzroy, Richmond and Collingwood Councils. The seminar brought together many individuals who 'battled' and 'brawled' side by side in the 1960s and 70s. It

---

[20] Gleeson, *Australian Heartlands*, 44.

was a moment in time at which, entering the new century, residents were ready to reflect. A common observation, expressed in numerous iterations, was the almost-embarrassed truism that purchasing a house in the inner city in the late 1960s was, far from being a 'trendy' or financially canny decision, virtually an absurdist act. One participant, Paul Coghlan, recalled:

> I guess I was an economic refugee in Fitzroy in 1969 when we first married. I suspect we couldn't have afforded to live in our own home anywhere else. We paid $9750 for a house in Rose Street, North Fitzroy with $2000 of our own that we managed to scrimp together with help from our families and $7000 or something from the bank and repayments of $54 a month and you could manage.[21]

Another (unidentifiable) participant suggested that even the 'professionals and academics' since identified as gentrifiers could be categorised as economic refugees, opining that 'a lot of my acquaintances and friends, we basically came from working class backgrounds ... Was it because we came from a working class background that we were comfortable in this locality?' Others grappled in differing ways with the ironic reality of, as one participant put it, 'the massive social realignment which has made areas which were once targeted not so long ago as slums into some of the most valuable real estate in the city'. Another suggested that 'what we are hearing from is the group of people who have been the stayers in the inner suburbs ... if we left out of the account the effect of all those other sometimes fairly transient groups which had a powerful effect in catalysing movements at particular moments, then I think we've missed part of the story'.

For many of those 'stayers' present at the seminar – few of whom had a non-English speaking or postwar migrant background – the question of whether they, or their activism had usurped the postwar migrant was still a matter of concern. David Beauchamp suggested that:

> I'd come from New Zealand, the Grimshaws had come from New Zealand, George Tibbits had come from Colac, Chris Molan had come from Mildura, Cathy Sanders from Shepparton, Trevor Huggard from Mooroopna and we were another migrant wave but we were a migrant wave that had obviously chosen to come here. We hadn't come here because that was the only cheap housing, we'd come here because this

---

21   Transcript of 'The Challenge of the Inner Suburbs: Social Inquiry and Community Action in the 1960s and 70s' Richmond Town Hall, 1 April 2000, 14.

was the suburb that had attracted us and we were prepared to work to keep that suburb the way we wanted it.[22]

Louise Elliott, formerly of the Fitzroy RAG, used a similar idea, describing herself as 'a migrant from Sydney. After a very brief period in Melbourne suburbs to complete my schooling, I moved into Carlton and then Fitzroy as a student and I have been there ever since. It felt my home, the rest of Melbourne didn't'.[23]

Others recalled that they, or members of their cohort, had migrated to the inner city specifically for its radical politics and the potential to try out new ideas in areas of real need. At the Richmond seminar Brian Howe recalled:

One day a very smart Jaguar pulled up in the front of the house, a black jaguar and a couple of fellows got out and one of them was Pete Steedman, who at that time was apparently keen on those sorts of cars and the other was Bruce Hanford. Now, Bruce Hanford really was an émigré from the United States, a draft dodger I guess and he'd gone and left and finished up in inner Melbourne and he wanted to be part of the action. He saw what was happening and Pete Steedman had really just come back from London where he played, as I found out later, quite a significant role in Save Covent Garden movement. So in a way you're talking about a little bit of globalisation. People really are immigrating in a sense or travelling and getting the experiences we're talking about ... this is a period in which people, like Winsome McCaughey, have been in New York and gets involved in a whole kind of neighbourhood child care movement that she's seen operate in New York.[24]

Vivienne McCutcheon was similarly inspired:

This was one of the things that we brought back or captured from perhaps places overseas like Chicago and London and talked a lot about and it was about a notion of empowering local people. It was what the Brotherhood was on about and why it moved from very unsuccessful attempts to import a notion of having one social worker to one family out where the Camp Pell families had moved into Preston, to them changing to the Family Centre Project. There's a sense in which there's

---

22   Transcript of 'The Challenge of the Inner Suburbs', 5.
23   Transcript of 'The Challenge of the Inner Suburbs', 8.
24   Transcript of 'The Challenge of the Inner Suburbs', 3.

that conversation about empowerment, about people being in control that was both exciting and was also a struggle for us.[25]

Still others identified a brand of inner-city activism that was, in essence, interested in the preservation of buildings rather than communities. As has been seen elsewhere in this book, this concern was a considerable motivating factor within, for instance, the Parkville and East Melbourne associations, and was a major activity for groups such as the Emerald Hill Association. John Power was the first president of the Balmain Association, formed in 1965. He saw organistions such as that at Balmain as a blend of community empowerment with conservation:

> I think that what was new was that the professional middle classes were congregating together in the inner suburbs and I think that they were really particularly concerned to introduce something along the lines of what John Dryzek in his book calls discursive democracy. But what was unusual, what was novel about these organisations was that they were like traditional National Trust branches … They required or demanded a civility in the way they were treated and they wished to be involved in planning processes but they had a relatively narrow set of interests; heritage, amenity, civility and a great deal of socialisation as well or socialising. But when the need for protests emerged they were prepared to go along and it's quite striking that the green bans originated so thoroughly in as upper class a community as Hunters Hill.[26]

Winsome Roberts, a self-styled 'migrant to Melbourne from Western Australia' suggested that 'the Fremantle Association was not dissimilar to the picture that John [Power] sketched in Sydney, that is the Fremantle Association was run along the lines of a National Heritage body that would protest but was basically a heritage movement'.[27]

A range of motivations were also discovered by Davison and Rowden in their interviews with Subiaco residents, where the Fremantle and Subiaco environments – sometimes conflated into one style by informants – were identified as commensurate with 'community': 'spatial form, heritage, architectural style and building materials were key themes'[28] and such an environment contributed to discussion of 'character' for encouraging

---

25 Transcript of 'The Challenge of the Inner Suburbs', 12.

26 Transcript of 'The Challenge of the Inner Suburbs', 3–5.

27 Transcript of 'The Challenge of the Inner Suburbs', 16.

28 Davison and Rowden, '"There's Something About Subi"', 198.

walkability, social capital and 'three conversations' in any stroll down the main street.[29] This 'village' society continues to be valued, and sought after, in Subiaco, Fremantle, Fitzroy, South Melbourne, Battery Point, North Adelaide and numerous other inner-city areas, and its appeal has been articulated as such in Australia for almost half a century. As Mayne and Zygmuntowicz affirm 'You can *still* feel you are part of a "village" when you live in Carlton'.[30] The critique made of Sydney's Paddington's inhabitants in 1968, that they 'resembled Mallee fowl, an enclosed community ... with rituals and ways of living specifically its own',[31] still seems current in comparable areas today. Yet a 'village' lifestyle is hardly the exclusive province of the inner city; middle-class middle-ring suburbs (particularly those with nineteenth or early twentieth century shopping precincts), new urbanist suburbs, country towns – particularly those which serve in part as dormitories for the metropolis; peri-urban mountain districts such as the Dandenongs, the Blue Mountains, and the Perth and Adelaide Hills, all feature communities which pride themselves on what they see as a village lifestyle. Villages, it should additionally be noted, are often settlements lacking in privacy, where gossip and judgment thrive, and residents might easily abandon civility for self-interest. It is a credit to the inner-city communities of Australia that such a scenario rarely manifests, at least in public. The battle which concludes this chapter may be an exception that proves the rule.

The Right to the City

> Later this week, various venues around Fitzroy will host an 'anti-gentrification festival' hosted by the 'radical craft group' Craft Cartel. Their aim, as they describe it, is to celebrate their presence in the city before they are driven out by what they describe as 'crazy living costs'. They've even got hold of the stinky, sticky carpet from the much-loved, mourned, dead and soon-to-be resurrected Tote and are making exhibitions, fashion parades and souvenirs from it to raise money for local charities.[32]

---

29   Davison and Rowden, '"There's Something About Subi"', 196.

30   Mayne and Zygmuntowicz, 'Changing Fortunes', 51 [present authors' emphasis].

31   Anon, 'Raising Hell Every Day' *The Bulletin*, 2 March 1968, 39.

32   Marcus Westbury, 'Artists Kick-Start Gentrification' Melbourne *Age*, 7 June 2010, 17.

Urbanist, broadcaster and writer Marcus Westbury, author of the above, was philosophical and perhaps even cynical about Craft Cartel (a self-styled 'posse of radical crafters'). 'It's easy to criticise this kind of approach. It seems a little naive. It's certainly neither the first nor the last time that artists in Melbourne and other major Australian cities have complained of being forced out of their stomping grounds by yuppies, developers, nimby regulations, and rising property prices', he wrote in 2010. Craft Cartel's iconisation of the much-loved Tote, a hotel in Collingwood, was in this context an example of scattershot protest; the Tote's brief closure was the result of government licensing laws in response to a broader problem of alcohol violence, and entirely unconnected to noise complaints or other issues surrounding live music in the inner city. Indeed, Westbury might well have pointed to the influential collection *Into the Hollow Mountain*, published the year he was born, in which noted Melbourne poet Π.O. published his diatribe 'Get out of Fitzroy'.[33] When the book was launched in November 1974, John Stevens' coverage in the *Age* was given the title 'Fitzroy versus Trendies'. Stevens wrote 'The old residents are digging in against the invading middle class people who want to turn their down-at-heel refuge into a fashionable suburb'.[34] The various authors compiled within *Into the Hollow Mountain* would no doubt have taken heart from the knowledge, logically unattainable in 1974 and seemingly unlikely, that there would still be a substantial, vocal portion of the inner-city population railing against the 'trendy twees'[35] thirty-five years later. They are not an ethnic group – with rare public housing exceptions, new migrants to Australia in the twenty-first century now contribute to enclaves further afield than the unaffordable inner city – but self-styled artists and musicians, particularly 'alternative' cultural producers, who need to be situated where the culture manifests. Kate Shaw has argued that alternative scenes (and 'alternative people') need centrality for interaction and assertion of their rights[36] and it is such an understanding which has led to recent tirades against the gentrifiers of Australia's inner cities. Indeed, many of the conventionally desirable inner-city pockets of the early twenty-first century have all the attributes – comfort, affluence, inward-looking exclusivity – of the suburbs

---

[33] See Chapter Three.

[34] John Stevens, 'Fitzroy versus Trendies' Melbourne *Age*, 14 November 1974, 17.

[35] Logan, *The Gentrification of Inner Melbourne*, 11.

[36] Kate Shaw, 'The Place of Alternative Culture and the Politics of its Protection in Berlin, Amsterdam and Melbourne' *Planning Theory and Practice* 6 (2) (2005), 149–169.

so despised by those who 'colonised' the Victorian streetscapes of North Melbourne and Balmain in the 1950s and 60s.

Ben Eltham's call for artists to move from the inner city to relatively 'depressed' areas is based in part on calling the bluff of Richard Florida's 'creative class' rhetoric, but also on an eminently understandable rubric of the low-income status of many art practitioners and the preference of 'creatives' to live with their own. He writes:

> For every high-art gallery priced out of its own building, there are dozens of hollowed-out warehouses and shopfronts being rehabilitated along the public transport spines of our capital cities. These are the deep suburbs that Australia's so-called "elites"—those left-leaning, latte-sipping figments of the right's imagination—are supposed to despise. In fact, many of them are well on their way to being rehabilitated, not only by artists but by an entire demographic cohort of 20- and 30-somethings priced out of the housing market but nonetheless diversifying the neighbourhoods where they rent.

There is no reason, he argues, that 'the state should intervene in the property market to ensure that arts institutions, which began their lives as sites for the edgy and the undiscovered, should survive in a particular locale'.[37] Indeed, one could argue that rather Park and Burgess' Zones – so simply laid out in a model diagram with the transitional region at the heart of the city – are now scattered into numerous zones. For migrants to Melbourne, suburbs such as Box Hill and Springvale now function in this way; the artistic suburbs of Melbourne are yet to fully form, but will undoubtedly do so in the near future. They will probably emerge in middle-ring areas such as Reservoir which, in an urban cultural landscape abounding with ironies, is ironically the suburban area from which a considerable number of the 1960s and 70s' iconoclasts have escaped to the inner city.

Eternal Vigilance

In 2004, editor Peter Yule and the Carlton Residents' Association – not the original 'CA' but a group formed in 1996 in response to the council boundary changes instituted by the Kennett state government – produced *Carlton: A History*. Contributors – including some of the authors of this book, and some founder members of the Carlton Association – detailed many facets of the

---

37   Ben Eltham, 'Hey Latte-Lovers, Art Works Just As Well on the Fringe' *Crikey*, 3 June 2011.

history and present state of this small yet eminently valued urban space. It is clear from the Yule book there is only one universally tolerated view on Carlton, which is that there have been, and continue to be, many Carltons.

The film *Struggle*[38] outlines the coming together of residents, unions and students to prevent the erection of a warehouse on railway land in North Carlton. In NSW in 1971 the BLF consciously went forth to prevent the development of Hunters Hill bushland for apartment blocks – that is, the question of whether it was a union's business to assist in the conservation of a middle-class area was argued on class terms. The previous year, as is clear from *Struggle*, the notion of North Carlton as anything but a deprived area was not countenanced. Footage of children riding bikes and playing in cramped streets of terraces was paired with actual verbal descriptions of the area as working-class – certainly, the schools of Carlton neighbourhoods were notoriously overcrowded at this time. The Carlton Association's role in calling for the retention of the railway land as open space was not minimised, but nor were the full implications of the motives of the activists – as discussed by Logan above in relation to the motivation of the activists in Lee Street – teased out.

The same land was again the focus of media attention and protest in 2010, forty years after the process began to prevent its use for industry. The Hardy Gallagher reserve is now a linear park and part of the Inner Circle Rail Trail. Local residents objected to a proposal put forward by the City of Yarra – the LGA responsible for North Carlton, the region having been bisected by the Kennett boundaries – to place a community garden in part of the park. "Council is intending to take 1300sq m of open parkland, available to all the community, and fence and lock it off as a community garden for use by a few," Chris Fraser, of the Friends of Hardy Gallager Reserve told the Melbourne *Leader*.[39] Online comments from the period in which the community garden proposal was heavily in dispute are diverse yet revealing. Critics objected on the basis that a community garden would take up too much space, would 'privatise' a section of the park, would attract vermin, would be ugly or would force passive users and cyclists into each other's space. 'Chris – park user' wrote that:

> It's interesting logic that those wishing to fence off the park for a few
> to grow vegetables are referring to those wanting to keep the park open
> to all as selfish!! It's also interesting that those who wish to use public

---

[38]   See Chapter Six.

[39]   'Fenced Out of Carlton North Park' Melbourne *Leader*, 1 February 2010.

open space rather than their own back yard are suggesting that others have the NIMBY problem!! There is no economic need for most Princes Hill residents to grow vegetables, particularly with the fabulous Queen Victoria Market within shouting distance, therefore we are talking about a limited number of people wanting to use fenced off and locked away public land for their hobby which they also want the rest of the residents to fund.[40]

'Lin kwong' wrote:

Australia is a very lucky country but very difficult to understand. I work 2 job and last year I bought a flat near the park so I can be close to my day job at the university. My neigbor said that the council will spend $100,000 to make a vegetable garden near my flat. I pay so much money to the council to live here. I do not want to work 2 job but I have to. I do not want my money to throw away for people hobby ... I hope I can take the vegetables I will be pay for.

'Dylan' asked whether open space should be replaced with a community garden – both of which offered advantages of community interaction – 'just because a kitchen garden is the latest groovy thing for one section of the community?' This same commentator worried about the 'privatisation' aspect of the garden proposal: 'surely its not just about claiming your own piece of the inner city?'

Others claimed their objection was essentially to the lack of consultation. Peter Cunningham wrote:

Before they're out of nappies, all competent practitioners of public policy development learn well that ongoing, broad, open, inclusive consultation is essential for a satisfactory public policy outcome. It is mind boggling to think that the bureaucrats have managed to engineer such a divisive issue.

Others, such as Catherine de Saint Phalle, tied history to the present with eloquence and wordplay:

The Hardy-Gallagher R. has already been fought for. It should be heritage listed rather than divided into plots. This time walled beds

---

40   This and subsequent online comments from 'Have Your Say: Fenced Out of Carlton North Park', Melbourne *Leader*, accessed 14 August 2012, http://melbourneleader. whereilive.com.au/news/story/don-t-fence-us-out-of-carlton-north-park/.

are robbing its trees instead of a Kleenex factory. The earth is full of railway scraps surely a sign to desist? Tap water is to be used instead of environmentally aware native plants and beds of copper red bark. How can the council be conned into such a witless, inconsistent act, causing dissension in the community? Thanks to the council, innocent parkland has become a bone of contention! Isn't gardening supposed to be in sync with nature? Is there pleasure in planting seeds in such an atmosphere? Yet, the most different human beings have been brought together to protect the beauty and serenity of the park. People who maybe would not have much in common otherwise have come to respect and in some cases deeply care for each other ... Why not make this an opportunity for a better community instead of a bitter one?

A few minority voices cut through, such as that of Marcus Liddle, who lived near the park space in question and claimed to have 'NEVER seen anybody using it' for the range of passive recreations detailed by others. He wrote:

I cannot believe the selfish, narrow-minded comments I am hearing ... Yes, I see people using the bike path but never on the grass. Especially when there is the whole of Princes Park less than 50 metres away!

It is not like they are taking away parklands and turning them in to a hockey centre or a car park. It is going to be a garden. A garden. When did that become a bad thing?

All of the arguments put forth here are just feeble excuses for Not In My Back Yard. I can only assume that the neighbourhood is more worried about things like the view from their front window and real estate prices than ideals like community or sustainability. It is all very well for those home owners living in houses with backyards and gardens but what about the rest of us? You can drive your car to the supermarket to buy your vegetables, but I want to be able to walk across the road and grow my own.

It really makes me lose faith for the future, the future that has already been ruined and now we cannot even begin to make better in the tiniest of ways.

Ultimately the City of Yarra reneged from what was, in any case, only one of a range of proposals and the Princes Hill Community Garden group announced via its website in May 2012 that it would not proceed with any of the initially proposed sites for its garden, ostensibly the best of which was in

Hardy Gallagher Reserve. The statement editorialised on 'two Princes Hill residents' who 'have waged a divisive campaign to sabotage the process by promulgating misinformation to local residents and the media on the aims of our group and the process we have followed'.[41]

The forty year gap between responses to two incarnations of what Logan calls an 'environmental intrusion'[42] on this open space is a valuable gauge of the way that Carlton has changed over time. It also, of course, demonstrates how protest itself has changed over time – from the physical presence of protesting bodies to the aggregation of virulent commentary on the internet. That said, 100 people did physically assemble under the Friends of Hardy Gallagher Reserve banner in the heat of late January 2010 to show their disapproval of the community garden proposal.

There is no longer, of course, any discussion of the value of open space to Carlton's working-class residents, or even to children as a group (notwithstanding the ten year old who commented: 'I hate vegetables, never touch them and do not want to look at them. Can I ride my BMX over the vegetables?'). Commonalities across the almost half-a-century include the rhetoric of lifestyle and community (one of the major complaints was that the nature of the consultation process instituted by Yarra, and the lack of information provided to locals, was dividing the community). In certain ways the stories by residents provided in their comments were, in part, life stories: these protestors came to Carlton in search of a particular kind of existence, one which a community garden might to some extent spoil. In that regard, their stories are part of what is now a tradition in Carlton, as seen from the older activists' stories at the Richmond seminar: that they relocated to the inner city to pursue a life which they are willing to ardently defend – even from each other.

The Logan study of 1985 drills beyond census-derived neighbourhood groupings into specific streets and blocks to find evidence of enclaves demonstrating degrees of gentrification behaviour. An in-depth study of the antagonisms and affiliations in North Carlton might go even further than this, into small sections of street, and perhaps even within households. That the dispute has been concentrated around public space is a historic commonality that has maintained a premium in this densely-packed suburb; that it has become perceived by many not as Carlton under attack

---

[41]   jb2, 'Update No 5: 'No Community Garden for Princes Hill', *Princes Hill Community Garden*, 1 March 2012, http://www.princeshillgarden.com/.

[42]   Logan, *The Gentrification of Inner Melbourne*, 193.

from outside forces, but as an area threatened by people within it (people in thrall to a 'groovy thing', no less) may well suggest a changing culture of entitlement within a community, particularly one in which the story often comes with details of the price paid to live in the area. It may also merely be a sign of an open, democratic and educated cohort ready to debate and, indeed, fight for what it believes in: in that sense, the spirit of the Carlton of the early 1970s lives on.

Logan's 1970s study of gentrification was an analysis of housing occupancy that found residential change best described as replacement rather than displacement. Forty years later, given the scale of redevelopment and construction of new apartment buildings in Melbourne's inner city, a study of population change would have to be based on a broader analysis that included the sources of finance capital and investment decision-making. Clearly the inner city is a construct that changes over time.

Chapter 10

A NEW PARADIGM?

TRENDYVILLE IN THE TWENTY-FIRST CENTURY

In an article in the British Town and Country Planning Association *Journal* in 1973, Gordon Cherry wrote confidently of a new paradigm, that public participation in planning had heralded a new partnership between planning and democracy.[1] In the same year the Interplan consultation process over the City of Melbourne Strategy Plan had also resulted in optimism for the future of participatory planning in Melbourne. The election of Rupert Hamer as premier at the end of the year and his announcement that no further freeways would be built added to this optimism while the Brooks Crescent conflict had marked the end of the Housing Commission urban renewal program. Sheila Byard recalled that:

> community organisations in Melbourne had a sense of power as a result of victories in campaigns directed toward reversing State government policies on freeways and "bulldozer" urban renewal. There was a heightened sense of the gains which might come from a more participatory planning process'.[2]

This optimism seemed confirmed by the spate of legislation passed by the Hamer government, including the establishment of a Planning Appeals Board, a Heritage Act and an overhaul of the Town and Country Planning legislation. Nor did the Hamer government proceed with the two controversial Urban Renewal Acts, which had both been subject to detailed critiques by the residents' associations, especially the Carlton Association.

---

[1] R. Howe and D. Nichols, 'A New Relationship Between Planning and Democracy? Urban activism in Melbourne, 1965–1975' *International Planning History Society Conference Proceedings*, Barcelona, July 2004.

[2] Sheila Byard, 'The Citizen's Action Plan for North and West Melbourne 1973' in *The Public and the City Plan*.

End of Century Realities

Despite the gains of the early 1970s, twenty-five years later, at the 'Public and the City Plan' seminar held in 1998, which was an evaluation of the CAN process, there was a less optimistic assessment of participatory planning. The CAN report remained 'an inspiration for the community and in many ways a model for action',[3] but the consensus was that the implementation process had resulted in very few gains for the CAN group. Although the MCC Strategy Plan had been adopted in principle, implementation had been thwarted by the political influence of developers and businessman. It marked the beginning of a long and fraught battle in the MCC during the 1970s and 1980s between community councillors representing the Carlton and North Melbourne wards and the CBD councillors. In 1981–82 the council was sacked by the state government and administrators appointed. This has been interpreted as a failure on the part of the residents' associations, who 'went underground' with the sacking of the council.[4]

The influence of the residents' associations declined on inner-city councils. In Fitzroy there was increasing dissatisfaction among new more affluent residents towards the influence of the ALP on Council policies. A significant turning point was the narrow defeat (on the Returning Officer's casting vote) of FRA/ALP candidate Onella Stagoll by the independent Angela Ireland in the Fitzroy Council election of 1991, a defeat regarded as significant enough evidence of the erosion of ALP influence in inner-city Melbourne to receive national news coverage.

Conflict between state and local government over control of planning meant constant pressure from both major political parties for the amalgamation of small inner-city municipalities. A Cain government inquiry in 1985, chaired by Stuart Morris, a lawyer and former member of the Planning Appeals Board, was unsuccessful in achieving amalgamations. In 1995 the Kennett Liberal government appointed administrators to undertake a large-scale reorganisation of local government in Victoria. The division of Carlton between the City of Melbourne and the new City of Yarra (which included the former Collingwood, Richmond and Fitzroy councils) had the intended effect of reducing the political influence of the residents' associations, especially the Carlton Association, now divided between two municipal areas.

---

3   Angela Munro, Conference Introduction, *The Public and the City Plan*.
4   Byard, 'The Citizens Action Plan for North and West Melbourne 1973'.

The community plans of the residents' associations had not anticipated the extent of the structural shifts in the inner city following de-industrialisation and the very rapid movement of the Australian and migrant working class from the inner suburbs. This shift was an international phenomenon and, as discussed in the previous chapter, explanations have been dominated by gentrification/displacement theories. In Melbourne, Miles Lewis was a critic of gentrification/displacement analysis, arguing that those homeowners who moved benefited both from rising inner-city house prices and relocation to suburban areas closer to work. CURA's study, *The Displaced*,[5] one of the few studies of inner-city displacement in Melbourne, found most displacement was caused by the large number of homes demolished by the HCV and inner-city road developments as by gentrification. It also found that home owners were not disadvantaged by moving, although it was a different story for low income and elderly marginal renters.

As gentrification moved from a cottage industry of DIY renovators to a global reworking of the city in the 1980s, the inner city became the focus of new employment opportunities and the profits to be made from property investment, and redevelopment ushered in a new wave of gentrification. Home owners who had moved to the inner city in the early period found they had little in common with the new investment-led urban change, but chastised themselves for paving the way. The North Sydney study identified this change as a result of 'over success' by residents' associations in fostering more liveable communities: property prices went up the more desirable areas became.[6]

Nor had the Melbourne residents' associations anticipated the extent and impact of economic restructuring. They had done little to encourage industry to remain in the inner city, apart from, in the case of the FRA, cooperation with factory owners in the Brooks Crescent struggle. Most new residents were ambivalent in their attitudes to industry, especially given the inner-city pattern of small often polluting and traffic-generating factories embedded in residential areas. There were constant complaints from nearby residents of the smell from the Italiano family's Perfect Cheese Factory in Fitzroy, despite the family's cooperation with FRA projects. Smell and traffic also elicited complaints about the National Can factory in North Fitzroy and the Rosella tomato sauce factory in Richmond, while residents'

---

5   Centre for Urban Research and Action, *The Displaced: A Study of Housing Conflict in Melbourne's Inner City* (Fitzroy: CURA, 1977).

6   Margaret Park, *Designs on a Landscape*, 19.

associations had supported the movement of large polluting industries from the Flemington/Kensington areas. It was not until the mid-1980s that steps were taken to develop regional strategies for strengthening the economic basis of the inner city with the formation of the Inner Metropolitan Regional Association of Councils and the appointment of Peter Tesdorpf as executive director to plan an industrial and employment strategy for the inner suburbs.

Nevertheless, the urban protest movements of the 1960s and 1970s had made important contributions to the future of Melbourne. Bruce Hanford thought the Melbourne movement not Marxist but reformist: 'It was the left-wing ALP type of level'. With hindsight, Caroline Hogg regretted the limitations and unanticipated outcomes of the reformist agenda. 'We did not think that at the time, we did not recognise that at the time but I think it would be absolutely true to say. We fought for community languages in schools and migrant education and all those things, you know, but I reckon we were the start of it and it drove us out'. However, asked if she was proud of the outcomes of her community activism she replied:

> Yes, that's all I can say. Not overwhelmingly so, there's probably more we could have done but certainly that little group, we worked hard to do what we could in Collingwood. We never turned our backs on the ideas and ideals that we had. Some of us then tried to, through Labor governments, take those ideas further still. I mean, if you look at Brian Howe's Better Cities Program, I guess that's the quintessence of what we were trying to do and wanted to do.

Howe established the national Better Cities Program in the 1990s, while a minister in the Keating ALP government, as a demonstration of urban place-making achieved through the cooperation of all three levels of government.

In his interview, Peter Hollingworth listed the later careers of the urban activists who moved on into government, welfare agencies, the public service and academic life, including the large number who were influential ministers in the Cain ALP government, and concluded that 'they've all done well. We've all done well'. Andrew McCutcheon, himself a reforming minister in the Cain ALP government, thought the contribution of the urban protest movement was that it

> got people articulating what's important and [gave] them skills. In the period before we were in government in the late '60s and through the

'70s, there was a lot of work done on community organising and giving skills to people to help organise causes. When the Labor Government got in, it employed a lot of those people to help implement the program.

Hanford thought that although there were many in the residents' associations who were 'complete twits', a particular strength of the Melbourne associations was their emphasis on values. The Crows were insistent on putting community values first in urban planning, while the inner-city churches and religious-based organisations such as the BSL and CURA were committed to value-based programs. There was 'that doctrine of Christian perfection, the sort of notion that if ... you'd put a little time and effort into the works of the congregation, that the world could be a better place. That's the sort of thing I would like to believe, I still would like to believe it'.

Doughnut City to Café Society

Lorna Hannan of the North Melbourne Association thought that an important contribution of the inner-city residents' associations was that despite the extent of de-industrialisation in Melbourne's inner city they had not developed into the 'rust belt' feared by the MMBW:

> There was something particular in the 70's ... that gave us the energy to push forward on a lot of fronts for the next couple of decades, a sort of confidence that people had then that they could do things. Without the activists of this period Melbourne would be a doughnut with an empty hole in the middle.

Although Hannan overstated the influence of the activists, Hal Kendig's 1977 study of the inner areas of Melbourne, Sydney and Adelaide had showed that these areas did not decline or stagnate, although as with most global industrial cities they had experienced loss of population, incursion of universities and hospitals, decline of manufacturing and large-scale public and private flat development. In contrast to Kendig's study, the MMBW in the same year produced an inner-area *Position Statement*[7] arguing that the inner suburbs were headed for an American 'rust belt' future without widespread redevelopment. However, twenty years later

---

[7]   Melbourne and Metropolitan Board of Works, *Melbourne's Inner Area: A Position Statement* (Melbourne: MMBW, 1977).

the publication of *From Doughnut City to Café Society*[8] showed that the predictions of the *Inner Area Position Statement* had not been realised. There had been extensive de-industrialisation in the inner city, but the loss of employment in manufacturing industry had been offset by growth in finance, the cultural and entertainment sector, health, education and services. The residents' associations, in curtailing HCV developments and focusing not just on saving houses but also on the importance of community development, had contributed to the emergence of the inner-city region as an important social and economic force in Melbourne. The economic drivers of Melbourne were no longer the factories of industrial suburbs but the hospitals, universities, offices, restaurants and entertainment venues of the city and inner suburbs.

The urban activists had contributed to transforming the image of the inner suburbs from a zone of industrial slums, migrant enclaves and red light areas. But beyond image-making they also helped save large areas of traditional housing and community buildings from redevelopment. As Bruce Handford observed, the residents' associations had recognised

> that a lot of the housing stock that was there was actually very good, very appropriate, and gave people privacy and independence and spaces they could call their own rather than shared with other people. Somehow it allowed the layers of the city to continue on and contribute to how we see urban life, rather than knocking it all down and blasting it off the face of the earth. Melbourne has got a fantastic sort of Victorian housing stock. A lot of that could have just been demolished.

Michael Jones, in his 1978 paper 'Economic Patterns and Alternatives', found Australian inner-city areas 'incredibly healthy', with

> valuable housing stock saved and renovated with little cost to the tax payer. This has been something that is quite unique in many ways to Australia. American cities because of racial problems, tax problems and other things really have become 'doughnut' cities. The 'doughnut' is nonsense when applied to Australian inner suburbs.[9]

The spate of planning and heritage legislation in New South Wales and Victoria, introduced as a response to the urban protest movements,

---

8   Department of Infrastructure, *From Doughnut City to Café Society* (Melbourne: Dept. of Infrastructure, 1998).

9   Michael Jones, 'Economic Patterns and Alternatives' in *The Inner Suburbs*, 39.

contributed to the maintenance of the inner-city areas of Melbourne and Sydney physically, economically and socially.

Also important had been the support of the union movement, a distinctive feature of Australian urban protest movements. This support had been essential in retaining housing and public buildings and in ensuring that redevelopment projects were socially inclusive. In their analysis of the influence of the union green bans on Sydney, Meredith and Verity Burgmann argue that the support of residents' associations by the NSW BLF had reduced the scale of social displacement in the inner city.[10] In The Rocks, BLF intervention ensured the retention of historic areas and the provision of well located community housing. Andrew McCutcheon, who worked on the redevelopment of The Rocks after the BLF had ensured that the state government's plan did not go ahead, recalled that

> it's very hard to control all the forces at work and the economic ones are the ones that are hardest to resist. When we did The Rocks redevelopment we actually took some of the sites for public housing … and there are still people today screaming there shouldn't be public housing, they're too valuable, we should give them to the wealthy to look down the harbour.

Urban protest movements emerged at an important time for unionism as unions turned their attention to concerns beyond wages and working conditions. The Burgmanns conclude that the outcomes of the NSW green bans supported Manuel Castells' 'optimistic depiction of urban social movements as forces leading to change in the underlying economic or social structure'.[11] The Burgmanns also point to the international influence of the green bans and their political influence which attracted the interest of members of German politicians who visited Mundey in Sydney. Petra Kelly, who later formed the German Green Party was especially impressed with the working class linking with the middle class over environmental issues. This contact later led to Mundey undertaking a European tour supporting the formation of Green political parties.[12]

Although the focus in analysis of urban protest movements has been on the role of the BLF in Sydney, the breakaway unions from the Melbourne Trades Hall Council were also significant actors, with a comprehensive

---

[10] Burgmann and Burgmann, *Green Bans, Red Union*, 282.

[11] Burgmann and Burgmann, *Green Bans, Red Union*, 56.

[12] Burgmann and Burgmann, *Green Bans, Red Union*, 56.

social agenda. No such union support for urban protest movements on this scale was forthcoming in American or British cities. The Melbourne unions saved many buildings under threat of demolition due to their ability to act quickly and prevent maverick demolitions. Certainly union bans contributed to the saving of historic Collins Street, along with protests from architects and the actions of the newly formed Historic Buildings Council chaired by Professor Graeme Davison.

By the mid-1970s the support of the union movement was beginning to wane as economic conditions changed and members worried about losing work, especially on the large construction sites in Sydney. Looking back on this period in Melbourne, Norm Gallagher recalled the growing opposition to bans among union members concerned at the impact on employment in the construction industry. Demands for development projects in a period of uncertainty about the future of the economy became more insistent and harder to resist.

Losing the Fight?

Changing economic and political conditions also hindered local government efforts to discourage gentrification and maintain a population mix in the inner city. In the 1980s and 1990s St Kilda Council (absorbed into Port Phillip Council in 1994) had put council funds into securing well located sites (some on the Esplanade, a prized location) for building public housing and low-rental accommodation. Fitzroy Council (absorbed into Yarra Council) introduced policies protecting boarding houses and subsidised rental accommodation for low-income residents. Such housing policies were increasingly difficult for local government to implement given the lack of resources and the growing powers of state governments over planning.

These growing pressures are traced in the last chapter of the North Sydney planning history, ominously entitled 'Losing the Fight: Planning Chaos and Confusion'. Until the mid-1970s, 'the rise of the resident action movement and the election of sensitive new aldermen introduced to the chamber propelled North Sydney council into new directions with a whole sweep of changes'.[13] But the heavy pressure for development made it increasingly difficult for the council to cope, causing delays in decision-making and conflict with the state government which wanted (and increasingly held

---

[13]   Park, *Designs on a Landscape*, 147.

the planning powers to insist on) the development of flats and commercial areas. Despite the election as mayor of residents activists Carole Baker in 1979 and Ted Mack in 1980, community-based policies were not supported by new members of council who did not have a residents' association background. The increased powers of the state government under the NSW Environment Planning and Assessment Act (1979) and the demand for increased densities from the Department of Environment and Planning introduced a long period of conflict. Although the extent of local support was such that Ted Mack was elected as an independent federal member for North Sydney in 1988, even this stellar achievement did not greatly assist the North Sydney residents association in the battle to resist the state government's planning powers and development policies.

In Victoria from the late 1980s large developments were taken out of public scrutiny, in favour of direct negotiations between developers and the state government. The restructure of local government by the Kennett government in the 1990s further restricted the planning powers of local councils, who found it increasingly difficult to control development.

At the 1998 conference in North Melbourne on the CAN report, Colin Long outlined the massive expansion of real estate development in Melbourne's CBD and surrounding areas from the late 1980s and the view of the inner city as a driver of economic growth compared with the community-based and participatory view of the activists. The objectives of planning had changed in the face of economic restructuring and stagnation, with emphasis on the need for growth and development and the need to stimulate economic activity. 'Seldom had the agendas and interests of governments and developers been so compatible. Local government planners were overlooked or seduced by a State government determined to reduce the power of elected councillors'.[14] This change was achieved by privatising the functions of local government, amalgamating municipalities and introducing performance-based planning schemes. The new era was epitomised by Jeff Kennett revering the former premier Henry Bolte, the nemesis of the activists, as his hero, even rescuing Bolte's desk from the basement for his refurbished premier's office. The contributions of Victoria's progressive Liberals, Rupert Hamer and Alan Hunt, were ignored.

There was a backlash in response to these changes. In 1997, when all Victorian municipalities were required to prepare and adopt performance-based planning schemes, the TCPA adopted a Charter for Planning drafted

---

14   Colin Long, *The Public and the City Plan*, 4.

by a working group led by Miles Lewis.[15] Lewis was also involved in the establishment of the umbrella group Save Our Suburbs (SOS), as residents action groups were established in response to development pressures spreading to middle ring suburbs. Lewis described SOS as challenging the dogmas of the political parties and the orthodoxies of professional planners. 'In doing so it represented ... the quintessence of democratic principles at work'.[16] However, despite the comprehensive and detailed Charter for Planning, SOS had limited influence in mobilising residents of the middle ring suburbs or changing prevailing views that residential densities must increase, that development was inevitable and that the free market should prevail. The focus of most SOS groups was on amenity issues and protecting neighbourhood character, unlike the broader social objectives of the 1970s urban protest movement. The urban economist Mike Berry, who had been active in the Save Collins Street movement, rued the 'cargo cult' commercialisation of the street in the 1980s, in which 'growth, development and progress, the new trinity of self-styled pragmatic and responsible governments concerned to "get the economy going again" is opposed to and seen to override those earlier social issues and environmental concerns'.[17]

There was little emphasis on the value of community planning or participatory democracy. An important example was the change of the Planning Appeals Board, established by the Hamer government, to allow third party community groups access to the planning process, to the less accessible Planning Division of the Victorian Civil and Administrative Tribunal. Pat Grainger, in an article on 'Participatory democracy as a means of manipulation', argued that 'the process of participatory democracy has become a tool of power, enabling Government to rationalise questionable actions arising primarily from economic considerations'. Consultation could involve one public meeting, one glossy brochure, one discreet notice in the press or a two-volume technical document available on the ninth floor of a city building with limited time to respond.[18] Consultants and market research firms were increasingly brought in to undertake 'consultations' on planning proposals. A recent low point in the cynical manipulation of consultation was the leaking of an email from the minister for planning in the Brumby

---

[15]   Miles Lewis, *Suburban Backlash*, 267–269.

[16]   Lewis, *Suburban Backlash*, vii.

[17]   Mike Berry, 'Cargo Cult in Collins Street' in Kate Shaw, ed., *Bayside Views* (East Melbourne: The Author, 1988), 32–41..

[18]   Pat Grainger, 'Participatory Democracy as a Means of Manipulation: The Consultative Process at Work in Victoria, or, What Happened to Democracy?' in *Bayside Views*, 9–16.

government on proposed manipulation of the consultation process relating to plans for the redevelopment of the heritage-listed Windsor Hotel, a sad end for the 'new paradigm' in planning.

However, urban protest has successfully moderated some recent large developments. The early stages of the huge Barangaroo development on the Sydney Harbour foreshore revived memories of The Rocks redevelopment and 'even in this complacent self-indulgent age there has been an extraordinary reaction against the proposed Barangaroo design. Public and professional concern has triggered the formation of action groups on a scale not seen since the 1970s'.[19]

If any urban activist group still active resonates with the ambitions and ideals of the early 1970s, it may be UnChain St Kilda. While in truth St Kilda is an exemplar of the gentrified Australian beach suburb it nonetheless can justifiably be said to retain the fighting spirit of an earlier age. UnChain St Kilda has retained this spirit in the context of similar protest campaigns – such as the tenacious Save Albert Park movement, active since 1996 – in which state governments have proved largely unmoved by local interests.

As in the case of the Princes Hill Community Garden, the issues that led to the creation of UnChain St Kilda were connected to a desire for community input – or rather, an awareness that the community was being denied involvement in planning decisions. The 'St Kilda Triangle', a small piece of crown land between Jacka Boulevard, The Esplanade and Cavell Street, was earmarked for development. The proposal, long in conception (beginning with the St Kilda Foreshore Urban Design Framework of 2001) was in its initial stages for a complex including a hotel, a restaurant, a supermarket, event spaces, a cinema, live music venues and the William Angliss Institute of TAFE. This design was later amended with certain features removed – primarily to increase public amenity – through the machinations of UnChain St Kilda, formed in 2007 and operating in a style which would have been familiar to the activists of 1970: 'community rallying, instigating and attending protest marches, submitting objections, petitioning ... attending community and council meetings and displaying banners throughout St Kilda with captions such as "Too Bloody Big"'.[20] Key UnChain activists were Anna Griffiths and her husband Don Gazzard, who had played an important role in the resistance of Sydney's Paddington

---

19   'No Place for the Timid: Barangaroo and Bust, or a "Better Barangaroo"?' *Cityscape News Blog*, 15 July 2011, http://cityscape-news.com/?p=327.

20   Meghan Sweeney, *An Analysis of the St Kilda Triangle Planning Process* (Honours Thesis, University of Melbourne, 2008), 45.

Society to the widening of Jersey Road, forty years earlier.[21] The Rolling Stones donated $5000 each towards the anti-development campaign, in recognition of the pleasure they had taken in playing at the Palais, adjoining the triangle, in 1965; other celebrities added their weight to the anti-development protest.

In 2008, the fate of the triangle site yet undecided, the UnChain protesters took their campaign into the realm of local politics. Dissatisfied with the local (Labor) council, the group proposed its own candidates, among them the Alsace-born photographer Serge Thomann, President of UnChain. Once elected, Thomann professed to understand St Kilda as 'an incubator of rich ideas, a unique place in Melbourne's landscape, and a connected engaged community'. The initial design was abandoned by Port Phillip in late 2009, and a new one launched in 2012.

It is a badge of honour to Thomann and his fellow UnChain councillor Jane Touzeau that they are not members of a political party, believing as they do that local issues are for local members, not 'political party careerists'.[22] In this regard UnChain deviates significantly from its predecessor groups of the 1970s: it will not engage with party politics. Thus, it is divorced from any more widely applicable ideology, and it does not need to examine its motives or platforms beyond those specifically sculpted for what is deemed the good of St Kilda.

The Future of Trendyville

The notion of the 'trendy' has been discussed in previous chapters, and gives us the title of this study. It is too easy, however, to say that Australia's gentrification was only ever really 'Trendyville', just as it is too simple to suggest this has now given way to 'Legoland'. Certainly, the 'trendies' have long been a bone of contention and, like so many similar derogatory terms, the 'trendy' has always been a term to use against someone, lest it be used against you. Kaye Hargreaves recalls that when Race Matthews moved to Falconer Street, North Fitzroy, in the early 1970s, 'some locals graffittied "Fuck off trendy" on his Jag, parked out the front'.[23] When South Melbourne's mayor, Bruce Cormick, lost office in September 1975, he blamed

---

21 Don Gazzard, *Sydneysider: An Optimistic Life in Architecture* (Boorowa: Watermark Press, 2006), 59–62.

22 'Unchain', *Unchain*, http://www.unchain.org.au/index.html.

23 Kaye Hargreaves, 'My Memories of Alan Jordan', *Kaye's Universe*, April 2012, http://kayehargreaves1.wordpress.com/personal/my-memories-of-alan-jordan-akj/.

the 'trendies' with their 'wealth, academic qualificiations and resources' for his defeat.[24] But the perceived anomaly in the early-to-mid-1970s of middle-class consumers, interested in fashion and consumption, living in working-class neighbourhoods, is no longer compelling or peculiar. Towards the end of her life Ruth Crow was reputedly appalled by the time inner-city residents spent drinking coffee and indulging in idle chatter. Though Crow herself was not averse to conversation, hers always had a purpose.

Melbourne, along with other global manufacturing cities, has undergone great and continuing change in the past forty-five years. In *Melbourne Remade* Seamus O'Hanlon traces the profound and complex changes in the inner city, increasingly gentrified and with rising housing costs. He notes the irony that the public housing estates of the HCV are now the main providers of low-income housing in inner-city Melbourne. However, O'Hanlon says many reacted to his book with shock that he didn't lionise the old working-class inner city and 'see the new economy of consumption and spectacle as somehow less authentic, less moral than its manufacturing predecessor'.[25] His view is that the Australian and migrant working-class and their children and grandchildren were beneficiaries of the change and that the diversity of the new inner city opened up opportunities for women, gays, lesbians, artists, professionals and entrepreneurs. The inner city is increasingly culturally different from the rest of the metropolis, with different attitudes and voting patterns reflecting the complexity of the post-industrial economy.

The Unchain response in Melbourne demonstrated that community based urban protest movements can still influence large-scale development decisions, drawing on the traditions and tactics of the earlier residents' associations. Nevertheless the influence of the urban activists had peaked in the mid-1980s, indicating the difficulty protest movements have in developing an on-going positive agenda. Their decline left a political vacuum which in the inner suburbs of Sydney and Melbourne has been occupied by the Greens. The Greens have roots in the environment movement which gathered momentum following the battle in the late 1970s over saving the Franklin River in Tasmania. The new environment organisations drew their main support from the inner and middle ring suburbs of Melbourne and Sydney but had links with the urban protest movement, especially through Jack Mundey in Sydney who had contributed to the development of a broad green political agenda, and David Scott in Melbourne who had encouraged

---

24   Richard Goodwin, 'Trendies Beat Me, Says Mayor' Melbourne *Age*, 1 September 1975, 6.
25   O'Hanlon with Dingle, *Melbourne Remade*, 6.

the formation of the Australian Conservation Foundation and the emergence of protection of the natural environment as a political issue.

Political support for the environment movement increasingly came from the younger generation of inner-city residents. Whereas the political strategy of the urban activists had been to influence the policies and structures of the established parties the younger generation of inner-city residents has turned to the Greens. The Greens have also attracted left-wing supporters, especially in Sydney where the Mundey influence was strong and following the demise of the Communist Party of Australia (CPA). Inner-city political discourse is now dominated by the Greens and includes not only environmental issues but also global issues such as gay rights, climate change, immigration, and nuclear non-proliferation. Politically the Greens have been most successful in gaining representation in inner-urban local government, Legislative Councils in Sydney and Melbourne, and at the Commonwealth level in the Senate. In recent elections they have been successful in attracting votes from the ALP in lower-house inner-suburban seats in State parliaments and recently elected and then re-elected Adam Bandt in the seat of Melbourne as the first representative of the Greens in the House of Representatives in the Commonwealth parliament.

Another significant change has been in the area of public housing policy and the unforeseen outcomes of the bitterly contested housing policies of the 1960s and 70s. In Sydney the policy of the NSW Housing Commission to locate families in outer suburban areas to the west and south of the city have resulted in concentrations of areas of social and economic deprivation, exacerbated by the decline of regional employment. In Melbourne, the high-rise tower estates built in inner-city slum areas are now located in areas of prime real estate. The estates provide homes for the elderly, disadvantaged families and low-income residents, giving them access to the employment and social advantages of inner-city locations. Such advantages are not available to most low-income residents increasingly forced to locate in suburbs on the edge of the city. While the inner-city high-rise estates have provided well located housing for low-income residents, the concentration of disadvantage and unemployment combined with a lack of community facilities has isolated residents and prevented them capitalising on their locational advantage.

These factors have led to proposals by Victorian governments for major redevelopment of the inner-city high-rise estates. Assisted by grants from the Commonwealth government, the ALP Brumby government in 2009 proposed partial redevelopment of public housing sites in Kensington, Carlton, Prahran, Richmond and Fitzroy, with the aim of introducing social mix through the provision of medium-density housing largely financed by non-profit housing associations and designed by Melbourne's leading architectural firms. Plans for estate redevelopments included the provision of community facilities such as education hubs, health centres and child care centres. These developments were to be accompanied by some refurbishment of the high-rise towers and demolition of most remaining four storey walk-ups, to be replaced by medium-density apartments built by the private sector and available for sale as private residences or for social housing. The current Victorian coalition government is considering further development on inner-city estates that would include commercial developments and private sector housing. Rumours that the demolition of some high-rise towers was being contemplated were denied by the government. Ironically, these contemporary re-development proposals have similarities with the models for mixed and medium-density developments advocated by the urban activists almost forty years ago in the Carlton Plan, CAN and the plan for Brooks Crescent.

The change in value of the sites of inner-city public housing developments and the conflict in St Kilda which led to Unchain are indications that Melbourne, along with other twenty-first century global cities, is undergoing another period of urban transformation, prompting reconsideration of the achievements of the urban protest movements of the 1960s and 70s. When Melbourne was awarded the accolade of being the world's most liveable city in 2003, former planning minister Alan Hunt reminded people that this award was no accident, rather the title was earned.

> For more than 30 years, despite enormous pressures of rapid growth. Metropolitan Melbourne's charm and character have been protected and enhanced by planning and environmental policies specifically designed to do so ... All these policies were developed and refined with considerable public participation and are generally accepted by the community.[26]

There are now substantial barriers in challenging development investment decisions involving powerful global capital institutions. Consultation and transparency are no longer priorities in planning decision-making as the inner suburbs are absorbed into the central city as an economic unit for planning. Compared with the earlier period there is no sense in twenty-first century Melbourne that this is an exciting and optimistic time. William Logan, reflecting on his research on gentrification in Carlton, observed that

---

[26]   Alan Hunt, 'World's Most Liveable City No Accident' Melbourne *Age*, 29 April 2003.

in the 1960s and 70s 'there was an optimism that the popular will could be expressed in social movements and actions and that our governments will be persuaded to listen, an optimism about politics that I fear has gone out of the Australian scene today'.

In 2008 the Municipal Art Society of New York held forums and an exhibition on 'Jane Jacobs and the Future of New York' to mark forty years since the publication of *The Death and Life of Great American Cities*. The event was prompted by the striking contemporary parallels with the early 1960s, with redevelopment taking place in New York on a scale not seen since the days of Robert Moses. Jacobs' issues of scale, economic diversity and public participation in the planning process had suddenly returned to the fore. The forums aimed to rejuvenate Jacobs' legacy, which over the years had come to be seen as obstructive and NIMBYism rather than as engagement and empowerment, and concluded that proactive communities and neighbourhoods, ensuring cohesion and stability, were still important goals for the city.[27] Perhaps this book will encourage a similar rejuvenation of interest in the Melbourne residents' associations of the 1960s and 1970s and a recognition of the ongoing importance of participatory planning in ensuring a liveable and socially inclusive city.

---

[27]   'Jane Jacobs and the Future of New York', The Municipal Art Society, January 2008.

INDEX

INDEX

INDEX